M

m

M A N

d

e

JEREMY P. TARCHER • PUTNAM
A MEMBER OF
PENGUIN PUTNAM INC.
NEW YORK

m
MAN
d
e

A Memoir of My Body

Ken Baker

Most Tarcher/Putnam books are available at special quantity discounts for
bulk purchases for sales promotions, premiums, fund-raising, and
educational needs. Special books or book excerpts also can be created
to fit specific needs. For details, write Putnam Special Markets,
375 Hudson Street, New York, NY 10014.

What follows is a true story. The names of certain characters have
been changed in order to protect their privacy.

Jeremy P. Tarcher/Putnam
a member of
Penguin Putnam, Inc.
375 Hudson Street
New York, NY 10014
www.penguinputnam.com

Library of Congress Cataloging-in-Publication Data

Baker, Ken, date.
Man made : a memoir of my body / Ken Baker.
p. cm.
ISBN 1-58542-083-2
1. Men. 2. Masculinity. 3. Gender identity. 4. Sex role. I. Title.
HQ1090.B348   2001   00-050796
305.31—dc21

Printed in the United States of America

1 3 5 7 9 10 8 6 4 2

This book is printed on acid-free paper. ∞

BOOK DESIGN BY DEBORAH KERNER

FOR BROOKE

Prolactin: A HORMONE THAT
WOMEN SECRETE TO PRODUCE
BREAST MILK.

PROLACTIN LEVEL IN THE BLOOD OF
AN AVERAGE MALE
= 10 NG / ML*

PROLACTIN LEVEL OF
A NURSING MOTHER
= 200 NG / ML

AUTHOR'S PROLACTIN LEVEL ON
OCTOBER 16, 1997
= 1,578 NG / ML

(ng = nanograms/ml = milliliter)

INTRODUCTION

My body was at war with itself, and on a summer morning in 1998 my brain surgeon brokered a peace agreement. While his steady hand removed a tumor from my brain, it could not halt the haunting, emasculating memories that came rushing forth as I lay recovering under the fluorescent glow of the hospital's intensive care unit. Those memories have allowed me, after spending my entire adult life trapped in a gender netherworld, to finally tell my story.

A little more than two years later, I'm sitting in front of the computer in my home office. Reflected in a mirror across the room I see a thirty-year-old man from whose head a surgeon cut out a tumor as wide as a chestnut. Though a large tumor, the size wasn't so much the problem as the havoc the clump of cell tissue had been wreaking on my masculinity since I was about fifteen years old. As the tumor grew, my body was flooded with massive amounts of prolactin, a hormone that women secrete to produce breast milk but that men, who possess only trace amounts, don't need at all.

With too much prolactin, a man's testosterone level will plummet. As such, my sex drive diminished; my nipples grew sore and swollen, and they eventually started leaking a milky fluid; my poor muscle tone, from my abs to my legs to my arms, left me feeling soft, ill-defined; I had scant body and facial hair, whiskers that I needed to shave only once every couple months; I suffered near constant pain in my forehead and temples that sometimes forced me to conduct business calls while at home lying in bed with an ice pack on my head. On those rare, anxiety-filled occasions when I worked up the courage to get into bed with a woman, I could not achieve an erection, the single most cherished male bodily function.

I was so distraught by my deterioration that there were times I would rather have died than live another day as what I perceived as an inadequate, impotent, useless man. My erectile dysfunction (which, in the days before Viagra, I knew only as not being able to "get it up") made me cower in the face of sexual expectations and performance pressures. I resented my traditional gender role: sexual aggressor, initiator and virile protector. The more physically attractive the woman, the more I loathed the thought of forcing myself to attempt sex with her. Self-denial and abstinence became my coping method.

In order to exist as a biochemically normal man today, I must take a prolactin-suppressing medication—in the form of a white pill resembling a Tic Tac—twice a week, probably for the rest of my life. What will happen if I stop ingesting these tiny yet potent pills? The same hormonal demise I know too well.

Luckily, though, so far the medication *is* working, and I *am* a hormonally healthy man. And there are none of the signs of my disease— the impotence, fatigue, depression, heightened emotional sensitivity, milky nipples, gender confusion, sexual performance anxiety, splitting headaches—that I experienced before I went under the knife. As a result, I am free of the shame and feelings of worthlessness that sexual dysfunction causes in men, and I no longer must carry the additional burden of inflicting the confusion, concern, guilt and self-doubt that my disease created for women I loved.

Ignorant of the prolactin-secreting invader growing three inches behind my eyes and a few centimeters from my brain's speech and language center, I dealt with my struggle to be "normal" as I believed any real man should: I drew a line in the sand and waged a battle—against an enemy that I mistakenly thought was my own psychological weakness. Blaming my self-regarded "pussy-ass" disposition on an imagined subconscious reaction to having been raised as an overachieving, hockey-playing son of a hypermacho father in upstate New York, I set out to conquer my sexual demons as a climber would Everest. Like many young men, I had been taught that one's manliness was gauged largely by his ability to overcome adversity. Dad, my brothers, my hockey coaches, the entire culture, passed this myth of manhood on to me. With enough strength and fortitude, so our culture's man-as-hero myth goes, I could be the fisherman in Hemingway's *Old Man and the Sea,* becoming better through surviving life's hardships; the Jack London character braving subzero temperatures in the northern woods; or the apostle Paul my Sunday school teachers talked about, who walked hundreds of miles to spread the good news of eternal life through faith in that model man, Jesus Christ. Along with the direct influence of my parents, these characters—and the countless other images of manhood in stories and the popular culture—helped form my idea that manhood means strength, manhood means stoicism, manhood means overcoming hardship and destroying the enemy.

But what should a man do when that enemy is his own body, inside of which hormones are making such manly behavior increasingly difficult to act out?

Sadly, I refused to acknowledge that I was in a fight that I couldn't win alone, that I couldn't survive without revealing my pain to someone else. And throughout my decline I lost more than sexual function. As a teenager I was a top-ranked goaltender in the United States Olympic ice hockey program. Reared in a large working-class family outside of Buffalo where men were consumed by the macho world of beer, chicks and hockey, I was a young man whose success and happiness in life had always depended almost entirely on his body's athletic ability. I eventually fell out of love not only with hockey but with the macho culture in which I was raised. I came to feel alienated from the manhood that society had defined for me and groped helplessly to find comfort in my male identity. No matter how influential my macho *nurture* had been, my increasingly effeminate *nature* prevented me from behaving the only way I understood. And I kept my pain a secret.

With those years remanded to memories, I can now view my hormonal crisis as a gift. By possessing more than 150 times the normal level of prolactin, and experiencing the related effects of testosterone depletion, I was able to journey to a biological place few men will ever know. My entire being approached a state of biochemical femaleness, and my manhood today is stronger because of it.

As such, I feel a sort of kinship with women. I, too, was once confounded and frustrated by that seemingly foreign brand of human being: men. I, too, spent a lot of time trying to understand why so many men acted so different than me—from slapping waitresses on the ass, to cheating on girlfriends, to getting into fistfights over who stole their parking spaces. I used to resent how society seemed to reward maleness more than manliness. Yet, I also respect and appreciate the innate gifts of being a heterosexual male: my affection for women, my testosterone-fueled physical strength, my renewed athleticism and my sex drive.

I cherish my ability to procreate and raise a child, and, using the lessons that my father and my subsequent illness have taught me, I vow to help my son, should I have one, avoid making the mistakes I did.

I've never heard a father tell his son to "be a male." For most guys, being male is the easy part; it's being a man that poses the real challenge. Having a normal composition of male hormones makes being a man in our sex-obsessed culture much easier because sexuality and manhood, according to the laws of nature and rules of society, are not mutually exclusive.

No matter how "normal" I am today, I remember the days when I muddled through life in what seemed a moribund state of androgyny, when I viewed the relationship between maleness and manhood as an unattainable quid pro quo. I've come to realize, however, that maleness is the shell; manhood is the soul.

I have spent my career as a journalist writing about other people—in essays, academic papers, newspaper and magazine articles. But I was only able to start writing this book after I made a series of life-changing vows: no more silence, no more telling other people's stories while avoiding my own, no more trying to hold back the flood of memories that rushed to me as I lay in a sterile intensive care unit. Surgery healed my body; writing will heal my soul.

m

MAN

d

e

AWAKENING

I'm groggy, but the fog is lifting. I can see clearly through the window at the foot of my bed to the nurses' station in the hall. I lift my head an inch off the pillow, just enough to inspect the yellow, blue and white maze of wires connecting the bleeping box to the tiny round patches stuck to my bare chest. I assume they are heart monitors.

Taking inventory, my eyes stop at my thigh area, where I notice a clear plastic tube poking out from beneath the blanket. The tube, slithering between the blanket and my leg, curves down toward the floor. I can see a yellowish fluid dripping inside. For the first time since I came to, I bend my arms, slowly lifting the blanket off my gown-covered body. Nudging chin-to-chest, I struggle for a better view. Scanning past my stomach to my groin, I pull my gown up, and I cringe. Oh, God . . . it's a catheter.

Glancing down, I see my penis shriveled, tiny as a garden slug, stuck to my thigh with white medical tape, its tip swallowing the narrow, straw-size tube snaking up to my bladder. I swallow another glop of blood as I, peering over my oxygen mask, stare at my limp dick, gray and lifeless—so unsexual, like half a sausage link topped by a wilted mushroom.

This tiny nub of tissue, numbed by the trauma, this is what women crave and we men deem the paragon of virility? The stability of our fragile male psyches depends on this pathetic little body part? Viagra, penis envy, penis pumps, phallic national monuments shaped in their honor. Count the

number of English words we have for it and you realize its assessed impor-
tance. Dick, prick, cock, schlong, peter, penis, pecker, poker, prick, hammer, rammer, rod, dink, dong, the high hard one, Mr. Happy, the
baloney pony, the one-eyed snake, the main vein. *Now look at it, rest-*
ing there helplessly, an involuntary exitway for my urine, an inch of fleshy
tissue getting in the way of the catheter and my bladder. This medical nui-
sance, so easily rendered impotent by a tumor, brought me so much grief for
so many years? I've just risked a stroke, brain damage—my life!—so that
I can get hard, make babies, please a woman and please myself. But now I
can barely lift my arm, let alone harden this pathetic-looking penis.

I plop my head back onto the pillow and stare at the ceiling. I want to
cry, but I am too tired. I can only think how I wish every man could see his
private pride-and-joy in this vulnerable, emasculated state. Only then might
we witness an alarming drop in White House sex scandals, child pornogra-
phy, murder rates, abusive boyfriends, cheating husbands, wife-beaters,
AIDS, prostitution, gang-banging, domestic violence, hubris, schoolyard
shootings, terrorism, war. Also, then we might see fewer people like me, a
young man who, until sniffing the wafting reek of death in a hospital's in-
tensive care unit, had been convinced that, no matter how hard he tried, he
could never be a real man.

KEN BAKER

When Drew Barrymore invites you to a party, you go—especially when you are a twenty-five-year-old (wannabe) Hollywood hipster and have been celibate and single ever since you were unceremoniously dumped by a girl almost four years ago.

If I don't attend Drew's soiree, I might as well relinquish my Hollywood press corps credentials. *People* magazine's Hollywood bureau chief expects me—hey, he even gives me a corporate AmEx card for the very purpose—to schmooze as much as possible with nubile A-listers and any other glitterati I may meet while trolling the streets of Los Angeles for the scoop, the dish, the dirt.

Therefore, as soon as the courier arrives in the office lobby and hands me the fancy-shmancy cardboard invitation to Drew's fundraiser for a southern California wildlife refuge, I phone over to Drew's production office on Sunset Boulevard and, intoning the cockiest voice I can muster, I inform the movie star's perky assistant that I—"Ken Baker, from *People* magazine"—am RSVP'ing for tonight's bash.

Later, I stare in my cluttered bedroom closet, a palpable pre-party anxiety oozing from my naked body, which I do not glance at in the wall mirror because I would rather not see what I regard as my disgusting, womanly figure: my Jell-O abs, puffy breasts, narrow shoulders. This is perhaps the most vital moment of any night out in

3

Hollywood, because it is when I choose a battle armor that will conceal my unmanliness from the opposite sex.

What to wear, what to wear, what to wear. Hmmm . . . let me do some fashion math: *Cool = Black.* So I don black Banana Republic jeans and a loose-fitting black T-shirt (to hide my man-breasts) with black Kenneth Cole shoes, under which I will wear black Gap dress socks. My invited partner for the evening is Kelly (a guy), who is my roommate. Across the hall of our two-bedroom apartment in his bedroom, Kelly does a sartorial copycat maneuver, going black, too, although he adds a few beaded chain necklaces of dubious cultural origin just for mysterious effect.

Then, before my sun-lightened hair dries, I squeeze a viscous glob of L'Oréal Anti-Stick Invisi-Gel into my palm and smear it through my long, straw-straight hair, which I have grown as a protest to the buzz-short hairdos that the so-called cute, hot guys on *Friends* are wearing these days. Lastly, I dab a speck of flesh-colored Clearasil on a red pimple conspicuously placed in the middle of my tanned forehead. Once I'm made sufficiently pretty, we depart for downtown Hollywood.

A typical evening. It's about seventy-five degrees, clear skies, the residual smog and city lights muting the glow of the stars. My red Saturn inches down the crowded boulevards, which are packed bumper-to-bumper with status symbols far more mobile and of much higher status than my own. Porsche convertibles. Mazda Miatas. Shiny BMWs. Of course, black is the coolest color of all.

Outside the club—natch, there's curbside valet—I leave my keys and the requisite five dollars with the red-vested boy. Once inside, Kelly and I stride self-consciously across the room and into the hobnobbing courtyard. *No eye contact . . . detached coolness . . . be the man.*

I head straight for the patio bar, where I elbow myself a space from which to holler out my favorite cool-guy beverage while flapping a twenty-dollar bill in the air like the lazy palms shrouding the patio. "Martini—make it strong, dude."

"Look, Kel, there's that redheaded guy from *Politically Incorrect*. What's-his-name . . . "

"Uh, Bill Maher. . . ."

"Hey, man, isn't that the guitarist from Hole?" Kelly asks.

"Which one?"

"The skinny blond guy."

"I think so," I say. "But I didn't think he was that tall." I jab Kelly's upper arm and add, "Now that's gotta be Courtney Love."

"Kinda bad skin, huh?" he says.

"But she's hot. I grabbed her leg once at a concert."

"Seriously?"

"I'm not shitting you."

A gulp—one glass closer to achieving a buzz that will make me feel less uncomfortable in my non-celebrity skin.

Because it is my job as a *People* magazine correspondent, because it is the sport of hipsters in Hollywood, I scan the crowd for yet another celebrity.

"Isn't that older chick sitting at the table—that dye-job blonde over there—Nina Blackwood?"

"Who's she?"

"Who is Nina Blackwood? An old MTV veejay, dumb-ass."

Mental note: Write a "Where Are They Now?" piece on Nina Blackwood.

But where is the hostess of the evening, the golden-blond goddess I've had a crush on since I was twelve, when her love for E.T. made me cry?

Though only twenty-one, Drew is already a screen legend, and I have bitten raw the cuticles around my fingertips in nervous anticipation of this event. I am in awe of her vast life experiences: breast-reduction surgery, drug and alcohol addiction (since third grade), a suicide attempt, her own film-production company, a bare-ass-naked spread in *Playboy*, an autobiography (*Little Girl Lost*, ghost-written by my friend Todd, who has filled me in on Drew's likes and dislikes). If all these accomplishments aren't impressive enough, Drew has even flashed her naked breasts on network television before an eye-popping David Letterman—and me, who was sitting at home desperately trying to recall the last time I had seen a woman's bare breasts in person.

So where the hell is she, anyway? Maybe she won't show. Maybe she's just another phony starlet who flirts with me during an interview, hoping I will tell millions of People *readers how great and real and nice she is, but then, ten minutes after I leave, can't even remember my name, let alone how sensitive and charming and what a good listener I am. Maybe our interview, in which she and I chatted for over an hour, wasn't as meaningful to her as it was to me. Or maybe it's just that I really do look like the dork that I feel like on the inside.*

This being a Hollywood party hosted by a Gen X icon, however, virtually everyone on the patio is young and attractive, with faces and bodies right out of a Baywatch *episode or a Calvin Klein ad. Except, it seems, for me . . .*

A mini-skirted female server presents me with a tray of fried eggplant and saucy stabs of chicken satay. I decline, because, well, I think I'm too fat. I suppose *fat* isn't the right word. I'm about five foot eleven and not even 175 pounds. On paper, it's a respectable height-to-weight ratio, but I *feel* flabby, soft around the edges, not strong, unsolid—sort of gelatinous. I am puffy. Puffy face. Puffy chest. Puffy neck. Puffy stomach. No matter how much I rollerblade up and down the Venice Beach bike path, no matter how few calories I consume (usually about a thousand a day—no bread, no fried food, no sweets), no matter how much older I get, my body stubbornly refuses to harden into manhood. It's depressing.

I have been avoiding looking at my body in the mirror because my physique is a far cry from what I believe it should look like at my age, what with my athletic background and starvation diets and all. I want—no, I need!—a hardbody . . . like that blond guy over there with the perma-tan and volleyball-guy broad shoulders who is standing so studly surrounded by the ladies while I stand over here with Kelly like a loser.

Stop whining like a little sissy.

Why did I—*I said stop being a pussy-sissy-chicky-wimpy mutant!*—have to move to ground zero of a popular culture obsessed with accentuating the visual extremes of gender definition? Bulging biceps and tight butts. Big dicks and big boobs. Hard cocks and tight butts. Chiseled chests and hairless legs. Steroids. Liposuction. Pec implants. Dick implants. Personal trainers. Collagen injections. Boob jobs. Eye jobs. Dye jobs. Nose jobs. Ear jobs. Tummy tucks.

I am ashamed of my manhood because my version of it doesn't look or feel at all like the manhood my dad, brothers, hockey coaches, team mates, friends, girlfriends, or billboards, magazines, TV shows, movies—the entire goddamn popular culture—tells me is manly.

I am supposedly in the prime of my life. Meanwhile, gorgeous women, probably dreaming for a not-so-bad-looking, Ivy League-educated guy, swarm around me in their little skirts and tight tops and bodies to die for. I just watch them. *Bzzz. Bzzz. Bzzz.* They're all around me! Not only can't I catch them, but I am not so sure I want to.

It's easy to understand my shame, my fear of sex and walls of self-denial, when you consider the fundamental mechanics of human reproductive biology that I am lacking. I've spent a lot of time thinking about this male-female mating game. A healthy person, with a sex drive and perfectly functional genitals, doesn't have to ponder such things, I believe. I bet their genes have them acting on sexual autopilot. I'd imagine that, for them, sex is as easy and uncomplicated as the whole process is confounding for me. Women have it even better than men. While our penises must perform a hydraulic feat just to get an erection, a woman only needs to lubricate—and that can be done artificially. There's a lot of pressure on guys to perform, especially guys like me who aren't comfortable with sex. High-tech fertility technologies notwithstanding, a sufficiently hard penis is the first step in a sexual reproductive process that keeps our genes in circulation. As an impotent man, what do I have to offer?

I am disabled, an outsider. I am a backup goalie, sitting on the bench, watching the game being played by others with more strength and talent. I don't belong. I am probably the only guy at Drew's party who hasn't even desired to have sex in almost four years, although I soon stop calculating the length of the dry spell to avoid falling into an even deeper sexual depression.

In one sense, though, I do fit in. Like at least half the guys here, I am an actor—only I'm acting as if I have not a single neurosis, not an ounce of insecurity about my fear of getting intimate with a woman, about my subdued sex drive and, most of all, about my lame, impotent slag of penile tissue.

Finally. About time, Drew.

There you are, over there by the bar, ordering a drink. Oh, those cute dimples, that porcelain skin. And that smile, so gleaming, so white and pure and womanly. You're puffing on a Marlboro. After seeing what they have done to my dad, I hate cancer sticks, but I'm willing to make an exception for Drew Barrymore. Only you could make sucking on a lung tumor delivery device an act of sexual seductiveness.

I absolutely, positively must approach her. The validity of my manhood depends on it. If I don't go over to her right now and say hello and flirt and hit on her, then, well, I deserve to be the celibate freak that is this "Ken Baker from *People* magazine."

I am Man; Drew is Woman. This is a test of my manhood, and I must pass it.

But I will only fail, as always.

Stop it right there. Control your thoughts. Don't think. Zen Ken. Remember? Just like you did with hockey: Let it happen. Especially don't think

about how afraid you are of women, of failure; instead, think about those
quotes on courage that you've tacked up on your bedroom wall:

"You must do the thing you think you cannot do."
— ELEANOR ROOSEVELT

"Courage is resistance to fear, mastery of fear—not absence of fear."
— MARK TWAIN

"Don't be afraid to take a big step if one is indicated.
— DAVID LLOYD GEORGE

Empowered, I walk over to Drew.

Nonchalant. Devil-may-care swagger. A take-her-or-leave-her gaze.

Chest out. Shoulders back. Stomach clenched tight. Marlboro rugged. Confident. Just what the girls want. Be the man. *I can do this.*

"Ken?" Drew says, tapping my shoulder. "Hey, there."

"Oh, hey, Drew. I didn't recognize you with your hair up like that."

"Yeah . . . well. Do you like it?"

"Uh-huh. Definitely. It's . . . it's very cute."

"I'm so psyched you could make it. I really enjoyed chatting with you the other day—"

"So did—"

"—and it's really—"

"—I."

"—nice to see you here tonight."

She sips from her glass, probably annoyed at my eager interrupting of her sweet voice.

"I have to admit, though," she continues, "the whole idea of your article is pretty embarrassing."

"Why?"

Cradling her drink, she explains, "Because how can someone say I am one of the quote-unquote fifty most beautiful people in the world? I mean, what qualities must a person possess to be on a list like that?"

"A lot of qualities, Drew."

"Like what?"

"Well, for starters, they should be sensual."

"Ooooh." Her blue eyes expand like perfectly rounded seas. "I like that word. It is *such* a great word. You know, I've recently started reading the dictionary just so I can learn new words—I am self-educated, not having gone to college or anything—and the word *sensual* . . . wow, that's just an excellent word."

"Yeah," I say. "To be sensual is so much more attractive than just being sexual."

Her eyes now are so big and blue I could dock a ship in them. She's sipping, she's puffing her smoke, she's smiling!

"I like writers," she says. "Words are, like, their paint."

Is she hitting on me? Or am I just fantasizing this? Is this meeting going to end as tragically as all of mine do, just like the one last month with Linda, that girl from Chicago, whom I had met at a Beverly Hills party brimming with good-looking TV faces. In town for a couple days, she gave me her hotel number. Gambling that even if my penis didn't get hard I wouldn't have to see her for the rest of my life, I phoned her, we dined in Venice, walked on the beach. Later on, we strolled through downtown Santa Monica. Her blond hair blew in the warm Pacific breeze. A kiss under the moon. A quick drive to my apartment. The make-out session on the couch. Her attack on my zipper, her tongue's lustful assault on my limp penis. Her confusion, my devastation, my embarrassment, my fruitless attempt at manually jump-starting my supposed sex organ. Date over. Night over. If I had had the balls and the gun to do it: game over.

My face, my lips. Drew's face, her lips. I'm not even a foot from her; I can smell her sweet perfume.

What do I do if Drew likes me? What if she invites me back to her house? What if we start kissing, touching each other, tearing off each other's clothes? What then? Will my dick get hard, or will it—as usual—dangle lifelessly between my legs? Now, that would be a fucking disaster. I would rather never try to have sex with Drew Barrymore than to try and then fail to have sex with Drew Barrymore because I couldn't get it up. Now what, Eleanor, Mark and David?

"Drew, it-it-it was great seeing you," I stutter.

Seventy degrees? It's gotta be at least a hundred on this patio.

"Um, thanks for inviting me," I say with a quiver. "But, uh, I really gotta be going now. Maybe I'll see you around again later."

"Uh, sure, no problem. Sorry you have to leave so soon, but . . ."

"Me too."

" . . . thanks for coming, Ken. It was really nice to see you."

At the curb, I hand the valet guy my ticket. Sweat blotches circle the armpits of my shirt. I wipe streaks of sweat from my forehead as I hustle into my car. I am light-headed and sick to my flabby fucking tits and stomach.

As I am about to pull away, Kelly opens the door and plops down beside me.

"Why you leaving?" he asks. "Drew was so into you. Are you fucking crazy?"

The answer—although I don't yet know it and just think I am psychosexually inept—lies somewhere between yes and no.

Kelly gets in and I steer us back to our Brentwood apartment, barreling down the passing lane on Sunset Boulevard—past the hard-body models on the billboards, past the hookers advertising their product in high heels, past the black-clad Gen-X'ers waiting in line outside of the Viper Room, past Drew's office.

My chest feels tight and sore, perhaps from the jagged crack that has just split my heart in two.

And, suddenly, I feel sixteen again.

(PROLACTIN LEVEL: 200 NG/ML)

I'm snuggling in bed with my girlfriend, enjoying the hockey game, when the commercial pops on: *Got the Buffalo blahs? Come visit Toronto's glamorous Sutton Place hotel for a romantic get-away weekend!*

It's nose-hair–freezing cold outside. And, as usual, our furnace is on the fritz. It's a night in western New York State in winter, when the shadows grow long at two in the afternoon and when my dad chisels ice off the windshield of our rusted, American-make jalopy and grumbles, "It's colder than a Siberian nun's tit out here."

I don't know where that might fit on the Fahrenheit or Celsius scales, but I do know that Jenny's runny nose feels cold to the touch tonight, even though she and I lie fully clothed under at least two blankets, one of which is electric. On January nights like these, with relentless bands of "lake effect" snow blanketing the frosted tundra, the television doesn't only provide entertainment, it's a heat source.

As the commercial continues, Jenny's brown eyes crack wide open like walnuts and her ears perk like Spock's. Her dark, thick hash of eyebrows curve downward like crawling caterpillars, and her pale, freckled face contorts so much I think she either has been startled by the cheesy commercial or her acid-washed jeans are clinging too tightly to her nineteen-year-old body.

My normally subdued girlfriend fixes a laser stare at the screen, listening to the British-accented announcer tout the hotel's *deluxe accommodations* and *breathtaking views of the Toronto skyline.* This voice-over montage, set to mellifluous Muzak right out of a Holiday Inn elevator, is accompanied by shots of a happy couple prancing hand in hand through the hotel's opulent lobby, flirting beside candlelight, toasting glasses while submerged in a bubble bath. *All this . . . for just $89.99 a night!*

The low-budget commercial—which, by the way, is only getting in the way of my hockey game—finally ends, and Ted Darling, the sonorous "Voice of the Buffalo Sabres," bellows his play-by-play commentary from my black-and-white's tiny speaker.

Jenny, however, is no longer interested in watching the boxing match disguised as an ice hockey game. Instead she wants to play tongue hockey, heretofore the only game we play when cuddling under the blankets. So Jenny pulls my head toward her lips. A minute later she comes up for air and makes an announcement: "Let's have sex."

"Right now?" I ask. "Right here?"

"No, silly."

She points at the flickering TV and adds, "We should go to Toronto and stay in that nice hotel for your birthday."

As huge a piece of news as this is, I still have trouble processing what has just transpired in my frigid bedroom. So let me get this straight: For the first time in our four-month relationship, my normally nunnish girlfriend is actually suggesting—no, she's practically *demanding*—that we have sex. In a foreign city! At a world-class hotel where champagne-sipping white people take bubble baths!

Jenny rips the stack of blankets off her body and, clutching each of my shoulders, emphasizes her every syllable as if I am one of Jerry's kids.

"We—are—going—to—have—SEX," she romper-rooms me.

I can't contract the throat muscles necessary for locution. Cotton mouth has disabled me.

Jenny's caterpillars furrow. "So what do you think?" she asks.

What do I *think*? It's January 1987, I've never had sex with anything other than my right hand, I'm a dude, and my seventeenth birthday won't arrive until April eighteenth, which—duh—is over four months away. *I should have gotten this over with a long time ago!* is what I think. Everyone, it seems, is having sex but me. It is time.

But I don't say this to her. I don't want to pressure Jenny, nor am I prepared to drop my long johns and do "it" right now, on the spot, upon her command like a ball-chasing Labrador retriever. I may be a virgin, but, well . . . I'm a *nervous* virgin. That means I first must get some ducks in a row: (a) Since I have never bought a condom, I will have to embarrass myself in front of the druggist and buy some Trojans, and (b) having never done it, I don't really know how to perform sexual intercourse. It's not like anyone has ever told me: "Okay, Kenny, you stick your thing into here, then move like so . . ."

I don't dare show Jenny my sexual insecurity, though. I fear she may change her mind and decide not to do it, which could mean yet another year or two of being a virgin, and I cannot enter college without having had sex. That's unheard-of!

Our upcoming Canadian sexpedition is not only going to be about losing my virginity. No way, man. Sexual intercourse, that biological feat of penile performance, will—with an official testosterone stamp of approval—mark my entry into manhood.

Suddenly my room doesn't seem so cold anymore; actually, I already feel a little more manly.

The irony isn't lost on me later that night when, after Jenny has fallen asleep, I watch a player fire a wrist shot past a goalie's outstretched arm, which prompts Ted Darling to verbally ejaculate: "He shoots, he scoooooores!"

I've always envied how girls can instantly know they have become—biologically, at least—young women, while for boys sexual maturation, I think, is much more mysterious. At the onset of puberty, most girls have breasts and have begun menstruating; consequently most of them are able to deduce that they have reached sexual maturity: You know, they can have sex and get pregnant. We boys, however, don't receive such clear and present signs that our bodies have become capable of sexual reproduction.

My physical development was more gradual, mysterious and thus, I believe, more anxiety-inducing. Around age thirteen, I noticed that pubic hair had started growing in strange places. Then my voice began deepening, which was preceded by a girlish squealing before anything sounding remotely manly vibrated from my vocal cords. My body lost some of the baby fat it had been carrying around. And then one night, perhaps a year or two after these manly changes began, I ejaculated for the first time, scaring and amusing me at the same time. I took this to mean that my gun had been loaded, and now I could truly begin obsessing about firing my weapon (and, as my friends, my brothers and my father had led me to believe, it would be a *war*).

I can only assume that fueling this obsession—with the high school neighbor-girl who likes to lay out in her bikini, with the cheerleaders and the girls on the school soccer team, with every girl in that J. Geils Band "Centerfold" video on MTV—was a sharp rise in the amount of testosterone, which starts coursing through the veins of most boys before they turn fifteen.

Testosterone, according to my health teacher, is the hormone that, chemically, most makes a man a man. Doctors call it "the big T," because it does all the big male stuff: It grows hair, builds muscle, produces testes and penises, deepens voices and stimulates the kind of aggressive behavior that inspires perhaps nine out of ten high school cafeteria brawls and just about every fight my father picks with my mom. In addition to turning males into grunting fools on occasion, it woos women and turns boys into men. Last but certainly not least, the big T also allows males to have erections.

Ever since I possessed enough pelvic coordination to spell my name in the snow, I have been awaiting sex—the Big Kahuna of teenage-boy life. I have already done the other guy things that are expected of me:

Machismo: I *never* cry in public; when provoked, I have punched kids in their snotty little faces; and, perhaps most evidentiary, I am a hockey player.

Not-gayness: I have called non-macho guys "fags" (mostly so my friends won't think I'm gay); I talk about how much I love "tits" and "asses" and "pussies" and, when other guys brag about what they want to do with these body parts, I pitch in with my own immature chest-thumping.

Stoicism: I rarely show pain or weakness of any kind. Like the commercials say, *No pain, no gain. Never let them see you sweat. Just do it!*

Despite my impressive list of gender-proving accomplishments, I'm fully aware that I have not crossed into manhood, because I haven't proven sexual ability. When I do this, though, I will definitely become a man. I'm fully aware that this manhood-proving business, Buffalo style, is pretty absurd stuff. History teachers have taught me about feminism—universal suffrage, Susan B. Anthony, the ERA. Plus, I grew up watching *The Phil Donahue Show* with my mom. Even so, that doesn't make it any easier for me to rise above its stupidity.

As a teenager, though, none of that societal evolution, *vis-à-vis* gender equality, seems to matter much to the guys I know. Most of them hail from families where moms still stay at home and dads work and work and work and watch sports on the TV and mow the lawn on weekends and drink Genny Cream Ale and then maybe go bowling on Friday nights at Leisure Land. Women generally don't rock the boat; men don't exactly encourage them to even climb aboard the boat. In fact, most of our neighbors—the steel-plant workers, the truckers, the bartenders, the cops, the uniformed workers with their names printed in cursive over their breast pockets—cling to traditional gender roles like icicles to a gutter.

I live in the easternmost notch of the Great Lakes rust belt, just south of Buffalo, New York, where there isn't much socially liberal dogma to speak of, especially when it comes to male-female relations.

In my own family life I have only a handful memories of my dad even kissing my mother, let alone Romeoing her. Sure, my parents would go out for dinner a couple of times a year, leaving me and my four brothers with a baby-sitter. Then they'd return a few hours later, a few drinks in them, holding hands, and disappear into the bedroom.

I may be intimidated by my pubescent transition into adulthood, especially when it comes to hanging out with sexually experienced kids my own age or listening to my older brother Keith tell me, "You don't know shit until you get laid."

The ice rink, however, is my sanctuary, a 200-by-85-foot sheet of placid ice enclosed by Gothic-cathedral-strong boards and Plexiglas, where I can escape from the real world, where I can find peace from the pressure of my dad always pushing me to play better, of my brothers driving me to act older than I am, of having to lose my virginity. Behind my goalie mask, I'm whoever I dream myself to be. On the ice, I can transcend my off-ice insecurities about always feeling one step behind everyone else on the sexual maturation chart. I can be a warrior, a hero. The slippery ice, the bulky equipment—they serve as equalizers, allowing me to play as tough as the tough guys, to masquerade as a cocky sonofabitch, even though I am not. I chop the backs of player's legs with my heavy stick. I make lighting-fast glove saves. I send players to their bench shaking their heads at their inability to score on me. It feels good. Someday hockey will be my ticket to a better life, but it already is an escape from the life I know.

Because Jenny isn't exactly a sexual dynamo either, I have been able to make it to sixteen without having sex, which, while a burden, is also relief because I believe it is the most frightening of the teenage rites of passage.

Jenny fears getting pregnant as much—or more—than I do, which is a lot. My father, who often says he probably wouldn't have married my mom if she hadn't gotten pregnant with my oldest brother, Kevin, has always told me that women can "fuck up your life." Although she is two years older than me, is a college freshman and has already slept with her two previous boyfriends, Jenny says she feels she was more used than loved by those guys. Jenny dreams of marrying a nice guy like me and becoming a clinical psychologist who helps people with their problems. To do this, she reasons, she must have as few problems herself as possible. Pregnancy would be a problem.

Jenny doesn't want to take birth control, because she's absolutely convinced it will only encourage us to have more sex, which she just *knows* will get her pregnant. "You know," she says, "the pill is only ninety-nine percent effective."

In adhering to her strict evacuation-from-Buffalo plan, during the week she earns straight A's at the local state college and on weekends deep-fries chicken wings and makes subs and bakes pizzas at Molino's. Meanwhile, she despises the pallid, hairsprayed young women with no apparent aspirations beyond mere existence who lurk around town like the bloated, chalk-white corpses in *Night of the Living Dead.* These sorrowful yet plentiful Buffalonians are reminders of her fate should she have the misfortune of getting pregnant.

Jenny constantly is telling me she loves me, but in the next breath she laments living in Buffalo, my hometown, which she views as, basically, a prison with snow drifts and small-mindedness for bars. Driving past dormant smokestacks, abandoned steel mills and rusty railroad tracks overgrown with weeds, she often wonders aloud, "Why would anyone choose to live here? If they know there are warmer, nicer places to live—with jobs, with sun, with actual fun things to do—why don't they move there?"

I really can't blame her. In 1970, the year I was born, the city of

Buffalo prospered on the heels of its robust blue-collar economy. It had 463,000 residents, making it the nation's twenty-eighth largest urban area. By 1990, the city's population had shrunk to 328,000, meaning in my lifetime the city had lost nearly a third of its population. Moreover, the city had physically shrunk, from 41.3 square miles to 40.6.

One of the worst economic blows came in the early 1980's when the region's largest private employer, the Bethlehem Steel Corporation, which in its mid-century heyday forged steel for the nation's biggest construction projects, from Manhattan skyscrapers to major bridge projects throughout the East, laid off nearly all of its employees. It now sits by polluted Lake Erie in apocalyptic desertion. Unemployment has surged, to over twenty percent in some of the hardest-hit neighborhoods.

Adding psychological insult to economic injury, despite nearly twenty seasons of trying, the Buffalo Bills, the Incredible Shrinking City's crown cultural jewel, still have not won the Super Bowl. Lately some of the city's own loyal inhabitants, who long ago dubbed Buffalo "The City of Good Neighbors," have started calling it "The Mistake on the Lake."

Clearly, things are getting grim. It's as if people suddenly have started realizing it isn't a good thing for "down south" to mean Pennsylvania; that keeping their snow tires on until May isn't exactly ideal; that when they want to put down residents of another city to make themselves feel better, after thinking long and hard for a less desirable locale, they can only come up with Cleveland or Rochester.

My hometown of Hamburg (population 52,000) sits about ten miles downwind of Buffalo's brick smokestacks, which line the Lake Erie shoreline like sentinels guarding the city against warm weather. Hamburg is situated on the glacial flatlands that ring all of the Great Lakes. Hamburg is greener and generally more pleasant (in the summer, at least) than the decaying core city ten miles to the north. The town marks the beginning of Buffalo's southern suburbs. Roadside welcome signs proclaim it "The Gateway to the South Towns," but, really, it is a middle-class sprawl of fast-food joints, strip malls, chain retailers and cloned housing subdivisions where the dread of another harsh winter lingers like a barrel of benzene buried below Love Canal (the famously polluted neighborhood near Niagara Falls from which my town is also downwind).

Although it's a more family-friendly place to grow up (murders are extremely rare) than Buffalo, and it has a lot of trees (in the summer, at least), the town of Hamburg isn't exactly home to the country's best and brightest. That's a nice way of saying my town has its fair share of racist steelworkers and trailer-trash mamas still young enough to use Clearasil.

Hamburg can be the kind of place where one day you'll see a skinny sophomore sitting in trig class cracking her gum and twisting her hair, all girlie-like and stuff; then, maybe a year later, you see the same girl at the grocery store, obesely large and in charge with a drooling baby on her shoulder, purchasing two-for-ninety-nine-cents hot dogs and a stick of beef jerky with food stamps. "I'd rather die than live like that," Jenny grouses.

I really can't blame her.

Jenny is my first love, and I find her obsessive desire to leave Buffalo one of her most attractive traits, mostly because, in that respect, we are in total agreement. To make ourselves feel better about our geographic hardship, we will talk about how we are better than the underachieving losers around us, that we are destined for a greatness that is impossible to achieve in a city where an unspectacular NFL team is the most cherished cultural institution. Maybe we put down everyone around us just to build ourselves up. But my reasoning is that if it motivates us to move on to bigger, better, brighter places, then it's worth all the cynicism.

According to my master plan, I will enter the National Hockey League upon graduation. I have been a member of the U.S. Olympic hockey team development program since age fourteen. Every summer I fly out to the Olympic Training Center in Colorado Springs, where clipboard-clutching Team USA officials evaluate my skills. The nation's top players fire pucks at me at 100 mph; coaches videotape my on-ice moves and, later, study them in slow motion. Being invited to train at the center, the officials tell me, means I have a legitimate shot at making the 1992 Olympic ice hockey team, which has been my dream ever since I sat in the living room with Dad on a Saturday night in February 1980 and I saw my country defeat the Russians on its way to winning the gold medal.

Announcer: *Do you believe in miracles?*

Me: *I believe!*

The players on that team—Mike Eruzione, Jim Craig, Mike Ramsey—were regular guys from regular northern towns with regular dads. *I could be them.*

Some adolescent boys may receive their most influential sex education from teachers or doctors; a few may even learn about sex from their parents. But I'd bet most men-in-the-making learn from sex-ed. sources more like mine: movies, television, friends, porno magazines and rock stars. In fact, the first woman I ever see fully naked is Vanessa Williams in an issue of *Penthouse* that one of my brothers brought home one afternoon in 1984.

Among my earliest sexual influences is a perverted musician from Buffalo named "Dr. Dirty." His real name is John Valby. But that's too vanilla of a name for a performer whose parodies of American pop and folk songs make "Weird Al" Yankovich look like a Christian rock star.

I am first exposed to Dr. Dirty's hallowed discography at age twelve, while playing on a hockey team composed of potty-mouthed thirteen- and fourteen-year-old guys obsessed with sex and hockey— in that order.

It's around Christmas time as we sit on wood benches in the locker room lacing up our skates for practice. Quiet Riot, or some other hair-metal band, blares from the team's suitcase-size radio. (A decade from now, it will be chic for kids to own tiny radios, but at the moment a radio isn't cool unless it's the size of a small car and has more switches, levers and buttons than the cockpit of the Space Shuttle.) It's a few minutes before practice. Just as my teammates and I are ready to strap on our helmets and head for the ice, a player walks over to the mammoth tune box and ejects the tape. The guys begin yelling at the player to *put that fucking tape back in.*

The object of their scorn slips in another cassette and presses play.

At first, we think that the dweeb has put on sissified Christmas carols, since all we hear is a piano playing the melody of "Santa Claus Is Coming to Town." But then a male, off-key lounge singer bellows:

Santa's whore is comin' to town!

Dr. Ruth Westheimer might be at her peak of popularity, but my teammates instantly decide they prefer Dr. Dirty.

As high school graduation nears, I have grown increasingly concerned that if I don't clean my pipes *pronto* the guys may start questioning my adherence to the unwritten code of sexual behavior. Yeah, I spent the summer before my sophomore year making out with Sophie, a French foreign-exchange student who was living with a family down the street. I am going out with Jenny, but since I'm not Mr. Horny like most of the other guys, I am just as afraid of being a "faggot" as I am of being called one.

The source of my anxiety is that I simply can't understand why most of my friends use metaphors like exploding rockets and boiling pots to describe the urge they feel to have sex. The pressure to have sex is more of an external force (mostly fraternal and peer pressure) than an internal one bubbling from my loins. I don't sit around all day dreaming of naked girls undressing me. My friends talk about masturbation as if it's as much a part of their daily life as brushing their teeth. Tommy, Geoff, Mike and Rich brag about getting laid as if they had just found the cure for cancer. It such *a big deal.*

I may not be a sex maniac, but at least I am a romantic.

As corny as it sounds, Jenny and I can identify with the characters John Cougar Mellencamp sings about in "Jack and Diane." In fact, whenever that acoustic tune comes on the radio, we crank up the volume on her Ford's stereo and belt out car karaoke: *Little ditty, 'bout Jack and Diane . . . Two American kids growin' up in the heartland . . . Changes comin' around soon will make them women and men.*

Although we are in love, we still aren't having sex. "If we can love each other without having sex, then we will know we really are in love," Jenny has explained, usually as we lie in bed naked. My mind tells me that I have to get this sex thing over with, but my groin agrees with her. I really don't need to have sex. So I never pressure her. Instead, I assure her I am content with the occasional rub and a tug—for the time being, at least. "We've got a lifetime," I say. "I'm not in any rush."

The truth is (and I would never tell my hockey pals this) that it just isn't that difficult for me to abstain. First of all, Jenny's concerns in many ways only reinforce what my dad has been telling me for years about girls: "Don't knock one up. They'll ruin your life." That makes Jenny not only a celibate option but a safe one. The last thing I want to do is fuck up my life by creating Kenny Junior. And neither of us want—nor can pay for—Jenny to get an abortion if she got pregnant.

I feel like I should have sex only because everyone else my age seems to be making such a big deal out of it. My Hamlet-esque quandary—to do it, or not to do it—only grows more and more vexing as, one by one, my buddies proclaim their "pipe cleaning."

Guys on my hockey team have said they have dumped girls because they wouldn't go all the way. One fellow has even boasted that he kicked a girl out of his car one night because she wouldn't swallow. Most of them are probably lying in the way adolescent boys do about sex, but I don't know this. Since I believe them, it seems like all of my friends are having sex, my older brothers are having sex and hardly a

TV show or movie appears without people having sex. Message: Everyone is having sex. And so should I.

To ward off any of my friends calling me a homo, I emit as much machismo as possible. I wear my baseball cap backwards. I listen to hard-rock music, like Bon Jovi, Bryan Adams and ZZ Top. I wear the coolest acid- and stone-washed jeans my mom can afford and don the white high-top Converse sneakers with the red, fat laces untied at the top. I preemptively combat their calling my masculinity into question by concocting fictional sexual encounters, plagiarizing material from what I can cobble together from my older brothers and stories I've been hearing older guys tell in the locker room since I was ten years old. Now, or so my fledgling male ego rationalizes, all I need to do is turn my creative tales into equally titillating nonfiction.

Yet, behind all my bravado is the truth: My saccharine sex life, sadly, could appear uncensored on *The Facts of Life*. Jenny and I may make out on her parents' couch for several hours into the night, until my lips are sore and my testicles ache, but, still, we never have sex. It doesn't matter if my thirty-two-inch-waist jockey shorts lay crumpled around my ankles, she grabs my groping hand and breathlessly says, "No, not yet, Kenny."

Jenny fears that sexual intercourse will turn what she believes is our "special" relationship into nothing more than the kind of hedonistic humping that everyone else is doing. She thinks most relationships are about using, not loving, each other. Although I wouldn't admit this to my friends, I agree with Jenny, and even though I can't wait to get the having-sex thing over with, I really don't mind keeping it in my pants.

And the reason why I am not unzipping my pants enthusiastically to end my dry run is that if I have learned anything, it's that reproducing, if not planned, can make for one big unhappy family of parents and children—in my case, two incompatible parents and four male monsters.

"Kevin, uh, Keith, Kyle, uh . . . K-K-K-Kenny! Come in here, will ya?"

Penciling in newspaper crossword puzzles while sunken in her musty La-Z-Boy recliner, Gramma often will run through each of my brothers' names before finally calling me to the living room to seek my help on a particularly troubling puzzle query.

I am the fourth of the five Baker children—all boys—and for no apparent reason other than my parents, Larry and Marcia (go figure), like the eleventh letter of the alphabet, they have given each of us names starting with K. As a youngster, I learned that our overabundant K's confuses my mother's mom. Gramma is a caring woman who bakes me cornbread and makes fat omelets packed with slabs of Velveeta in her iron skillet, but she has been borderline senile and hunchbacked for as long as I've known her. Unable to keep us "rascals" straight, Gramma ends up hiding a cheat sheet next to her chair, stuffed in her eyeglass case. An investigative journalist in the making, one day I find a piece of notebook paper, on which what appears to be her attempt at listing us Baker boys in the correct birth order:

Kevin ✓

Keith ✓

Kyle ✓

Kenny ✓

Kris ✓

Kevin, the oldest of the Baker boys, is the inaugural draftee into Dad's manhood military. Unfortunately—for Kevin and Dad—Kevin isn't a good soldier. Kevin hates Dad's hard-ass parenting methods. In the summertime, I often watch Dad play catch with his eldest son till dusk, coaching him on his baseball technique. How to pitch a curveball, a sinker, a knuckleball. How to field a pop fly. How to pick off a guy on first base. How to steal second.

Dad sometimes teaches with great patience. I feel then like we are one of those happy TV families where the dad is a kindhearted, unconditionally loving gentleman and the sons are compliant and respectful. Just as often, though, Dad's coaching sessions degenerate into a shouting match between two hardheads.

One time Kevin, who was twelve, complained that his throwing arm was getting sore.

"Let's take a break, Dad," Kevin whined.

Dad has always hated whiners. He rocketed the ball even harder into Kevin's glove, punctuating his bullet by saying, "I've been working my ass off all day, and I'm not tired."

Kevin dropped his mitt down and stomped toward the house. Dad chased after Kevin, shouting into his face, "Quitter!"

Kevin—surprise, surprise—soon goes AWOL from my father's army and drops out of organized sports altogether. He decides he instead wants to be the lead guitarist in a rock band. Ted Nugent, not Ted Williams, becomes his idol.

Kevin takes me and Kyle to a Kiss concert at the dry-ice–shrouded Buffalo Memorial Auditorium. As Gene Simmons is spitting blood onto the audience, I sneak a glimpse of Kevin puffing on a joint and handing it back to a girl sitting in the row in front of us. *Holy . . . shit! That is so illegal.* "If you breathe in deep," he shouts to me over the music, "you can catch a contact buzz." I am nine years old.

Kevin has spent his teens growing things—his hair, midway down his back, and a forest of marijuana plants in his basement closet under a heat lamp, just as he read about it in *High Times*. Dad never finds the plants or the magazines. Kevin is lucky: Dad probably would cut his balls off if he ever knew that his son was growing the best copycat Colombian in western New York right below his bedroom.

Keith, who is christened Dad's favorite until he follows in what Dad calls Kevin's "druggie footsteps" in his early teens and starts having sex, smoking pot, dropping acid and skipping school, ends up officially on Dad's so-called shit list the year he quits baseball.

Kyle, a year older than me, possesses a personality 180 degrees opposite of mine. Despite being a year apart, we have very different relationships with our father.

Dad has never been Mr. Affection with any of us. Never once do I remember him saying "I love you" to me or my brothers. We never got a good-night peck on the cheek (that was Mom's job). Out of our hundreds of childhood photos, never is Dad pictured hugging or kissing any of us. In fact, the most intimate photo is from when I am three, standing shirtless on the beach holding a fishing pole after having just caught a fish. Dad is resting his arm on me, his wrist awkwardly curled around my upper arm as if he's hugging Pig Pen.

The only time I've ever heard of Dad changing a diaper was when he had to baby-sit me and Kyle, who was about two years old. As the family legend goes, my mother was away for a day and Dad was watching us. Shit started leaking from Kyle's diaper as he butt-bounced down the carpeted stairs from the second floor to the living room. Dad had to change Kyle's diaper and wipe up the mess, probably for the first time in his married life. He shouted at Kyle so much that day that, according to both my mom and dad, Kyle did not talk to my dad for about the next five years.

As pre-kindergartners, although Kyle is the sweetest kid on the block, he is as clumsy, shy and introverted as I am active, friendly and outgoing. Kyle loves animals. He enjoys catching tadpoles and watching them grow into frogs, and likes trapping turtles. He's got a gentle touch with nature; I'd rather play with a ball.

Growing up, the single greatest thing Kyle and I have in common is our white-blond hair. When I'm four, Kyle, carrying his perpetual hangdog expression, mopes around the neighborhood so quietly that I feel obligated to speak on behalf of the Baker boy most everyone assumes is a deaf-mute.

"Would you like some soup?" our neighbor, Mrs. Parker, asks Kyle one day during a visit. He gives his usual response to strangers' inquiries: He sucks his thumb and stares down at his untied sneakers.

Usually, older brothers protect their younger brothers. Standing a little over half his height, though, it is I who looks out for my older brother, mostly because I hate it when people think he's retarded. "Kyle doesn't like soup," I protectively tell Mrs. Parker. "He likes cheese sandwiches." Mimicking what I had heard Mom explain to other adults, I add, "He's just shy."

My mother tries like hell to turn Kyle into a walking, talking human being like the rest of his extroverted brothers. And Dad? He shows love the only way he really knows how: He makes Kyle play sports.

First up, baseball. Bigger than the other kids, Kyle initially can slug the ball over the outfield fence and throw harder than anyone. But by the time he turns twelve—when other kids get quicker and more competitive—Kyle, who had earned the nickname "gentle giant," lags behind and soon quits.

The same thing happens with hockey. After I begin playing at age eight, Dad signs up Kyle for the beginners' clinic. While I whiz around the rink, skating and stickhandling circles around opponents, Kyle glides along the boards, ankles bent inward, simply struggling not to crack his tailbone when he crashes to the ice like a sack of bricks. Dad probably thinks that lavishing me with praise will motivate Kyle to get better. It doesn't. Kyle quits after just one season.

Kyle stays inside most of the time, reading sci-fi novels, watching *Star Trek* and sketching apocalyptic cartoons in his sketchbook. He's an earnest, well-behaved kid; yet, soon Dad all but stops paying attention to Kyle.

While playing in the side yard one afternoon, I overhear my parents arguing in the kitchen.

"You can say all you want, Marcia, but I think your kid's a gaylord," I hear Dad say, talking so loudly I wonder if he wants Kyle to hear him. "He sits up in his room all day long playing with himself like a freakin' fairy."

Mom may not enjoy confrontation as much as Dad does, but, much to my father's consternation, she certainly doesn't play the role of obedient housewife very well. It helps that she is only an inch shorter than my dad; when they argue, she can go eye-to-eye.

"Larry," Mom whispers, "just because he doesn't like sports doesn't mean he's gay. He has different interests than the other kids. He needs your support. Did you ever think that maybe he's alone up there right now because you're not with him?"

The argument ends like most of theirs: Dad lets out a condescending grunt and storms out of the house and peels out of the driveway, leaving behind a fresh scent of burnt rubber and my mother crying at the kitchen table.

Mom signs Kyle up for private art lessons, which gives him an expressive outlet but further alienates him from my dad, who, of course, says, "Art is for faggots."

The less attention he gives Kyle, the more Kris, the baby of the family, and I receive. It's not exactly a shock that by age fifteen Kyle becomes a stoner (following in the freak footsteps of elders Kevin and Keith) and wants nothing to do with Dad and everything to do with enjoying the feel-good escapism of Mary Jane and Jerry Garcia's jams. A week after Kyle graduates from high school, he leaves Buffalo to travel with the Grateful Dead for a summer. Dad calls him a "loser."

Dad constantly reminds me that, at any time, I, too—with enough stupidity—can end up on his shit list. Whenever I do something remotely bad, like stay out past my nine-o'clock curfew or get a D in math or skip hockey or baseball practice, my father makes sure to remind me that the minute I start misbehaving—or "fucking up"—he will write me off as well.

Dad doesn't so much as say it, but I realize there are several things I can do to lose my father's respect. I can quit hockey, do drugs or—and I surmise this is the worst thing because it hits so close to home for him—knock up a girl.

Kevin and Keith haven't been the best of role models for me in that department. I have grown up watching my two oldest brothers love 'em and leave 'em—often in the span of one night, without even leaving their basement bedrooms. Their late-night trysts usually involve sneaking a girl into the basement sometime after midnight. As my dad, exhausted by carrying three hundred pounds on his five-foot-eight frame, snores upstairs—their green light that the coast is clear—the two young lovers will tiptoe down the stairs, their steps in such perfect sync that they sound like one person walking.

Though two years younger than Kevin, Keith beats our older brother on the sexual conquest count by a margin of at least five to one. Keith is such a Casanova that Kevin has nicknamed him Fith, which stands for "Fucking In The House."

I know my older brothers' sexual scorecard so well because I sometimes gingerly tiptoe downstairs a few minutes after I hear Keith or Kevin, and usually some cute girl, creaking down the wooden staircase to the basement, where I then secretly listen to them through one of their padlocked bedroom doors. When they don't crank up their Van Halen, Aerosmith or Grateful Dead tapes, I can hear the girl groaning and grunting as if she's pumping iron, leaving me wondering just what my brother is doing in there. I have an idea, albeit a vague one.

I grow adept at hiding in the dark, behind an old couch that sits wedged into a corner of the basement, listening surreptitiously to their festivities. Copying a tactic I saw on either *Three's Company* or *The*

Brady Bunch, I sometimes place a drinking glass between my ear and the bedroom wall to amplify the noise coming from inside their bedrooms. It works like a charm.

My spying goes undetected for months until one night, thanks to our hyperactive black Labrador, Rocky Balboa, as in the cinematic boxer. Rocky doesn't like closed doors; he yelps and scratches mightily until you open it and let him in. And whenever Rocky hears what to him sounds like someone in pain or trouble, he faithfully trots over and offers an ambulatory paw and tongue. I know this is a sweet quality, and I usually appreciate his adorable doggie demeanor, but this time I can do without the canine's caring heart.

Freaked out after hearing one of Fith's girlfriends moaning, Rocky won't stop barking and scratching on the bedroom door.

"Shhh, Rocky, shhh," I whisper from behind the couch. "Quiet, boy. C'mere."

Damn dog.

Shirtless and sweating, Keith swings open his door and shoos Rocky away with a swift kick to the doggie ribs. The last thing Keith wants is for Rocky to wake Dad. So Keith grips shut Rocky's mouth and kicks him again, right in the doggie ribs.

As Rocky yelps, I huddle red-faced behind the couch, holding my breath, hoping Keith won't give *me* the Rocky treatment. Just then good ol' Rocky gallops over to my shadowy hiding spot and pokes his nose behind the couch and starts licking me. My cheeks now blue, I have no choice but to blow a loud exhale.

Busted.

Keith has what a psychologist might call "anger-management issues." His angst probably has something to do with the rest of us pointing out that he is the only one of the five Baker boys who has our dad's thick black hair and reddish-brown skin, a genetic remnant of my father's paternal grandmother, who was a tribal member of the Cherokee Nation. We all—even Keith—have our dad's high cheekbones and straw-straight hair. But while Kevin, Kyle, Kris and myself are blond and pale (thanks to our mom's Irish and Polish heritage), only Keith has the skin tone and dark hair of our dad. We like to remind Keith of his conspicuously Native American heritage, calling him "Indian Boy," which only fans the flames of his already flammable temper.

Blame it on our politically incorrect epithets, blame it on years of his being subjected to our dad's equally volatile temper or blame it on the closed-fist diplomacy of his big brother, Kevin, who has bullied Keith ever since their preschool fights over Tonka toys. Whatever its cause, Keith possesses a temper that, judging from the bestial look in his brown eyes, he is two seconds away from unleashing on me.

"What THE FUCK are you doing?" he says mounding the chest of my T-shirt into his hand. He lifts me off the floor, letting my legs dangle like a rag doll.

"I was just looking for something," I say, guilty as sin, scared as shit.

"Yeah, right," he says. "You were spying on me, you fuckin' homo."

Deeming past experience an accurate indicator of future events, I conclude that Keith plans to box my ears (which entails him simultaneously whacking my ears as if my head were a mosquito), or he is about to hold me in a Hulk Hogan headlock until I either faint or tearfully promise to never spy on him again. (Keith used to take twisted pleasure in lifting me up by the elastic of my underwear, so I started not wearing any, thus thwarting his patented "ball-busters.")

Before Keith can unleash his torture of choice, I rapidly scan my brain's directory for last-ditch pleas, and . . . *voilà!* I come up with the one and only verbal defense that can stop this bully in his fuming tracks.

"If you hit me, I'll tell Dad you always sneak girls down here."

He clenches his teeth. "No, you won't. Y'know why?"—he wrinkles his nose like a pit bull—" 'Cause then I'll kick your white ass, that's why."

"I don't care," I bluff. "I'll go wake him up right now and tell him."

I know that Keith, four years older and at least forty pounds heavier than me, can't risk having Dad find out about his in-house humping. He lets go of my shirt and slams me against the cellar wall, pursing his lips and exhaling his beer breath into my sweating face. But he doesn't box my ears, yank a ball-buster or place my skull in a death grip. I smell victory.

"All right. Fine. But if you say something, *anything*, to Dad"—he stops and re-grabs my shirt, which has torn at the neck—"I'll kick your ass."

I head for the stairs before he changes his mind. Halfway to the top, safely out of his reach, I muster the courage to shout, "Indian boy!"

Glaring up the stairs at me, Keith grunts, "KAK!"

KAK stands for Kiss Ass Kenny. When not calling me Little Shit, my charming brothers call me KAK for short. I've earned the acronym by, in the words of my brothers, being a "brown-noser," a "suck-up," a "momma's boy," and an all-around parental "ass-kisser," which is the primary etymology of KAK.

Mom penned in my baby book, "Kenny is a cutie—Daddy's shadow," when I was three years old. Ever since then, I've always shared a close bond with my father, viewing him as nothing short of God. I enjoy getting more attention than my other four brothers. I have come to crave it. That's why when Dad tells me to take out the garbage, I enthusiastically reply, "No problem, sir!" When Mom, standing with her hands-on-hips, complains that we're all a bunch of slobs who never clean up after themselves, I roll the vacuum cleaner out of the closet and suck up the mud clumps, the stale potato chip flakes, the pot seeds—basically, all the detritus of my brothers' various irresponsible activities. When Dad wants us home by nine o'clock, I make sure I'm home watching the cleavage-revealing country girls on *Hee Haw* (if it's a Saturday) with Dad in the living room at eight; if my brothers stay out past nine, thus infuriating Dad, then I will inform him exactly where they all are and what substances they were ingesting and/or inhaling the last time I saw them.

Sometimes I deserve their taunting; still, I hate the KAK nickname more than I hate Jerry Garcia, Kevin's and Keith's heroin-addicted hero. But I don't let them know how much their words hurt me. I can't show weakness. I learned early on that the more I let my brothers bully me, the more they will torment me. That means whenever they entertain themselves by, say, locking me in a closet, I just lie down and nap until they get bored and let me out. Whenever they pin me down and singe my hair with a Bic lighter—you know, just for kicks—I spit at them in defiance, trying my damnedest not to cry. Whenever they knuckle-punch my arm, I flick them the finger and run away, then hide in my bedroom and bawl my eyes out, watching, as if through a time-lapse camera lens, a red spot on my arm morph into a blue-green bruise. No one has to tell me to be tough and act like a man; I know I have to.

At age ten, I'm a chubby kid, with pipe cleaners for arms, sloping shoulders and a paunch that gives me the overall shape of a bowling pin. Safe to say, it's an unimpressive physique.

Other kids notice my plumpness, and as kids often do, they try to make fun of me for it. *Try* being the optimal word. For example, I remember when Tyler, a wily speed-demon of a kid in my fourth-grade gym class, shouted across the asphalt playground, "Hey, Chugalug!" because, during a game of kickball, I had been running with all the grace and speed of a sumo wrestler. I responded to Tyler with the form of diplomacy my brothers had taught me to practice: I calmly walked over to Tyler, smiled and, when he was least expecting it, punched him in the gut. I was suspended from school for the rest of the day, but at least Tyler never called me Chugalug again.

Although such bullying might work against pip-squeaks, it can't defend me against a couple of older brothers who are bigger, faster and stronger. When Kevin turns fifteen (and I'm nine) he weighs close to two hundred pounds. Dad likes to say Kevin is "built like a brick shithouse." Keith, meanwhile, lifts weights in his makeshift Muscle Beach, a corner in our basement rec room, for hours on end. He curls dumbbells until his biceps bulge and his long black hair sticks to his shoulders. "Curls for girls," he says, standing before a mirror.

He takes off his shirt. Sweat traces down his V-shaped back.

I grab a couple of five-pounders and copycat-curl them, losing my balance.

Mid-grunt, Keith glances over and quips, "Nice try, KAK."

I possess fightin' words, if not muscularity. I tell my brotherly tyrants that KAK is an acronym for *Kick* Ass Kenny, which I hope will stymie them because I high-mindedly assume they don't know what *acronym* means. It doesn't matter; they still abuse me.

Mom makes me feel better. She says my brothers are just jealous because Dad brags to everyone about my hockey talent and how I am generally "a good kid" who someday is going to make something of himself. My brotherly relations don't improve, however, when Dad starts spending most of his free time (when he isn't working at his printing shop, sleeping or watching TV) with me, which bothers my brothers, who, like me, were raised by our father to not show pain—be it emotional or physical. As Dad says, "Never let them see you cry."

I perfect the role of Kiss Ass Kenny, playing the Good Son, balancing out the badness of my older brothers.

In so doing I suppress my desire to party, have friends and, well, sometimes be bad just for the sake of being bad. Few kids want to disappoint their fathers. But the stakes are doubly high for me, because Dad is always reminding me that Kris and I represent his last hopes for a son who will achieve the athletic stardom that he never did due to his mom and dad being "a couple of rednecks."

Mom's always trying to explain to my father that there are more effective ways to get us to do things he wants than through profane threats, mind games and physical intimidation. It's no use, though.

Dad doesn't want to be a jerk. But his version of parenthood is one he learned from his own parents. He hails from a family whose effect on him—and, to varying degrees, on me and my four brothers—is depressingly textbook.

Six years after being born in Washington, DC, in May of 1943, Lawrence Leon Baker's parents divorced. His mother, Phyllis, a high school dropout turned waitress, took custody of Dad's younger brother and sister and moved to Silver Creek, a sleepy village about thirty miles south of Buffalo on the rocky shores of Lake Erie. "Little Larry," meanwhile, stayed in Maryland with his dad, Wally, who had quickly remarried a woman named Margie.

Wally worked as a bail bondsman in Maryland's Prince George's County, which saw its fair share of spillover crime from the seedier neighborhoods of the nation's capital, a few miles to the west. Wally loaned cash to criminals at inflated interest rates, then bullied them to pay up when they didn't repay their debt in a timely fashion.

By night, as my Dad proudly tells us, Wally ("a real ladies' man") tried to hump anything that moved. This, in my view, made Wally far from the model husband and father. On top of his extracurricular activities, Wally never played catch with my dad, never took him to the movies, never showed him much affection at all. If he did anything, Wally, an absentee father before there was a name for such deadbeats, unknowingly was motivating my father to pay more attention to his kids. Problem is, Wally didn't show him how to express love while giving that attention.

While Wally didn't get to know his son Larry that well, he did get to know a lot of hookers after bailing them out of jail. His dubiously benevolent acts of emancipation also earned him a few favors from his jailed ladies of the night—debts that, according to family legend, Wally gladly collected.

Understandably, Wally's extracurricular activity didn't bode well for a happy marriage with Margie; when not shouting at his father, Margie would beat Larry with a leather belt, often till his back bled. When he was thirteen, my father visited his mother in Silver Creek for a summer vacation. She saw the marks on his back and refused to let him return to Washington.

By the time my parents began dating at Silver Creek High School, Dad was one of the "bad boys" who strutted down the village sidewalks in blue jeans and a T-shirt, his black hair greased back and his black loafers spit-shined to perfection. He drove a red 1956 Ford, "a real hot rod," as he says. On weekends, as my dad fondly recalls, he drank beer and drove over to the neighboring town, Dunkirk, where Dad and his cronies "beat up queers."

My mother, meanwhile, was the Olivia Newton-John to my dad's John Travolta. Bookish and bespectacled, the Marcia Murphy one sees in Silver Creek High School's 1961 senior yearbook photo looks like a librarian. Marcia got straight A's and was the school's queen of extra-curricular activities: a member of the honor society, saxophonist in the school band, president of the Future Teachers club and a staff reporter on *Hi-Times*, the school newspaper. Larry was on the wrestling team, frequently skipped classes and smoked Pall Malls by the pack, which, à la James Dean, he stuffed beneath the sleeve of his white T-shirt.

In the summer of 1961, with the anticipation of life after high school as thick as the rising cornfields surrounding their rural high school, Larry Baker, then seventeen, penned a cursive love note to his steady girlfriend of the past year:

Dear Marcia,

A couple of more weeks and our high school days are over. You'll be going to college, and I'll be working "in heaven," at the Lake Shore News. I'll probably be using those pink ink removers your father got me on one of his trips. For some reason, I believe you and I will always remember Sunday afternoons!!!

We sure have had a good time in our senior year. I've had a hard time my senior year with my car. It won't be long now before it's back on the road. But your sweet mother is kind with her own car and considerate enough to let me use it. Not a bad mother-in-law, nor a bad car. What's more wonderful, I have a wonderful girl to go along with it. A fellow couldn't ask for a better girl, or the girl's family, than I have now and will have for many years to come. There is one night you will never forget!!! You know which night that was. Boy, were we ever lucky.

Well, I guess I'll close for now. This is our last year in school, but not the last year for us.

Love always,
Larry

Two years later my mother, who was studying to be a teacher, dropped out of Buffalo State College after getting pregnant with Kevin. My mother was a strict Catholic: Abortion was not an option. Neither was an out-of-wedlock child. So, before the disturbingly lifelike crucifix inside Our Lady of Mount Carmel Catholic Church, less than a mile from their childhood homes, my father, a printing-press operator, married my mom. A few months after that, they had Kevin. Six years after that, on the morning of April 18, 1970, I was born.

Although my parents in seemingly every category were as opposite as a proton and an electron, they did share one major bond: They came from broken families.

My mother and her younger brother, Ron, grew up seeing their father, a lanky Irish engineer named Herbert Murphy, one day a week, if that. Their mom told them that Herb wasn't around much because he "traveled a lot" for his job as an engineer building bridges from Buffalo to Alabama. On Fridays, Herb would show up at their house and hand their mom crisp twenty-dollar bills. Sometimes he'd spend the night; sometimes he wouldn't. Sometimes he'd take Ron and Marcia and their mom out to dinner; sometimes he'd just pop in, say hello and head off to his next "trip."

Her father's absence from her daily life became an embarrassment to my mom when neighborhood kids started asking her why she didn't have a dad. "I do have a dad," she'd say. "He just travels a lot."

Soon after my parents started dating, Larry, seventeen, grew curious about just where his girlfriend's dad was all the time. Something didn't seem right. Her brother Ron also had recently begun questioning his father's constant, mysterious out-of-town expeditions, but his mother didn't have any answers.

During one of Herb's regular Friday visits, Ron snooped through his father's wallet and found his driver's license. It listed an address of 35 Forest Drive in Orchard Park, a town located about thirty miles north of Silver Creek, just outside of Buffalo. That's strange, Ron thought. Why would his father list Orchard Park—not Silver Creek— as his home address? Maybe it was a boardinghouse, or a YMCA, where his father slept while on business trips. When Ron told my dad about it, the two decided to drive up there and find out for themselves.

So one Saturday morning, my father and Ron drove past the correct address on Forest Drive, which was a large white ranch-style home in a tree-lined neighborhood. My dad parked his '56 Ford down the street and, like a couple of cops on a stakeout, eyeballed the end of the driveway through the rearview mirror.

In those days, delivery men still brought baked goods to your doorstep. When the bread man walked by the car, Ron hopped out and, pointing to 35 Forest Drive, asked, "Who lives in that house, do you know?"

"Mr. Murphy and his wife," the bread man replied.

Ron's jaw dropped. He got back in the car and relayed the news to my father, who promptly made a U-turn and did another drive-by. This time as they passed the house, Herb was washing his Thunderbird in the driveway wearing shorts and a golf shirt. As they drove away, Ron realized that he had never seen his father in anything other than a business suit and that he didn't know his father owned such an expensive car.

They returned to Silver Creek and told my mom what they had discovered in Orchard Park. Then they confronted their mother about it. She confessed that, yes, their father was married to another woman, and, yes, Ron and Marcia were both illegitimate children. Suddenly, everything made sense.

I know scant details of my father's childhood until he takes my little brother and me on a summer family trip to his childhood home in Maryland. I am fourteen. Wanting to spend some quality time with us, Dad takes us on the week-long trip. Our first stop is the house he lived in with Margie and the man whom my dad conspicuously calls "Wally," rather than "Dad."

My father has been chain-smoking his unfiltered Pall Malls all morning, spitting tobacco shreds out of the car window. As he steers the white Mazda through the rundown alley of postwar cookie-cutter homes, many with tarpaper roofs, Dad remarks that he has not been back here in thirty years and hardly recognizes the neighborhood. A pizza-oven breeze is tossing my dad's graying black hair.

Residents are cooling off in their front yards and wooden stoops, and Dad practically dislocates his neck when we pass an African-American family barbecuing on a porch. "Niggers?" Dad, as racist as he is homophobic, says, locking his door with his elbow. "We never had niggers around when I lived here."

Dad flashes back, telling us about riding his bicycle through these streets, catching snakes in the woods over there. He points out a grassy plot that no longer has a diamond but where he says he used to play baseball all day long on summer days like these. His voice trails off to a whisper; clearly, he's talking to himself, not us.

Kris and I are used to his sports-related bragging, but Dad rarely talks about his past or his family, only in the most superficially negative ways. As in "My stepmother was a nut case" or "They're all a bunch of ignoramuses." *Morons* is among his favorite words, actually. But he never goes into detail.

We drive over the crest of a hill and park in front of a two-story clapboard house sorely in need of a paint job. Dad, who typically smokes three packs a day, has lit up at least ten nicotine delivery devices in the last twenty minutes.

With the car idling beside the curb, he stares past me at the house. The white paint is flaking, and the grass looks like it hasn't been mowed since my dad had last been here—in 1955. "This is where I lived when I was around your age, Kris," he tells my ten-year-old brother, bored in the backseat. "Just like I remember it," Dad mutters under his breath. "Same shithole."

He flings his thirtieth cigarette butt of the day out the car window and steps outside. Kris stays in the back, slackjawed and napping.

It looks like no one's home. He and I walk around to the backyard for a look-see. Attached to the back door is a rickety wooden porch with a two-foot-high crawl space underneath. Dad casts a steely glare at the porch and crosses his arms in front of his chest. Expressionless, he sparks another Pall Mall and sucks in its tarry smoke. He stares at the porch. The hot breeze is clapping the leaves on a backyard poplar tree as he inhales a few more puffs. "You know, Kenny," he says, "I used to sleep under that fucking porch."

Unsure how to react, I raise my eyebrows and nod, pretending not to notice as he quickly swipes a trickle from the corner of his brown eye. For the first time in my life, I see my dad cry. But I don't want him to know I've seen this happen. *Never let them see you cry.*

We walk to the car and drive back into the city to take a narrated tour of the capital on a tourist tram. Dad, in his shorts and T-shirt, sits in languid silence the entire tour. As the tram crosses the Potomac and rolls into Arlington National Cemetery, Dad sits as stone silent as the thousands of white grave markers lining the green hills. Perhaps he's trying to re-bury his childhood memories along with the remains of the men buried below us.

"Hey, Dad. Got the flu?"

"Nah. Just the fuckin' sniffles," he says, ever the stoic, ever the tough guy with the cigarette butt turning his teeth brown and fingers yellow and his lungs filled with phlegm that he has to hack out every morning in the toilet.

Just by listening to Dad's denials about his poor health, a total stranger may get the impression that he possesses Herculean health and strength. He will have a fever of 102 and snot oozing from his nostrils and gobs of phlegm lodged in his smoky throat, but he still won't concede illness or frailty of any kind; instead, at mid-cough he will place his hand over his heart and pretend he is having a heart attack.

"Oh, no, Kenny," he says. "You're right. I can't breathe." (He starts panting.) "I *am* dying. Quick, Kenny. Get me another cigarette!"

But he is a comedian crying on the inside.

After learning more about his abusive childhood, I start thinking that maybe Dad takes so poor care of himself because he thinks so lowly of himself. Maybe he can't express love because, when it comes down to it, he doesn't love himself. I start thinking that maybe he is so hard on us because he doesn't want us to make the mistakes he has made. "Your father used to always say that he was going to be rich before he turned thirty," my mother told me when I informed her of my post-trip assessment. "He hates his family; he thought they were a bunch of losers, and he always wanted to get rich and rub it in their faces. That's why he has always been a workaholic."

That he is. I've grown up hearing him talk about how he has never missed a day of work going back to age fourteen, when he had a newspaper route in Silver Creek; how he had to work at a printing company all through high school because his stepdad made him pay rent to live at home; how he didn't go to college because he couldn't afford it. But a college education, he believes, isn't what matters most. "The hardest worker will always outshine the smartest worker," he says.

When I'm seven, Dad, who has worked his way up from an ink-stained printing pressman to a tie-wearing department head, founds his own company, Port of Printing. He works fourteen hours a day, six days a week, managing its twenty employees. He eats pizza and Buffalo wings at his desk for lunch and dinner.

Even though he is loath to admit it, the job is killing him. He has been riddled with health problems from his mid-thirties onward. A few times a year an ambulance comes screaming into our driveway and picks up my father. He prefers the fattest, most sugary foods and never exercises but for the occasional game of catch in the side yard. When he rewards me with two Big Macs, large fries and a vanilla milkshake at McDonald's after hockey games, we have to go through the drive-thru because he is too fat to fit in a booth.

Not knowing when or if he will ever return from his increasingly more frequent hospital stays, my stomach knots up with anxiety. I bite my fingernails with the voracity of a rabbit eating carrots. I gnaw the skin around my fingernails. When the skin breaks, I suck the blood till it clots.

Obsessive nail-biting is a habit I have learned from my semi-neurotic mom, whom I can imagine sitting at home as a child, chewing her fingers raw, waiting for her "traveling" dad to come home.

Whenever I'm at a friend's house or at the park down the street and I hear ambulance sirens, I hop on my bike and pedal home to make sure it's not my dad being carted away to Our Lady of Victory Hospital. Ambulance sirens unnerve me well into adulthood.

Most of his emergency-room trips are for kidney stones lodged in his urethra. If the stone is small enough, he passes them. After one particularly excruciating urination, he returns home looking pale and about ten pounds lighter.

"Kenny," he calls out to me from the couch, where he's been resting continuously for the last few days. "Lemme show you something." His open palm cradles his just-passed kidney stone. It's a gray pebble, a little smaller than a pea.

"Ouch," I say, wincing.

"Oh, this is nothin'," he sighs, reaching into his pocket and pulling out another pebble, twice the size of the first one. He rolls the stone onto the coffee table. "Try pushing *this* boulder out of your dick."

Unsure whether to laugh or cry, I laugh. *Dad is Superman. He can pee rocks!*

"No, thanks," I say, shaking my head in horrified disbelief, feigning amusement with a nervous, disingenuous chuckle.

Dad's urologist warns him that his body will keep producing these acidic kidney deposits unless he changes his diet. That means he must cut out the two-liter bottles of Pepsi he sucks down every day. Predictably, Dad dismisses the doctor as being "a little light in his loafers."

Dad, who has always said, "You gotta die of something," ignores the dire warning. Seeing him make amazing recovery after amazing recovery, then joke about it, I actually think he may never die, no matter what he does to his body, so strong is his pugnacious personality. *He can pee rocks!*

Then yet another, more intense kidney stone attack strikes. This time he can't take the stinging pain, and it won't pass. He gets an X ray, which shows a perfectly round stone the size of an olive pit. With his kidneys on the brink of shutting down, he doesn't urinate for three days. His ankles, wrists and knees swell with fluid, his face bloats till his head looks like a pink soccer ball with eyes, a nose and a mouth painted on it. I'm chewing and spitting out my nails like a woodchuck.

Toxins are backing up into his system and his eyes start turning yellow. When it becomes clear that he is going to die right there in the living room, Dad, who heretofore wouldn't let us call an ambulance, finally relents. Later that day, a surgeon cuts out the stone from his right kidney, a procedure that leaves a purple, ten-inch scar on his side, from his hip to his belly button.

True to character, following the operation, sick of hospital "dog food" and "bitchy" nurses wiping his butt and constantly telling him what to do, my dad puts on his slippers and leaves. By the time Mom and Kevin arrive, he is sitting in a wheelchair in the lobby with his suitcase in his lap and smoking a cigarette.

I hear a car door slam and look out the front picture window and see Dad shuffling up the driveway in his blue hospital-issued slippers, wincing with every baby step. He isn't even forty years old, but his stiff body dawdles like an old geezer's. Seeing the man I've always considered the strongest, most invincible man in the universe lamely inching up the driveway unsettles me in a way that his fights with Mom, his arguments with my brothers, his threats to write me off, never have. This scene is different. My dad, the consummate tough guy who never complains of being sick, who rolls up his sleeves and flexes every time that Duracell commercial comes on and Robert Conrad dares the audience to knock the battery off his shoulder— if he can be this weak and vulnerable, what does that say about me?

I am eleven years old but still sleep with a stuffed bear (I hide it under my pillow so my brothers and father don't see it). I play tough on the ice, but beneath that bulky goalie equipment is a flabby boy with love handles jutting out wider than his shoulders who feels athletically inferior to every player he's ever competed against. When I flex my biceps, no muscles bulge. I also worry too much—like a woman, my dad says—about the Soviets dropping the bomb on us, about my older brothers getting hurt by my hot-tempered dad when he punches them in the gut for lipping off, about my little brother getting kidnapped whenever he goes to the playground without me. I worry about never amounting to anything in life and ending up stuck in Buffalo. I worry that my dad will die soon. Jagged fingernails and bloody cuticles are totems of my neuroses.

These worries haunt me as I watch the childlike man shuffling the soles of his feet on the blacktop driveway he poured himself on a humid summer day just a few months ago. Now look at him: near death, a pathetic ghost of the macho man I've always known.

The top of Mom's shoulder supports him under one armpit, Kevin's under the other, as he slowly makes his way through the front door and toward the three-cushion couch. I watch from across the living room, out of their way. They each shove a hand under one of his armpits as he readies to squat on the couch, which my mother has lined with a sheet, blankets and some extra pillows.

"I can do it myself," Dad says. "Let go of me." He can be the most belligerent man on Earth when he wants something. *This is a good sign. He's still tough.*

They let go of him—holding their hands inches from his side, just in case—as gravity plops his butt onto the sofa. Upon landing, Dad sucks in a pocket of air and bites his lower lip.

Ooooooooooooo . . .

"Larry," Mom, reaching for his side, says, "watch the bag!"

A yellowish stain expands on the side of his loose-fitting dress shirt. Mom unbuttons his shirt and grabs hold of a see-through plastic bag that is connected to a catheter implanted in his right side. The seal between the bag and the catheter has broken, sending urine rushing down my father's back, onto the fresh sheets Mom has just carefully lain down.

Kevin dabs the urine with a towel as Mom frantically searches my dad's suitcase for a fresh bag. I come over and offer help, but Mom barks at me to go to my room. I do. I run upstairs and bury my head under a pillow, silencing the moans coming from downstairs.

Once again, Dad's recovery is amazingly rapid, as if he has the ability to will his kidneys back to normal function. Within two weeks he is back at work, spending his usual fifteen hours a day at the office. But Dad never quite regains the strength he had before that surgery. The days when he plays catch with one of us become as rare as incidents of him and Mom kissing in public.

A year after his surgery, his right testicle balloons to the size of a tennis ball. An infection in his epididymis, a duct on the testicle through which sperm passes, has caused this most inhumane swelling.

Doctors inform my mom that this condition often—but not always—is sexually transmitted, meaning he might have gotten it from a woman. Mom tells me that she never has had any venereal diseases: She has only slept with one man—my father—her entire life. After the surgeon removes a portion of his testicle, my mom confronts Dad about the exact cause of the infection. He swears he has never cheated on her. Mom, one hundred percent financially dependent on my father, is totally unprepared to do anything about it if he has cheated on her. Understandably, she gives him the benefit of the doubt.

Her forgiveness, though, can't keep my dad from his own self-destructiveness. Following the testicle episode, he spirals into a deep depression. He snores away in the bedroom, with the door shut and curtains drawn, day after day after day. When he is up, he's watching reruns from the *Get Smart* era. They're sitcoms, but he doesn't laugh. He doesn't even go to work. He's not angry, he's . . . just . . . there.

"Dad's chewing Valium like candy," Kevin tells me one day. "I hope the miserable bastard OD's."

I don't know what Valium is, but I'm smart enough to know that it's not for happy people. I leave Dad alone. I try to cheer him up by bringing him a bowl of salt-and-vinegar chips—his favorite—or a glass of pop. "Thanks, Kenny," he says. "You're a good son."

As soon as Dad comes out of his "slump," he returns to working fourteen-hour days and snarling at Mom whenever they are around each other more than ten minutes.

They fight constantly, in fact. Their bedroom is next to mine. I hear all their bickering, word for dirty word. They call each other the worst names in the Book of Defamation (*whore, slut, bastard, fat shit*). I bury my head under a pillow to muffle it.

My mother, who has since tired of being just a stay-at-home mom, has begun working for the Hamburg Town Clerk's office, where she grants, ironically enough, marriage licenses. My father resents her job and the freedom she now enjoys after a lifetime of servitude to him, and to us. When she comes home late from work, he's convinced she must be having an affair with someone in the office.

My parents fight about everything: money, the car payment, the print shop, the dog shitting all over the side yard and no one picking it up. It's pathetic, really.

Judging from my hockey success, I believe God answers my prayers. So I start praying for another miracle: that He will put them— and Kevin, Keith, Kyle, Kris and me—out of their middle-aged misery with a heavenly annulment. . . . *God, I really hope you will make a lot of people happy by getting my parents divorced. In the name of the father, the son and the Holy Spirit. Amen. . . .*

Soon, through the paper-thin wall separating my room from theirs, I hear my parents talking—make that *shouting*—about getting a divorce. *Thanks, Big Guy.*

The morning after one particularly bombastic clash, however, Dad calls Mom at work, and I fear that God might have gone a little too far in answering my prayers.

"Marcia," Dad says calmly, "I have a gun in my hand, and you know what? I'm gonna blow my head off this afternoon." He's on the Indian reservation, thirty minutes south of us. "I'm going to make you and everyone else very happy today. I'm gonna blow my fucking brains out." Before hanging up, he closes with an inappropriately sunny, "Bye!"

Mom immediately calls the police, who promptly issue an all-points bulletin for his arrest. *White male . . . 40 . . . black hair . . . armed and dangerous.* The police suggest that my mother take me, Kyle and Kris to a safe place where we can hide out until they find the suicidal gunman that my father suddenly has become.

Mom picks us up from school and drives us straight to Gramma's house in Silver Creek. She cries the whole ride as we listen to the all-news radio station, anxiously expecting to hear breaking news about a mad gunman on the loose.

Mom parks the car behind a thicket of bushes in Gramma's backyard, so that our gun-toting Dad won't know we are there if he comes looking. We close the curtains and turn off all the lights. As we have always done at Gramma's, my brothers and I play war with plastic toy soldiers. The whole time I chew my nails while envisioning the carnage that will happen when he barges through the front door waving his pistol like Al Pacino in *Dog Day Afternoon*.

Kris doesn't understand why we have to hide from our own dad. I just tell Kris, who is seven, that we are only playing a game, sort of like hide-and-seek, only with Dad. I take him to the back bedroom, shut the door and place a flashlight on the carpet. We play war in the shadows until he falls asleep.

Later that night, "the game" ends. The cops call to inform my mother that they have found him sitting alone in his car by the lake. He hasn't shot himself; he is alive.

Dad spends the night detained in the county jail, under observation and heavy medication. The next day, a psychiatrist evaluates him.

Being the bullshitter that he is, Dad probably convinces them it was all just a big misunderstanding, that his wife, in order to get him arrested, made up the whole story.

Dad is renting an apartment and I don't see him for a couple of weeks, although we talk on the phone almost every day. He never mentions the incident. Neither do I. I'm afraid that the most important man in my life may say something unbecoming of the most important man in my life. And we leave it at that.

My father once told me, "The best thing about marrying your mother was that Lyndon Johnson couldn't draft me into Vietnam." Apparently, Kevin didn't get the message, because when he was twenty-one he impregnated his fifteen-year-old girlfriend. A few months later, I attended the young couple's wedding ceremony in the Hamburg village hall, Kevin's teen bride packing a beach ball under a maternity blouse almost as loose-fitting as the judge's robe.

Not too long after, Kevin, who by then had snake-and-dagger tattoos etched up and down his thick arms, found God in a Pentecostal church just down the street from a park where he used to lick LSD tabs like dot candy.

Kevin may be a born-again Christian, but free baby-sitting doesn't come with eternal life in heaven. Whenever his young wife isn't around and Kevin's away working for minimal wage as an aide at a home for the developmentally disabled, I take care of the baby, Josh. I am only fourteen and I spent the last few years as a sort of father figure to Kris, but I really don't know what I have gotten myself into until it is too late.

I quickly learn how to breathe through my mouth while changing a diaper. Forcing a fourteen-year-old boy to scrub his little nephew's butt crack with Baby Wipes is an effective, if underused, form of birth control. By the time I am sixteen and in a relationship with my first serious girlfriend, Jenny, I am fully fearful of equally fucking up my life by becoming a young daddy, like my brother Kevin, like my father. Changing dirty diapers provides just another reason for me to train even harder in hockey so I won't end up stuck in Buffalo the rest of my life.

Hockey continues to be my escape. And my success not only belies my unathletic body, it comes in spite of—and probably in reaction to—the mess that my family life becomes when my parents finally put themselves and all of us kids out of their married misery and split.

The day my parents split for good, on a cold Saturday morning in January of 1983, Dad is supposed to drive me to a game in Rochester. Instead, he spends the day loading his car with boxes of his stuff while I sit laconically in the garage watching him. Figuring that I am too upset to play hockey today (I cried into my pillow all morning), my parents suggest I stay home.

But we are playing the Rochester Americans, a pretty good team, and my team needs me if we are going to win. And I need them. I call my teammate Jay's father and ask for a ride.

During the entire hour-long drive I don't think about my dad's engorged veins popping out his temples, about his throwing a coffee mug into the dining-room wall, about how earlier this morning Kevin (who is now bigger than my dad) threatened to kill Dad if he even laid a finger on Mom, about how the next few years of my life are probably about to be made extremely complicated by my parents' marriage meltdown.

I block all of it out on the ice too. It's generally considered an excellent save percentage if a goalie stops at least nine out of every ten shots. I stop 63 of 64 shots, and we win by a score of 2 to 1. When I return to the de-fathered war zone that is my home, I lie in bed and write in my diary about the big win. I write about how I will kick just as much ass in my next game, how I won't let any of this family mess distract me from being the greatest goalie in the history of the game. After all, I have a learned a thing or two from my father about blocking out the past in order to survive the present.

. . .

My parents, now separated, put our house up for sale. It is a four-bedroom ranch-style home with an in-ground pool and a two-car garage in an upper-middle-class neighborhood with manicured green lawns and street names suggesting suburban loftiness. We live on Yale Avenue, which runs parallel to Harvard, Columbia, Dartmouth and Princeton avenues.

Dad is in the process of selling his print shop, partly because he is feeling burned out but mostly to avoid being forced into a divorce settlement in which my mother, whom he now despises, gets half the ownership.

Mom has won the dubious right to custody of us three youngest Ks, as well as the honor of becoming a single mom who, with an annual income of $15,000 a year, makes a little more than minimum wage but also has the burden of supporting three kids. Even with my dad's court-ordered child payments, she can only afford a $250-a-month duplex on Harwood Avenue that is located, like most every low-rent dwelling in Hamburg, within earshot of the railroad tracks. It's only five miles from our old place on Yale Avenue, but it may as well be five hundred miles away. The duplex's shit-brown (Kris's adjective) paint is drab and peeling from the siding; a hideous yellow coat of paint flakes underneath. Being a duplex, we live in, basically, half of a house. That means everything is half the size of a regular house. Our beds take up nearly all of the floor space in the bedrooms.

Keith and Kevin have moved into their own apartments in another part of Hamburg. My dad has rented a place with his new love a few towns to the east, in a much nicer neighborhood than ours, a fact that my mother regularly reminds us of. Kyle's a year older, but since he is so quiet and Kris considers me his true "big brother," my mother informs me that I am now "the man of the house."

My life is about as Dickensian as one can get in the suburbs. Mom's income is low enough for us to qualify for free school lunches and a monthly ration of government surplus cheese, huge blocks of cheddar wrapped in cellophane, which, until we've eaten it all, serves as the centerpiece of our diet. Grilled cheese sandwiches. Cheese omelets. Cheese and crackers. Macaroni and cheese. Mom has enough money to buy us new clothes for school every fall—usually two pairs of pants, two shirts, new shoes (but only if the tread is worn on our old ones).

About a week after we move in, Mom is down in the basement doing laundry when brown water starts leaking through cracks in the concrete wall.

"Kenny!" she shouts upstairs to the living room, where I'm watching television. "Come down here!"

The basement always smells musty, but once I reach the middle of the stairs I catch wind of an odor much ranker than the usual mold.

"It smells like shit down here," I say, pinching my nose.

Grimacing, Mom points to the wet wall. "It's coming from there."

Seconds later, Kyle and Kris have come down for a whiff. The four of us stand there with our hands over our noses. Mom is almost crying.

She stomps upstairs and calls Mister Slumlord. She tells him there's a putrid brown fluid seeping through the walls. "Maybe there's a septic tank leaking or something," she offers, listening to Mister Slumlord's tepid response. "Yes," she affirms. "Definitely. It smells just like shit."

Mister Slumlord sends a plumber over the next day to fix the problem. I spy on him from the top of the stairs as he sticks his forefinger into a crack and smells it.

"Pee-yew," he says, wiping the gnarly brown muck on his pant leg.

The plumber mops up the puddles of shit and fills the wall cracks with caulk. Thirty minutes after arriving, he tosses a few rancid sponges into the trash, packs up his tools and heads outside, even though the cellar still smells shittier than the town's sewage treatment plant, which, natch, is located about a mile away from our duplex, downwind of course.

I'm thinking, *You fucker! Do you have any idea how upset my mom is? Don't you realize she's probably up in her bedroom, bawling her eyes out, wondering how in the hell she is going to pay next month's rent, let alone keep the stench from killing all of us? If Dad were here, he'd kick your wimpy little ass from here to Rochester.*

As he walks to his car I step in front of the bespectacled little rodent and inform him the basement still smells like shit.

"Well, then, go tell your mother to put a fan down there," he says, annoyed.

"We don't *own* a fan," I fire back.

"Go buy one."

Thereafter, we smell our tap water before drinking, and I learn how to operate a caulk gun.

My new bedroom is roughly the size of a closet and has no wall insulation or finished floor. Mom helps me nail an old red shag carpet over the wood planks; for Christmas our first year there, I get an electric blanket. It's yellow, wired to a white control module with settings from one to ten, ten being the highest. On cold winter nights (which, I suppose, is redundant), if it is set below eight, it's not even worth turning on.

At least we don't need a clock, because we know that every thirty minutes a convoy of rail cars brimming with scrap metal from the Ford metal-stamping plant a half mile over the hill whistles by, rattling our windows, as if we need a reminder that we don't exactly live in Bel Air.

Still, I don't complain. I've grown accustomed to making do with the leftovers and hand-me-downs, and since both my parents grew up poor, I've been reminded my whole childhood that things could always be worse. Therefore, I try to view our duplex, with its squealing mice beneath the porch, its proximity to the railroad tracks, the moldiness permeating every inch of the house, its nasty fluids leaking into the basement, as a residential version of a used baseball mitt. Mom remains optimistic—*At least we aren't homeless; at least we have a home*—but I doubt our life in that duplex represents the kind of middle-class existence the Republicans on the Sunday-morning political shows have in mind when they proudly speak of the Reagan Revolution. Oh, well. As Dad, ever the macho cliché machine, likes to say, "Life's a bitch; then you marry one; then you die."

Shortly after moving to Harwood Avenue, Kyle joins the stoner crowd, much to the chagrin of my mother, who literally goes to St. Bernadette's every Sunday and prays that I, Kyle and Kris won't end up being, like her two oldest boys, doped-out Deadheads. Sometimes I accompany her, persuading Kris to come along. Not because I think the cardboard holy wafers taste good, not because I can understand the point of the old priest's rambling homilies, certainly not because I like the scent of old-lady perfume permeating the pews, but because my mother is feeling alone in the world. Keith and Kevin, it seems, couldn't give two shits about Mom's feelings. Kyle is either sleeping or out smoking. That leaves me and Kris. When Mom kneels on the prayer rest and pinches her eyes tightly shut, I silently utter a *Me too* to the Holy Spirit because I know what she's asking for.

Despite our ramshackle duplex, despite no longer living with Dad, I retain the optimistic attitude that Dad might have abandoned my mother, but he hasn't abandoned me. Mom does my laundry, she cooks my meals, she drives me to school when I wake up late. Although she is taking night-school classes at Buffalo State University to get her business degree, she finds time to be my daily caretaker. But as hard as she may try, Mom doesn't understand my obsession with hockey. She knows I'm pretty good at it, but she doesn't think it's my meal ticket to a better life. "You need to study more and play hockey less," she says.

Not Dad. It remains mostly Dad who drives me to hockey practice, mostly Dad who cheers me on from the stands, mostly Dad who has been telling me since I was eight years old that, with hard work and dedication, I will make it to the NHL, I will someday make enough money to wear the nicest goalie pads, rather than the tattered leather ones he can afford. Having grown up in Maryland, he never played hockey; he can't even skate. But he is my biggest fan, my cheerleader, my greatest motivator. I affectionately call him Coach.

Meanwhile, Mom's boyfriend, whom she met through a personal ad in the *Buffalo News,* is spending a lot of time with us in the duplex. Disgusted at the thought of some guy intruding into my life, at first I delude myself into thinking he's just a friend of my mother's.

His name is Norm. He is an electrician at the Fisher-Price toy plant. He hunts and he used to be a television repairman. He knows my game of hockey about as well as a I know his work with electronic circuitry. I have never seen my father go to work without a tie on, and Dad is a hockey junkie. The most my father knows about television technology is how to turn it on and off. With a résumé so unlike my father's, Norm doesn't seem like my kind of guy, and I am fully prepared to hate him. But I don't. Actually, I like the guy. Perhaps it helped the day he came to me in the living room and said, with the kind of respect a peasant shows a king, that he understands if I'm feeling a bit annoyed by him shacking up with my mother. He never tells me what to do and never says a bad word about my dad. A few months later, he teaches me how to drive in my mom's brown Mercury Bobcat. He's a good man—a brand of adult male I've seen little of so far in my life.

At fifteen, I tell everyone that I will never get married. I've seen firsthand what marriage is about. Even so, having grown up singing along to fifties- and sixties-era love songs with my father, I can't imagine not ever falling in love.

Although Dad's romantic history isn't something I want to repeat, Dad's support of me is heartfelt and admirable. He sings my praises from the bleachers, cupping his hands around his mouth and shouting, "Attaboy, Kenny!" He also has no compunction about bluntly telling me after a game when I have played lousy: "You sure shit the bed tonight." What he lacks in sensitivity, he makes up for with his unconditional faith in me as an athlete. It certainly is a hundred times better than how he treats my other brothers, so I don't ask for anything more, and I don't cross him.

After work at least three afternoons a week, Dad will drive over to our duplex to pick me and Kris up for our hockey practice, and on the weekends he drives me to games in Rochester, Toronto, Montreal, Detroit, Erie, Pittsburgh. He never complains, partly, I'm sure, because it's his only break from working.

Sometimes we log hundreds of miles on the highway in a single weekend, talking hockey and listening to oldies stations the entire way. Elvis. Del Shannon. The Supremes. Roy Orbison. Oh, boy, Dad *loves* Roy Orbison and his sappy ballads. Like "Pretty Woman." It sort of makes sense that Roy's lovelorn tunes resonate with Dad, who, while warning me of the dangers of having a woman in your life, flirts with every halfway attractive woman whom he encounters and remains as romantic (philosophically if not practically) as when he was a high school senior writing mash notes in my mother's yearbook.

But as a high school student I realize that he has a wandering eye that must have driven Mom crazy, although she's never said as much. As I've gotten older I'm noticing more and more that he checks out every woman's butt and breasts, even the girls my age. I'm not even checking out the girls my age! I tell him he's a dirty old man. To which he proudly concedes: "Guilty."

I used to think he was just enjoying the scenery, which of course he was, only the sexual kind. I am embarrassed by his ogling and pretend I don't see him staring. *Am I supposed to do the same? Is something wrong with me because I don't?*

Dad is a rink rat. If Kris or I am playing a game or a practice, which is on just about any given day of the week, chances are that he is in the stands watching. He even met his new girlfriend, Jan, a hockey mom, at the rink. I think they bonded over smoking. When not ferrying Kris and me around western New York and Canada for hockey games, he spends a lot of time with Jan, and the rest of the time trying to find a job that pays as well as owning his own business did.

He seems to have less money than ever. Before the divorce, I would ask him for money to buy something from the snack bar and he would hand me five bucks and not ask for the change. Now, though, he fishes for change in his pocket.

According to Mom, one of their "issues" is that Dad could never explain to her where all the money from the print shop was going. He would just tell her it was none of her business. It turns out that even amid the shop's period of peak profitability, around 1980, he was drowning in debt—from the building's mortgage, the presses, the thirty-foot cabin cruiser docked on Lake Erie, the three cars (including a 1956 Cadillac in mint condition), the Yale Avenue home that he bought a few years after starting Port of Printing. Mom says money burns a hole in Dad's pocket, that Dad has always been poor and doesn't know how to manage his money. She is right.

Now he has sold, at a staggering loss, the debt-plagued print shop and has filed for Chapter 11 bankruptcy. Dad sums the loss up for me one day while we're riding in the car: No more boat, no more house, no more family. "If that ain't a shit sandwich," he mourns, "I don't know what is."

But he still can afford drinking Pepsi-Cola by the two-liter bottle and eating chicken wings drenched in blue cheese almost every night. In fact, it seems like the more stressful his life, the more he eats. His sumo wrestler diet has expanded him to about three hundred pounds, in fact, which is an especially obese weight when you consider he is barely five foot eight. He goes from stout to downright *fat* in less than six months.

Soon after the divorce becomes final, Dad complains of a constant unquenchable thirst and blurry vision. He pees constantly. And for some reason—stress? middle age?—he has trouble getting erections. (I heard him tell his friend Russ this on the phone: "My pecker doesn't want to peck.)" I think to myself that maybe being impotent isn't the worst thing in the world for him.

Health problems plague his side of the family. His younger brother Jerry, a diabetic, died from a heart attack at age thirty-seven. His father, Wally, also has diabetes. It's no shocker when a doctor finally diagnoses Dad with Type II diabetes when he is forty-two years old.

If he doesn't take insulin injections, his doctor warns, he not only may become impotent but he is also likely to die before he turns fifty. Such a dire prognosis would scare most people into straightening out their act. Not Dad. For as long as I can remember he has never thought he'd live past fifty, anyway. Nor does he seem to want to. When his hair started turning gray in his mid thirties, he dyed it jet black. "I'd rather die than get old," he has said. He really believes people go to doctors for the same reason people (like my devout Catholic mom) go to church: because they are "weak sunzabitches."

Not so surprisingly, Dad ends up only occasionally taking his insulin pills and cuts his pop guzzling maybe in half.

(PROLACTIN LEVEL: 200 NG/ML)

When I was ten, I broke my index finger playing football. It hurt real bad, and the doctor put a splint on it to keep me from bending it. After a few days I found that it hurt less when I relaxed my wrist muscles and just let my hand dangle limply. Apparently my method wasn't manly enough for Dad.

"You're walking around like a fairy, Kenny," he said, staring me down from his horizontal perch on the couch.

"But, Dad, my finger is killing me, and this takes the pressure off it."

He grabbed my hand. "Instead of flopping your wrist down, why don't you just hold it up with your hand?"

"What's wrong with letting my wrist relax?"

"You look like a fucking fairy, that's what's wrong."

Mom came to my defense and, as usual, an argument ensued.

A few years later, while driving back from hockey practice, Dad glanced over at a guy walking down the sidewalk and said, "Look at that faggot."

"How do you know he's gay?" I snarled.

"I just know," he said.

"How would *you* know?" I said, tauntingly.

"What?" he bristled.

"Nothing," I said, staring out my window.

"That's what I thought."

I was at the age when you can no longer stay silent when your parents say ignorant things. And, as societal progress has things arranged, your ideas are almost always more liberal than your parents'. Although being gay is the last thing I would want to be, I had developed my own, more tolerant thoughts on homosexuality.

A few miles down the road, I couldn't hold back. "Even if he is gay, I don't care. I mean, what would you do if I was gay?"

Dad focused like a laser into the road ahead and said, "Then you wouldn't be my son anymore."

I suppose Kyle knows what that's like. As a shy homebody, my brother Kyle had very few friends and stayed home most of the time. As a Deadhead, though, Kyle goes to parties and brings friends over to the house all the time. Suddenly, Kyle has become more of a socialite than me.

Judging by my daily schedule throughout most of high school, I may as well live in a monastery:

7 A.M. — Wake up and take a shower.

7:35 A.M. — Catch bus to school.

8 A.M. to 1 P.M. — School. Mostly daydream about hockey, hiding the sports section in an open textbook.

2 P.M. — Eat lunch at home and/or then play my drums.

3 P.M. — Arrive at ice rink.

3:30 P.M. — Read through my Jacques Plante goaltending manual, which is my Bible.

4 P.M. to 6 P.M. — Team practice. Achieve that day's goals (i.e., fifty up-and-downs, fifty breakaway saves, ten sprints).

7:30 P.M. — Eat dinner.

8 P.M. to 11 P.M. — Watch TV or study (only if a test is the next day). Write in my hockey diary; set goals for next day. Do sit-ups and push-ups. Talk to Dad on phone. Hang out with Kris (playing Trivial Pursuit or sock hockey in the hallway).

11 P.M. to midnight — Doze off while reading magazine or practicing positive imagery (me stopping pucks) with Zen meditation, or watching Johnny Carson or Letterman if I can't sleep (which is par for course the night before games, when I am so tense and irritable everyone knows to avoid me).

Basically, I do anything but waste my time hanging out with neighborhood kids, whom I consider a bunch of losers.

One afternoon I emerge from my upstairs cocoon to get a drink of water. Kyle is sitting there with a few of his friends, among them a blond girl named Sheila and her brown-haired best friend, Tonya, who lives down the street.

She is one of the stoner kids in the Harwood neighborhood who sits in the back of the bus on the way to school. Tonya and her posse, from my ascetic, goody-goody, jock point of view, do little more than wear jean jackets and smoke a lot of pot. I don't yet know her sister Jenny, who is two years older and always working at the chicken wings joint.

Tonya has long brown hair tied back into a ponytail and adorable Howdy Doody freckles sprinkled all over her face. When Kyle barks at me to go back to my room, Tonya throws a pillow at Kyle and says, "Don't be mean." She pats the spot on the couch next to her. "Sit down, Kenny."

"So this is your mystery brother." Tonya says, beaming as I sit beside her.

"Why don't you ever hang out with us?" she asks.

I tell her I'm a pretty busy guy, explaining how I am basically the greatest goalie to ever come out of Buffalo.

For the next ten minutes she peppers me with questions. *Wow, you play hockey? . . . You're a goalie? Doesn't the puck hurt? . . . How come you never party with us?* As I smugly reply to her fawning, Kyle, who has been flirting with Tonya ever since we moved there, glowers, rolling his eyes in disgust. I, however, eat up all the female attention.

A few days later I'm home alone and the doorbell rings. I open the front door and find Tonya standing there, alone. She isn't wearing her usual stoner uniform of tattered blue jeans and a concert T-shirt. Instead, she's wearing cutoff jeans and a white halter top, without a bra. Lipstick glows from her lips.

"Is Kyle home?" she says, all cheerleader-peppy.

"No."

"Oh . . . uh . . . do you know where he is?"

"Maybe he's at the mall. I really don't know. Sorry."

She starts twisting her hair and steps backward off the porch.

"I'll tell him you stopped by."

"Okay, cool," she says, walking away. She turns around. "Hey, you wanna go for a walk?"

"Sure."

A year ago I discovered a magical thing about my penis, which involves that squirting thing I had always heard guys talking about. I'm more curious about sex than horny, and I look at my squirting penis as I did my ability to tie shoes when I was five: Since I *can* do it, I might as well do it.

Under the ruse of looking for Kyle, we walk up the street to the neighborhood playground. No sign of Kyle; no one is there. We sit at a picnic table and she says she can't believe a guy as "cool" as me doesn't have a girlfriend and that—hint, hint—she has just broken up with her boyfriend. I tell her I'm a busy hockey player, how I'm working hard to be a *professional* hockey player someday.

She places a menthol-flavored cigarette between her lips and, grabbing a lighter from her purse, offers me one.

"No, thanks," I say. "I don't smoke."

Sprinkles begin falling from the slate-gray sky, and she suggests we go to her house and sit on the porch. *I guess we're no longer looking for Kyle.*

Halfway back to her house it starts pouring, so we sprint to her porch, play-racing, and when we get there we collapse, huffing and puffing. Tonya brushes my stringy, wet hair off my face and looks me straight into the eyes, emitting something I've never sensed from a girl: *lust.*

I peer down at the pink nipples clinging to her drenched white shirt. She smiles. Then we make out, just like in the movies.

We kiss. French kiss. Lip kiss. Neck kiss. I've never done this before, but my body is operating on Darwinian autopilot.

A few minutes later I come up for air. "I thought you and Kyle had a thing," I say, petting her back. She shakes her head and sighs, "No. Kyle's very sweet, but we're just friends."

Just friends. Something tells me that Kyle feels differently. But that doesn't stop me from going back to making out. I can taste her minty cigarette breath as she guides my hand to her crotch and rubs it against her shorts.

Holy moly! Third base!

I've heard friends talk about "fingering" girls, but until this very moment, I have only kissed two girls, and I didn't touch anything below their neckline. My inexperience notwithstanding, I'm not about to chicken out, even though it is broad daylight and Kyle will kill me if he ever finds out about this. I handle the pressure like a breakaway in sudden-death overtime: I focus on the task at hand. I don't know where to go and exactly what do with my fingers, but I gently poke around her wetness using a vague image of a vagina I have seen in my biology textbooks as a reference point. She moans softly while keeping an eye on the street.

Soon it stops raining. Dinnertime. A hug. Another kiss. An awkward hug goodbye.

Once home I frantically dial the numbers on the phone and call my friend Dave, the quarterback of the junior high school's football team.

"You did *not* stick your finger in her pie," Dave replies. "You're lying."

Fortunately, I have kept the aromatic evidence of my act on my right hand.

"Oh, yeah. Come over and smell for yourself."

Ten minutes later Dave arrives. Tonya's femininity still fresh on my skin, I stick my unwashed right forefinger under his nose. He presses his nose flush to my finger. "You lucky bastard," he says. "You really did finger her."

Lucky indeed. I am so excited about my achievement that I stay up till 3 A.M. watching baseball highlights on ESPN, breaking into giggles every few minutes and smelling my still unwashed finger.

The next morning I see Tonya at the bus stop, huddling with her friends—among them (gulp!) Kyle—smoking cigarettes. She's ignoring me. I pretend not to care, but of course I do. When they look my way, I just know (or at least fear) that she is telling them I don't know how to kiss, or that I clumsily fingered her as if I were cleaning out a pumpkin.

Act tough, man.

The entire ride to school I bury my head in a book.

The following Saturday, while passing by Tonya's house on my way home from a baseball game, out of the corner of my left eye I see a guy running at me from Tonya's front yard. I walk faster, my cleats clomping like a Clydesdale. *This guy's definitely running at me. Do I bolt like hell? Or play it cool like a man?*

Before I can decide, the guy broadside-tackles me. I remember it in slow motion: My face scraping against the asphalt . . . my elbow taking the force of the fall . . . my baseball glove flying into the ditch.

I roll onto my back and see a guy who looks my age, only he is about twenty pounds heavier, all muscle, and four inches taller. He straddles my body like a cowboy over a steer.

Before he can hog-tie me, I jump to my feet. "What the fuck are you—" Before I can finish, Angry Guy kicks me back down to the road with a swift sneaker to the sternum.

Tonya comes running toward us from her porch screaming, "Leave him alone!"

"Get up, asshole!"

Ah . . . Angry Guy is actually Angry Boyfriend. Tonya must have confessed to cheating.

"I didn't know she was your *fucking* girlfriend . . . you *dick*. She told me she didn't have a fucking boyfriend."

This confuses Angry Boyfriend, who, with his dumb-guy face and beefy muscles, obviously has spent more time in the gym than the library.

As his feeble brain processes the data, I grab my baseball mitt, flash Tonya the evil eye and continue walking home. *Dad's right. Girls are nothing but trouble.*

A month later Tonya stands on the railroad tracks by our house and gets struck from behind by a speeding train. She dies instantly. No one knows for sure whether it was a suicide, but some of her friends think that she has been depressed recently, confused about her life and unhappy with her boyfriend.

Mom buys Kyle a new dress shirt and slacks for her funeral. I stay home.

(PROLACTIN LEVEL: 225 NG/ML)

"There are faster and taller goalies out there," Dad has told me more than once. "But no one works harder than you do, Kenny."

And after several years of monkish dedication—during which I choose hockey over girls, drinking, goofing off and all the other social activities most of my peers engage in—all my hard work starts to pay off when I am invited to train at the Olympic Training Center in Colorado Springs. I get on a plane for the first time in my life. None of my brothers has ever flown; my father has only flown once. *I knew I was better than them!*

There I play against the young ice studs who will go on to become National Hockey League all-stars: Jeremy Roenick, Mike Modano, Steve Heinze, Tony Amonte. At sixteen I'm ranked the top goalie my age in the country, meaning that I have a legitimate shot at making it to the big leagues, or at least earning a Division I scholarship, even though I have absolutely no career aspirations other than stopping pucks with my body, which, much to my chagrin, does not look nearly as impressive as the goaltending feats it can perform.

I am a junior in high school; yet, I can't stop thinking about how my sixth-grade health teacher warned us to expect biological changes over the next few years. Soon, she lectured, our childlike bodies would transform into adult figures. "All of you will start thinking a lot more about sex," she said, eliciting a chorus of giggles. She said that boys, bubbling with testosterone, would go girl-crazy; ovulatory and estrogen-infused, girls would go boy-crazy.

Whatever. Those health class lectures seem like trailers for movies that promise epics but turn out to be turkeys.

I have shaved only once, and that was just to see what it felt like, because I couldn't see any stubble, at least not without a magnifying glass. I have never had a wet dream, and while I have recently shot up to five feet eleven inches, I have spaghetti-thin arms and a belly that jiggles and a waist that won't harden no matter how many sit-ups I do or how many meals I skip.

I'm pushing 180 pounds, which would be fine if I had more muscle, which is denser (thus heavier per square inch) than fat. I learn this sad fact at a junior Olympic tryout in Colorado Springs in the summer of 1986. The first day of camp, the coaches line us up in a gym and ask the players to strip down to our underwear. It's time for the official weigh-in, they announce.

I have been dreading this moment, running five miles a day at the high school track and skipping breakfast and dinner for the past month. I weighed 185 pounds on June 1 and wanted to slim down to 175 by the time I left for the Olympic Training Center on July 6, under the reasonable logic that they aren't going to pick a fat goalie for the Olympic team.

Two days before the tryout camp I step on my mother's scale in the bathroom. With all the nervousness of a roulette spinner, I cringe as the dial stops at the 181-pound mark. *What? I've hardly eaten for weeks. That's brutal!*

When my plane lands in Colorado Springs a couple of days later, I'm light-headed from starvation. In the last forty-eight hours I've ingested two cans of OJ, three pieces of toast (no butter), several glasses of water, one bite of American Airlines quiche surprise and a Coke. Jenny gave me an apple at the Buffalo airport, but I didn't even eat that.

Standing amid a pale sea of shirtless hockey prospects in their boxers and briefs, I gaze jealously at chiseled pecs that slapshots have shaped into rock-solid breastplates. Muscular thighs sturdy as tree stumps. Washboard abs. Adonis shoulders forming the wide top of V-shaped upper bodies tapering down to narrow waists. And there I stand, self-conscious, my boobies almost as big as my girlfriend's and that . . . that fucking *belly* hanging over the waist of my shorts like a fleshy Quebec tourist's on a Florida beach.

I contract my stomach muscles and suck in the gut, practically turning blue from holding my breath. I'm waiting for my turn to step on the scale, but about thirty guys are ahead of me. Most of them want to weigh as much as possible, to look big, strong and tough on the stat sheet, which is pored over by pro scouts. So many of the players were eating plateloads of bread and spaghetti and fatty desserts at lunch. A few guys had even planned on wearing ankle weights, an idea that they had to abort when the coaches made us take off our clothes.

My pal Jeff, a goalie from Minnesota, is standing in front of me. When he turns around, I cross my arms in front of my body. He stares me up, then down.

"Hey, Bakes," he says, "you on the doughnut diet or something?"

I tip the scale at 179 pounds.

Off the ice, being timed in the forty-yard dash and the push-up competitions, I feel sluggish and fat. But on the ice, my body hidden under thirty pounds of leather leg pads, a chest protector, arm pads and a goalie mask, I am lightning fast, letting in fewer goals than any other goalie. I make the cut. The last day of camp, the coaches call me into a training room. If I had any fingernails left, I would be chewing them. They hand me a Team U.S.A. folder and tell me congratulations. I am a member of the sixteen-year-old United States national hockey team.

· · ·

My goaltending achievements—rather than my feats of denial—earn me my first press, a feature story in an August 1987 newspaper article that runs just before the start of my senior year of high school.

The Bee prints with the story a photo of me posing in my pads and gloves with my official red, white and blue Team U.S.A. hockey jersey and a headline declaring, "Stopping the shot everyday occurrence for local youth." It praises me as a local boy poised to move on to bigger and better things. It certainly isn't Pulitzer material, but the reporter does a pretty good job at summing up my hockey career:

> *Division I hockey, the Olympics and the National Hockey League are all in the realm of possibilities for one local youth.*
>
> *Kenneth Baker recently came back from the United States Olympic Training Center in Colorado where he participated in the Select-17 camp, comprised of the best 17-year-old hockey players in the country. Of eight goalies at the camp, Baker was rated third and was told the competition was so close he could have easily been chosen as the top goalie in the country.*
>
> *At the age of 16, Baker attended the Select-16 camp in which he played against Quebec. It was the first United States gold medal hockey win since the 1980 Olympics. . . . At the age of 12, he played on the 13–14 year-old team. At 5-0 and 135–140 pounds, he was a large goalie.*
>
> *During his first game for the traveling team, Baker remembers playing his present coach Kris Hicks' team. Baker's team lost 8-2 but it was during that game he realized he wanted to play for Hicks.*
>
> *"I got a call from this guy wanting to know if I had open try-outs," Hicks said, referring to Baker's father, Larry. "When he came to tryouts I saw this little fat kid come out on the ice. I had two goalies from the year before trying out. But Baker was the best kid on the ice. He had the best reflexes of all the goalies. He didn't know anything about playing goalie, but he had the best reflexes."*

As a member of the Niagara Scenic Junior A Hockey Club based in West Seneca, Baker will have the opportunity to travel to Chicago, Detroit and Canada to play other athletes of his caliber.

Baker's immediate goal is to play for a Division I college. After that, he has thought about both the Olympics and the National Hockey League. Under NCAA rules, five Division I schools can transport Baker to their campus to encourage him to attend that school and receive an athletic scholarship.

All college correspondences Baker has received are alphabetized and put in a black box. If the correspondence is too large for the black box it is placed in a cardboard box. Baker, who will be a senior at Frontier High School, has been contacted by about 30 of the 41 Division I schools. The schools include Wisconsin, Brown University and Notre Dame.

Baker appears to have the world at his hands. However, he does not see himself as a great hockey player but instead looks at what he needs to do to improve. Next year, when the college decision is made and the NHL draft rolls around, Baker may obtain his goals.

"When he was eight, Kenny asked me how to become famous," Larry said. "I told him to take something he was good at and become the best at it. He had just started playing hockey and said, 'Well, I'm going to become a famous hockey player.' "

Reading this story now, some thirteen years later, I notice the omissions more than the accolades. The article doesn't mention that I have virtually no social life outside of hockey, that I have never attended a school dance and that I spend a fair amount of my free time doing hundreds of sit-ups in my bedroom, poking at my flabby stomach with disgust afterward. The reporter mentions that I don't consider myself a great hockey player, but she doesn't know—because I don't tell her—that I have such a low regard for my talents because I am a teenage per-

fectionist who mentally abuses himself *(You suck! . . . Piece of shit! . . .*
You could have stopped that shot. Get your ass in gear!) for several days
after letting in a bad goal or making a knucklehead play.

She doesn't know that when I was eleven, I decided one day that
what I really wanted to do was be a professional figure skater. My
mother had taken me to see an ice show, one of those Christmastime
ice ballets in which spotlights illuminate princes lifting princesses
above a dreamy mist of dry ice. I was mesmerized by the grace and
beauty of the figure skaters. Afterward I told my mother how much
more graceful these skaters were than hockey players. She suggested I
sign up for figure skating. "I bet it will make you a better hockey
player," she encouraged.

Back home, Mom told Dad that I wanted a pair of figure skates
and might start taking lessons. Dad wasn't so keen on the idea of seeing one of his sons carving figure eights into the ice. He probably
could taste the bile at the mere thought of his son wearing a pair of
spandex pants, a silk blouse and rouge smeared on his cheeks. Dad
came up to my room and poked his head through the crack in the
door. "Figure skating is for pussies," he said sternly. "If you do that,
everyone will think you are light in your loafers." I never took a single
figure-skating lesson.

Furthermore, the newspaper reporter doesn't know that ever since
my father left, I—not my dad—have taken care of my little brother,
whose anxiety has been so acute lately that he, at ten years old, still pees
his bed. The article also doesn't mention that, a few months before the
interview, my dad suffered another one of his bouts of depression after
yet another kidney-stone attack. These are the family secrets that don't
make it into that newspaper puff piece, the dirty little truths that scare
me, that motivate me, but that I don't dare tell anyone about, lest I reveal my weaknesses and vulnerability and risk not becoming famous.

I want people to think I have "the world at my hands," because my
dad has taught me that showing anything but confidence and
machismo and invincibility is unmanly. Dad tells me that I should en-

vision myself as Tom Barrasso (the Sabres' hotshot young goalie) and then play as if I am him.

"If you want to be the best, you have to think, act, walk, talk, eat, piss, *shit,* like the best," my dad says.

"What if I'm not feeling like the best?" I ask.

"Fake it," he says. "If you believe it, you can achieve it."

(PROLACTIN LEVEL: 250 NG/ML)

A year and a half after Tonya died in the train accident, I meet her older sister, Jenny, at a party Kyle throws in the half of a backyard behind our duplex. Jenny resembles Tonya only in her cute, brunette looks. Jenny doesn't drink or smoke pot. She also doesn't have a boyfriend who may tackle me for making out with her. Four months into our relationship, I still haven't told Jenny that I had been with Tonya. It's, well, a little too weird. It doesn't occur to me that maybe I am partially attracted to Jenny because she is a way of finding a sense of closure with her dead sister. I just think she is cute.

Although I have virtually taken a vow of celibacy and not touched another girl since the Tonya affair, I change my mind when I meet Jenny, because (a) Jenny seems too mature and sweet to screw me over, and (b) no matter how anxious I am about the whole idea of sex, I still want to put that magical squirt function of mine to its intended use.

I may not be boiling with carnal desire, but—thanks to that commercial for that Toronto hotel—at least Jenny and I have an agreed upon a location and a date for what Jenny has taken to calling "The Gift." She is giving something to me; I don't have to do anything. It kind of takes the pressure off.

The day after Jenny's epiphany, I call the Sutton Place and reserve a room with Jenny's dad's Visa number. I lower my voice to sound older. I reserve a room with king-size bed, reasoning that we will be spending a lot of time on it.

The next four months are spent preparing—logistically and mentally—for my inaugural romp. *Damn, it will feel good to get this over with.*

There's just one teensy-weensy little problem, though. Despite Dr. Dirty's best efforts, I'm still not clear on the biomechanics of how a guy actually goes about inserting his penis into a vagina. I mean, it isn't as if anyone has ever sat me down and showed me how to do it. Sure, I've seen porno magazines, but you can watch someone snow-blow the driveway and still have no clue how to do it yourself. Those mandatory health classes—with their sterile descriptions of birds and bees and ejaculations and menstrual periods—weren't very helpful, either. And my parental sex education has consisted of my dad calling me at home soon after I began seeing Jenny and initiating the following conversation:

"You like this girl, huh?"
"Yeah," I said.
(Uncomfortable pause.)
"Well, make sure you put a rubber on it."

Predictably, Dad's Archie Bunker School of Sexual Education hasn't brought me any closer to solving the whole penis-into-vagina insertion mystery. *Do I spread her legs? Will I need that jelly stuff? Or does she do that herself? How fast do I move? What if the condom slips off? And how do you put a rubber on, anyway? How will I know when—and if— she comes? Will she squirt all over me or something?* I have to figure these things out, but I'm sure as hell not about to humiliate myself by asking anyone.

I've got time. I have from January until April eighteenth—my birthday—to prepare for the nerve-wracking event.

. . .

My friend Garrett is not a hockey player, which means we can have actual conversations, not just the kind of tits-and-asses gabfests most of my hockey pals prefer. Yet, even Garrett, a sensitive folk singer whom I thought was as monastic in his musical pursuits as I am with hockey, almost chokes on his Coke when I tell him my secret. It's a couple of weeks before Jenny and I are supposed to go to Toronto for my birthday gift. I haven't told anyone about our plans for sex, and I think that Garrett may be able to impart some wisdom (he is a year older than me). We're sitting in the mall food court when I break the news to Garrett.

"You've *never* done it?" Garrett says. "But . . . but you told me you and Jenny screwed all the time."

"Yeah, well, I lied." It feels good to finally tell someone the truth. But I'm afraid he'll call me a lame-ass-loser-homo-faggot.

"Dude, how can you hold back?" Garrett asks. " I can't go a day without wanting to do it with my girlfriend." He's shaking his head, incredulous. "You must jerk off a lot, huh?"

"Not really."

"Get outta here." Noticing my dead-serious expression, he quickly adds, "Seriously?"

"Swear to God. We do some stuff, you know, but sex just isn't the most important thing to me right now."

"Wow. Hats off, dude. You're a better man than me. I could never hold back like that. You're going to have a lot of fun, man."

This conversation does nothing to boost my sexual self-esteem; neither does the entire popular culture around me that seems to be based on sex. The bottom line is that I'm a high school junior; I have a penis (over seven inches long, thank you; I measured it with a ruler one night in my room while on the phone with Jenny); virtually everything in the culture I see around me suggests I should be having sex. For example, *Fast Times at Ridgemont High* is, basically, about high school students having sex. Even Patrick "Johnny Castle" Swayze and Jennifer "Baby" Grey "dirty dance" and, afterward, have passionate sex.

The problem is that, unlike seemingly every other human on the planet, I don't feel an overwhelmingly hormonal urge to have sex. It just seems like having sex is what a young man is supposed to do to in order to become a real man; it is what the culture has informed me is a talisman of masculine power. But I have a very poor sexual appetite. I'm what an expert in such things would call a sexual anorexic, if there is such a thing.

Luckily my friend Paul has been having sex for several years (or so he claims), and, being well-versed in everything there is to know about girls, he serves as my coitus coach. Paul is a drummer in the high school band. In practice rooms, while tuning drums, we talk sex.

One afternoon Paul initiates a highly informative, sexually frank discussion as we sit in the percussion pit before band rehearsal.

"Before you do anything, man, you have to fabric fuck her," Paul instructs, air-humping like Michael Jackson in the "Thriller" video.

I tell him I don't know what a quote-unquote fabric fuck is. "Like this," he says, gluing his pelvis to a kettle drum and humping. "You fuck her through the fabric of your pants."

A few days later Jenny calls me at home from her dorm room. Her voice is quavering. She obviously is crying.

"I don't know if we are doing the right thing," she says, sniffling. "I don't know if we are ready for this."

"We don't have to do anything."

"I know. I'm just worried that, after we do it, things will change between us. I don't want our relationship to only be about sex."

"We only have to do it once. That's it. I don't even care about that. Whatever you want to do is fine."

She calms down and, before hanging up, says she loves me, and I assure her that I feel the same way.

April eighteenth comes quicker than expected. Hockey season is over; my junior year of high school is nearly complete. With no hockey until the summer league starts, I have little to do but work and obsess over losing my virginity.

My birthday arrives. I call in sick to my boss at Super Duper, the grocery store where I behead lettuce. I tell Dad I'm spending the night at Paul's house; no need to make the old man worry that I'm going to knock up a girl and ruin my life. This will be a secret trip.

For my birthday Paul has given me a twelve-pack of ribbed, lubricated Trojans. "The ribbed ones'll make her moan," he says, placing the box in my hand. "Trust me."

Saturday morning comes, a day before my birthday. I stuff the Trojans, a pair of jeans, an extra pair of tighty-whities, a couple of T-shirts and a heavy jacket (hey, we're going to Canada!) into my backpack. Jenny picks me up in the late morning, grinning from ear to ear. Two large leather bags are hidden under a blanket in the hatchback area of her mom's Ford Escort.

"What's up with two suitcases? We're only gonna be gone for a night."

"You'll see," she says.

It's a two-hour trip up the Queen Elizabeth Parkway from Buffalo to Toronto, and the whole boring ride up, all Jenny wants to talk about is The Gift.

"Guess what?" she says as we whiz down the freeway at a hundred kilometers an hour.

"What?"

"I'm at day five in my cycle. It's almost impossible for me to get pregnant tonight." She's gripping the wheel like she's riding a roller coaster. "I'm *so* psyched about that."

"Yep," I say, glumly, ambivalently staring out the window. I'm thinking that this trip may not be what I want. I recline the seat back and shut my eyes.

"What's wrong?" she asks.

"Just tired," I mumble.

She tries to cheer me up by telling me how we were going to wait till midnight, when I turn seventeen, before hopping into bed and "doing it." Naked even. "Don't worry about anything," she adds. "Just relax and let nature take over."

I am sick of talking about it, and, truth be told, I can't relax. I just want to get it over with.

At Niagara Falls, halfway to Toronto, I start biting my fingernails. By the time we pull to the valet curb at Sutton Place, I have gnawed them to the skin and they're bleeding.

Jenny checks us in at the front desk as I sit in one of the lobby's pseudo-antique chairs, watching tourists and businessmen bustling back and forth from the entrance to the elevator bank. The hotel sure doesn't look as glamorous as it did on the commercial. The floor is covered with fake marble tile and none of the workers speak with the kind of elegant British accent of the commercial announcer. Muzak oozes out of tiny speakers on the wall.

Jenny returns with the key and, holding hands like newlyweds, we ride the elevator to the sixth floor. Keeping with the hotel's less-than-luxurious accommodations, I separate the curtains and take in an entirely unimpressive view of a back alley. At least the bathroom comes stocked with free soap, shampoo and, as an elated Jenny notes, two terry-cloth bathrobes just like the ones that couple wore in the commercial.

I immediately collapse onto the king-size mattress. It's not even noon, but I'm feeling so tense about this whole virginity-ending ritual that I have exhausted myself. "Take a nap, big boy," Jenny says, petting my head. "You're going to need all the energy you can." If she's nervous about what's about to happen, she doesn't show it.

When I wake two hours later, Jenny is splayed beside me in her panties and a T-shirt, her button nose rattling with snores. Scanning her ivory-smooth legs, it occurs to me that this whole wait-till-midnight thing is silly. *I should just start kissing her, pull off her underwear, slap on a condom and get the damn thing over with.*

I don't even feel like having sex.

This is what I have been waiting for, the chance to experience that mysterious activity I've only seen done in my brothers' hard-core porno mags and heard about from Dr. Dirty. Something is definitely wrong. But I have to go through with this. What do I do when I don't feel like playing hockey but my team is relying on my goaltending? I grin and bear it. *This is what you've been waiting for, dude. Just relax and wait for tonight.*

I wait, but I definitely don't relax. Antsy, I shake her awake.

Jenny has made an eight-o'clock dinner reservation at a "romantic" restaurant on the waterfront, but after strolling through the downtown area we skip dinner and head straight back to the hotel. I'm so nervous that as we walk back, I suggest—more accurately, I mumble—that we cancel our sex plans for another night. "It's such a beautiful night!" Jenny exclaims. She hasn't heard me, and I don't repeat myself.

In the hotel room Jenny takes charge. "Let's take a bath," she says, kicking off her sandals. "Wait here." She takes all her clothes off and steps into the bathroom. Before closing the door, she quips, "But stay here."

A few minutes later she shouts through the door, "Okay, you can come in!"

I creak open the door and peek inside the darkened room.

"Ta-da!" she says, soaking seductively in the tub amid a pillow of cumulus soap bubbles. Two scented candles flicker on the counter next to a portable radio humming with classical music. I take off my clothes and squeeze into the tiny tub made for two—dwarfs, that is—displacing about a gallon of water onto the floor.

"Ow-eee!" I squeal. "Fuckin' A, Jenny. Why's it so boiling?"

"Hot water kills sperm. You know, the Chinese have been using hot water for birth control for centuries. You can never be too safe."

Maybe, I think, but you *can* overplan things.

By the time I have suitably soaked my testicles, it is almost midnight, and my much-ballyhooed birthday. We wrap ourselves in the hotel robes and head toward the bed. This whole do-this-do-that charade is making me feel more like a car on an assembly line than a guy on the romantic date of his life. I just want to get it over with.

Jenny carries the radio from the bathroom and sets it on the nightstand as I disrobe and sit naked on the edge of the bed as Jenny reaches into her top-secret bag and yanks out a handful of rubbers the way a magician pulls a rabbit from a hat, tossing them into a lazy pile on the king-size mattress. *This is really happening.*

Jenny—"I made a mix tape"—slides a cassette tape into the radio and presses Play. Just as she lets her robe drop to the floor and straddles me, the lead singer of Foreigner croons:

Feels like the first time
Like it never will again . . .

After rolling around the mattress for a few minutes, our lips locked, our naked bodies glued, Jenny gropes for one of the dozen or so rubbers on the mattress. She bites open the aluminum packaging and spits it out. I can feel her dripping wetness on my thigh.

Holding the condom in her right hand, with the free hand she grabs my penis . . . but it's limp. So she sucks on it. . . . When that doesn't work, she rubs it up and down . . . jerking it harder with every pump . . . but it still won't rise.

I lick the sweat dripping down my upper lip onto my tongue. Embarrassed. Pissed off. Frustrated. Disappointed. Humiliated. *I can't fucking believe it!* This is worse than letting a player score on me from the red line. I roll on my side, facing away from her, gritting my teeth in shameful disgust.

"It's okay. Really, it is," she soothes, stroking my wet hair. "You're just nervous is all. This happens to every guy."

"Yeah, right," I grumble.

"It's true. I read that—"

"Please, don't—"

"—it's common for a lot of—"

"Just shut UP."

The room falls silent except for the vibrating air conditioning unit and "Feels Like the First Time" still groaning from the portable radio. I knock the radio onto the floor.

I yank the blankets over my body and curl into the fetal position. I pinch shut my eyes, hoping to squeeze my brain into numbness, and I fall asleep.

A few hours later I'm awakened by Jenny slithering on top of me. Though half asleep, I'm sporting an erection—albeit a half-hard one. But it's enough. She slides my penis inside of her and lies still. "It's okay," she whispers in my ear and stroking my wet hair. "It's okay . . . it's okay . . ."

I keep my eyes closed and grip her swaying hips, waiting for it all to end.

AWAKENING

*The anesthesia is wearing off, which is good in that I can keep my eyes open,
but bad in that I am starting to feel an inescapable pain pulsating inside my
head. My skull is throbbing, my face is swollen and bruised, and, unable to
breathe through my nose, I'm growing anxious and uncomfortable—especially because I'm having a hard time trying not to choke on the globs of blood
that won't stop dripping down the back of my throat, my only airway. I'm
conscious, but I don't know the time or what day it is, nor do I care. I'm just
trying to breathe. Time inches by. Minutes feel like hours; hours like days.*

*When my eyes open, the southern California daylight no longer is
brightening my hospital room. Evening. All is quiet but for a wheezing old
woman struggling on life support in the room next to mine. In between
coughing fits, she won't stop moaning in Spanish, something I can't understand. Neither can the nurses, it seems. People are panicking, running in and
out of her room. I roll my head onto my left ear and peer through the divid-
ing window as a doctor rushes in, fumbles with a syringe and pulls shut the
privacy curtain. A minute or so later the woman lies silent.*

*I can't believe I'm here, that I let myself end up here, faceup, prostrate and
struggling just to breathe. It didn't have to be this way. I realize that. I
didn't have to get this sick. There were warning signs that my hormonal
household was not in order—that night in Toronto, for starters—but it's too
late for regret, too late to mourn the past. My life has come down to a series*

of moments, of phlegmy breaths. Please, God, give me the strength to get better, to get out of this bed. I promise I will never again neglect the life you have given me. I will pay attention to what my mind and body tell me. I will not deny the mortality of my humanity; I will not deny the fallibility of my manhood and the fragility of life. Please, just let me sleep, let that painkiller kick in, please just let me see black.

A nurse bends over and rubs my forehead, glancing at a rhythmically bleeping box beside my bed. She explains that I'm in the intensive care unit at Cedars Sinai Medical Center . . . my nose and sinuses are packed with gauze because my sub-brain surgical wounds are "draining" . . . I should breathe slowly through my mouth . . . let the oxygen mask do its job . . . just relax and everything will be okay.

The middle-aged nurse with a Spanish accent and a motherly voice then points to a button on the inside of the bed rail. "I know you can't talk, so just push this if you need me," she says soothingly, before turning and walking away. As she's about to leave the room, I grunt and point to my legs, which are still encased in rising and falling plastic leggings, covering me, like my hockey goalie pads did in a former, healthier time of my life, from my ankles to just above the knee. The nurse returns to my side. I crinkle my forehead, drawing panic lines, saying to my nurse with facial gymnastics what I can't verbalize: What the fuck are on my legs?

She—thank God—understands my primitive communication. "They're squeezing your legs, keeping your blood circulating," she says. "They'll prevent blood clots." Phew . . . that explains the incessant hissing. But I still don't like any of this. I want to move my own legs, circulate my own blood. I'm scared. I wish this was just a nightmare. I wish everything would go black again. And it does.

"We need a goalie, and we want you," Coach Terry Slater says in his Canadian prairie-bred patter. "We want Kenny Baker to play for Colgate."

Slater delivers me this news over the phone. It's late April of my senior year of high school and Colgate University's first-string goalie has dropped out of school to sign a pro contract, and since all the top college hockey programs have three goalies, they desperately need to fill their vacant goalie slot.

I have been receiving letters from Colgate's young assistant coach, Brian Durocher, since my sophomore year of high school, but they were always of the form-letter variety. *We're impressed with your talents and hope you will consider our school when that time comes . . . blah blah blah.* Terry Slater is a college hockey coaching legend. Slater has been coaching ever since he retired from pro hockey in the early sixties. Known as "Slats" in the cloistered hockey world, Slater first earned his reputation as a hard-ass while head coach for the Cincinnati Stingers of the World Hockey Association, the now-defunct rival to the National Hockey League that employed hockey greats such as Gordie Howe and Wayne Gretzky before merging with the NHL. So when *the* Terry Slater personally calls me at home one evening, I figure Colgate is very interested in recruiting me. And Slater does nothing to dissuade me from that notion.

As a dedicated reader of *The Hockey News*, I know that Colgate already has two goalies who will be sophomores next year. I respectfully ask Slater about my competition.

"Well, Kenny," he replies, "there's Greg Menges and David Gagnon. I can't promise anything other than you will have as good a shot as them. But I'll be honest with you, Kenny. I am not holding a slot for either of them. If you're the best one out on the ice, you'll be our starter."

I like how he sprinkles *Kenny* into every other sentence.

"Why don't you come out to campus for a visit," he adds. "We'll fly you out and take care of you for a couple days."

A week later I land at the Syracuse airport, where I am met by a driver in one of those chauffeur caps standing in the baggage claim area holding a cardboard sign with BAKER scrawled on it. The hour-long drive to the rural village of Hamilton takes me over several saddleback hills and narrow glacial valleys brimming with a springtime-green palette of oaks, willows and poplar trees. *This school must be in the boonies; okay, it's in the middle of nowhere, but it's still prettier than Buffalo.*

About two miles north of town, the hilltop campus and its stately brick buildings come into view. The driver, a self-described "huuuuuge" Colgate hockey fan, points out the various student drinking holes as we roll slowly through the village of Hamilton's quaint, one-block-long row of prewar storefronts. "That's the Back Bacon," the driver says, pointing to a hole-in-the-wall bar with a mural of a beer-swilling pig painted on the facade. "If you're like most of the hockey players I know, you'll be spending a lot of time there."

I don't tell him I'm practically a teetotaler, or that I am not the kind of cock-swinging jock he thinks I am. I like the attention, though. This is my first time in a limo. So I keep quiet.

"That's Kappa Alpha Theta," he says a little farther down the road, waving his right hand in the direction of a white two-story house amid a row of equally antiquated buildings that he calls Fraternity Row.

"A frat?" I ask.

"No, a sorority," he says with a *huck-a-huck* chuckle. "Prettiest girls in the school." He gazes back into the rearview mirror and crinkles a curious eye.

"You got a girlfriend?"

"Yeah."

"Too bad. Being on the hockey team, you won't have trouble meetin' ladies."

A few minutes later I meet Brian Durocher, Slater's amiable assistant, at the ice rink. Since the hockey season is over, Starr Rink sits warm and iceless; rows of wood bleachers are empty. I imagine the arena packed to the rafters on a frigid January night . . . the school band blaring the fight song . . . fans waving signs . . . I make a spectacular glove save with one second left in the game . . . rabid fans are chanting *BaaaKER! BaaaKER! BaaaKER!*

Brian tells me that the team had a pretty respectable season this year, finishing fifth in the highly competitive Eastern Collegiate Athletic Conference behind perennial powerhouses such as the University of Vermont, Harvard and Cornell. But, as Coach Slater had told me over the phone, the team's starting goalie has left, opting to go pro rather than finish college. "That means we're going to be weakest in the goalie slot," Brian says. "So we hope you like it here. Of course, we'd really like to see you next year wearing a Colgate uniform."

Brian and I walk across the trophy cases in the lobby over to Slater's windowless office. Black and white photos capturing Colgate hockey's highlights over his last eleven seasons line the concrete walls. I first notice Slater's hawkish, fifty-year-old face and piercing eyes as he sits talking on the phone, his forehead wrinkles squirming beneath a graying widow's peak of gopher-brown hair. Until now, I've only seen pictures of Slater, and in those he looked older and more intense than in person. When I sit before him, he smiles—something I've never seen him doing in the photos in the media guide they mailed to me. With the phone wedged between his ear and shoulder, Slater shakes my hand with a logger's grip. *This guy's not mean; in fact, he is downright magnanimous.*

I sit upright, poised. There's something about his rigidity that makes me feel like I'm addressing an Army general, which I later learn is exactly how he perceives himself, instructing players to call him "The General."

In 1977, Slater came to Colgate and turned around a losing hockey program that had up to that point been populated mostly with prep-school brats. Slater, a native of the Ottawa area who had played professionally in the Montreal Canadiens organization, used his fame and clout in Canada to recruit the top players from Ontario and Quebec. Harvard, Yale, Boston University and Boston College might have gotten the best New Englanders, but the Colgate Red Raiders started nabbing some of the best Canadian players. Americans, however, soon became token players who many suspected Slater kept on the roster just to please the mostly American alumni and athletic department brass. Out of about twenty-five players, in fact, Slater usually only had five to ten "Yankees" (as the Canadians like to call us) on the squad, making it among the least American squads in the league.

In his sales pitch, Slater never explains why he wants an American goalie; yet, flattered and respectful that they've flown me out to their campus, I don't bother asking.

"I'll get right to the point, Kenny," Slater says. "The goaltender is the most important player on the team. See, you're like the quarterback. And a team—I don't care how many hotshots they got scoring goals for them—is only as good as its goaltender, Kenny. That's why we've brought you out here. We've been watching your development for the last, oh"—he glances over at Brian, who offers "three years"—"yeah, three years," Slater continues. "You play in that butterfly-style, and I've seen your reflexes. You know, Brian was a goalie at one time himself"—"Boston University," Brian chimes in—"and he says you're the quickest goalie he's seen in a long time."

His flattery is working. This guy is good.

"The two guys we have now aren't very *quick* goalies, Kenny. They're big guys, and they've got a year on you, but I'm telling ya, you have got just as much a chance to be our number-one goalie as they do. I don't play favorites; I play the best, hardest-working players. Understand?"

"I do, sir."

"Good. Now I want you to have fun this weekend, talk to some of the guys, party a little, get a feel for our gorgeous campus here. You know, it was founded in 1819, so it's been around awhile." Slater laughs at his own joke, air pockets escaping his lungs like bullets from a tommy gun. "We don't expect you to decide right now. You have to test-drive a car before you buy it, eh?"

That's true, I nod.

"It's a big decision. But when you get back to Buffalo, I want you to talk it over with your father and let us know just as soon as you can."

If Slater were an Army recruiter, his charisma would have me signing the commitment papers on the spot.

Brian and I walk up to the student on center on the hill. Two players from Buffalo—Karl and Jeff—meet us on the stone patio where students, as they appear to do a lot of, lounge around like this plot of academia in Hamilton, New York, is the French Riviera. Brian tells me the sturdy junior players will be my tour guides for the weekend and, after handing me a few bills in fun money, heads back to the rink.

After touting the reasons to go to Colgate (the great education, the chicks, the great hockey program, the great chicks, the free booze, the chicks) during a walk through the leafy campus—*wait till I tell Dad the walls really have ivy on them*—Karl and Jeff take me over to the off-campus apartment of a cocksure player from Canada nicknamed "Boomer."

Boomer gets right to the point, to the core of what clearly is a recruiting message aimed at my most banal male urges. "You'll be like a kid in a candy store," says the muscular jock, who boasts of being the designated player for showing recruits a good time. "Free pussy. You won't even have to try, eh? The pussy will find *you*, my friend."

One of the first things I notice about Boomer is that, besides the fact that his top rack of superwhite teeth resembles a row of mint Chiclets, he, in a common conversational Canadian quirk, utters *eh* in every sentence, usually at the end, which turns just about everything he says into a question.

Boomer hands me a Molson and plops beside me on his ratty couch. The place reeks of beer. "Check out these babies," he says, thumbing through a stack of Polaroids like a deck of cards. The photos, he explains, are of a naked hockey groupie. "We fucked the shit out of this cum dumpster the other night," he explains.

Oh, I say.

The photos show a woman, probably in her early twenties, wearing nothing except for white socks sagging around her ankles. As if the images don't speak for themselves, Boomer enthusiastically describes every bare-ass shot of her laughing and grabbing her boobs, which dangle like a pair of plump watermelons. One picture shows her bent over, ass in the air, her pale butt cheeks that haven't seen sun in their lifetime forming a vertical smile for the camera. "Now that's a full moon if I ever saw one, eh?" he says. "But you know what they say: 'The bigger the cushion, the better the pushin'.'"

I laugh, too, and say, "*That's* for fuckin' sure," and then I sip some more beer, trying not to grimace from the bitterness.

Boomer spreads the pictures, solitaire-style, on the coffee table. My eyes pop open as he gives the pornographic play-by-play. *Check out those titties, eh? . . . I did her right there in the kitchen . . . Nice bush, eh?* Since I am a sexually inexperienced seventeen-year-old, and the only naked woman I've ever seen in person is Jenny, my curious eyes are glued to his personal pornography. I have never seen anything like this—so raw, so sexy, so . . . *wrong.*

Boomer makes it sound like my athletic grant-in-aid will come packaged with attractive—if not morally pure—women as a fringe benefit. According to Boomer, there are two types of Colgate chicks: (a) the "good to go" (any girl who will sleep with him), and (b) "bitches" (any girl, I quickly surmise, who has too much self-respect to spread her legs for some drunken jock). Later that night, I go from bar to bar watching drooling girls flirt with Karl and Jeff and Boomer and Dupe and Bish and Younger and Lillie and Davey and seemingly every other player on the team, who all strut around town like barnyard studs.

Without even seeing a classroom, I'm sold. Except for Cornell, Colgate, two hundred miles due east of Buffalo, is the closest NCAA Division I hockey school to home. That means Dad will be able to drive to see me play every home game. At breakfast with the coaches the next morning, I inform Slater that I will definitely play for Colgate. He has my word. Then I call Dad.

"You're sure, now," Dad says. "This is where you want to spend the next four years of your life?"

"Absolutely," I assure him.

"How much they offering?" he asks.

"A full ride."

A hundred or so students are filing into Olin Hall for the first day of Psychology 101. It's an unusually sweltering ninety degrees for an early September afternoon in central New York State. Students sit on the window ledges of Gothic-style residential halls and on the steps of the campus's dozen or so other sandstone monstrosities. I'm told they're academic halls. Sunbathers—I take note of the bikini-clad girls sprawled on blankets—lie in the grassy campus quadrangle, soaking up the rays and scoping guys through their hundred-dollar sunglasses.

In psych class, students are dressed more formally. This being the elite, private Colgate University, many of the girls wear designer-label tops and mid-thigh-length skirts covering the kind of sexy legs and backsides I've only seen in John Hughes movies. Likewise, most of the guys dress affluently cool, a campus uniform of either Dockers pants or pleated khaki shorts. Many of the guys wear Oxford-style shirts, unbuttoned at the top. They all look so *adult*.

Back home, in Buffalo, where I have to explain to my hockey pals (many of whom are attending community college or pumping gas or some other equivalent) that Colgate is not a toothpaste, I saw maybe a dozen or so girls in school whom I thought were as pretty as Jenny, and maybe two who even came close to TV-caliber beautiful. As I'm opening my spanking-new spiral notebook and fishing for my ballpoint pen, however, a gaggle of girls strut past me. The first one prancing down the aisle is petite with porcelain skin and brown hair. The next one, considerably taller, at least five foot nine, has long, tanned legs that glisten as if polished with Turtle Wax. Her long, black, shampoo-commercial hair bounces a dance of seduction along the top of her leather backpack. Then comes the Madonna blonde, who is laughing while telling a story that I can't hear over the classroom's hum of conversation. The blonde is barely covered in a tight, low-cut top. As they settle into their seats a few rows in front of me, I can't stop thinking that these are the kind of girls I've only seen in magazines and movies. These girls are *women.*

Most everyone is a freshman, including me, the pale dude with straight, sandy-brown hair parted down the middle—feathered bangs on the top, and mid-neck-length down the back. (A drunk girl at a party will soon inform me that my hairstyle is known as "hockey hair"—I had never heard that expression). Adding to my stylistic mishmash is a pair of acid-washed jeans and a white golf shirt with three buttons at the top, each of which I've fastened, thinking it is scholarly to do so. My mom probably bought the 50-percent polyester weave on a Blue Light Special a few weeks before I left for school, along with a pair of preppy "pleather" boat shoes and a few fresh tightie-whities and tube socks. "You're going to a preppy school so you'll have to dress preppy," Mom told me, a guy to whom clothing's purpose has mostly been to keep warm, not to make a fashion statement. She means well, but maybe if Mom, or anyone I knew for that matter, had ever stepped onto a the grounds of an upper-crust college she would have been able to warn me that the bright white tube socks (with blue and red stripes) she bought aren't supposed to be worn with the boat shoes. I learned this yesterday upon seeing a parade of guys with naked feet in real-leather boat shoes lounging at the dining hall. I took the socks off and stuffed them in my backpack before finishing dinner.

I need to go shopping.

Here in psych class, the trio of beautiful girls are casting an estrogenic spell on me that, even with my general sexual anxiety about being with women, and my increasing indifference about having sex at all, absolutely mesmerizes me. Just then, the professor stands at the bottom of the auditorium-style classroom and, clutching a fat black marker, flicks on the overhead projector. The class quiets down.

Naturally the professor starts at the beginning, the dawn of the discipline of psychology. He begins with a description of a German scientist named Wilhelm Wundt, "the father of modern psychology." The prof explains that if it were not for Wundt's (pronounced *Voont's*) historic studies on the machinations of the human psyche, there probably would be no Freud, no Jung, no psychobabbling self-help gurus selling books by the millions.

In the mid-1800's, the professor says from the podium, apparently from rote memorization, Wundt started teaching students how to study their conscious experience through a thought process he called "introspection." The prof then points out that this notion of introspection might have been groundbreaking in the horse-and-buggy days, but the idea of a person solving his own psychological puzzle by merely practicing introspection is considered an archaic notion.

The lecture doesn't strike me as particularly relevant to my life. Psychology is my father calling psychologists "no-nothing jerk-offs" when Mom informs him that she is consulting one. Psychology is for crazy people who don't know how to solve their own problems, to think them through logically, to endure their own mental anguish until they erase it with the power of positive thinking.

This opinion, of course, disregards my reality.

I spent much of my childhood obsessed with hockey and avoiding girls because I had to keep order and control over things while my family spun out of control. Beneath my veneer of confidence, though, I believe I am an unathletic fraud who hardly deserves a hockey scholarship, let alone to be the object of college townie idol-worship.

Ever since that failed night of sex in Toronto earlier this year, I have not even mentioned the word *sex* to Jenny because I am so embarrassed, so paralyzed by performance anxiety, that I'd rather be celibate forever than ever have my dick betray me like that again. A few weeks after we returned to Buffalo from our trip, Jenny and I finally did have sex—in her bedroom while her parents were at work—in a less pressured environment. In fact, we eventually did it maybe a half dozen times, each time a little more enjoyable and less nerve-racking than the previous one. Still, it was always Jenny who initiated. Now that I had lost the stigma of virginity, I felt relieved and content that it was over.

"You don't have to wait for me to jump your bones," Jenny soon told me in that instructive kindergarten-teacher voice of hers. "A girl likes to be mauled sometimes."

Yet, I never rip off her clothes like in the movies. Mostly, my penis doesn't seem to want to rise to the occasion so spontaneously. It usually takes my hand, or hers, or her mouth—and an investment of several minutes—to get me ready. Even then, sometimes my penis doesn't get hard and I try to brush it off by joking, "He's sleeping," when I'm actually beating myself up inside as if I had let in a puck that was shot from a hundred feet away. Sex is not that important to me, anyway. I don't think of my penis on a daily, even a weekly, basis (except when it fails me, at which time I can't stop thinking about why it won't work). Plus, I simply don't feel as if some unstoppable biochemical force were propelling me into a skirt-chasing frenzy. Sure, those three girls sitting below me in psych class are gorgeous. I can see them. I find them attractive. But the last thing I am going to do is go and talk to them. I'm too intimidated, too afraid that my dick will not do what I want it to. Furthermore, I don't much feel like getting naked in front of girls right now. I need to get into better shape, become more manly-looking. Now it's *really* starting to bother me that, even as a supposedly hotshot college hockey player and Olympic team prospect, I don't carry any more muscle tissue on my frame than I did before I started growing pubic hair, which came in almost two years after other friends my age. Despite my insecurities, I will *not* let them infect my on-ice activity. As always, the rink is a sanctuary—a reality unto itself where I rise above my petty little insecurities.

So, then, why am I taking psychology? It's just a class that most freshmen take. I signed up, so here I sit. I haven't yet realized that classes—like books—often find you.

I scribble the gist of what the prof is saying into my notebook, rushing to finish before he moves on to the next topic. I am far too slow of a scribbler and far too preoccupied in my own thoughts, however, to fully grasp the point he is making. I'm too busy trying not to look like a fool. I'm afraid the professor, or maybe those pretty girls in the front, will see me for who I really am: a boy from Buffalo who is getting a $20,000-a-year scholarship to attend a prestigious liberal-arts college because he can stop pucks—not because he is particularly smart.

I fully realize that some students may (rightfully) look at me as undeserving, a dumb jock, a cliché. Many of them come from elite prep schools that I've never heard of—Exeter, Choate, Andover and Deerfield. I saw them driving their Saab convertibles and hand-me-down Volvos and drop-top Euro-racers into the parking lot this morning. Their parents are stockbrokers, lawyers, doctors, bankers, millionaires. I bet they have never worked a hard day in their life.

Me? I graduated from a suburban public high school outside of Buffalo, New York, with barely a B average. Last summer, I bagged groceries at Super Duper for $3.35 an hour (and that's before subtracting my food-worker's union initiation fees). My car? I don't even own a bike, let alone a car, although in my junior year I will finally save enough money from my lawn-mowing summer job to buy a car: a 1978 Ford Granada with a beige vinyl top and a hole in the driver's-side floor.

And while I feel certain that most every Colgate student has read the great works of American literature, I prefer *The Hockey News, Hockey Digest,* as well as hockey instruction manuals and the occasional issue of *Mad* magazine. Although Dad reads the newspapers and Mom reads *People* magazine and mystery novels, our family spends more time watching the boob tube. Which is why I can summarize, with frightening accuracy, entire episodes of *Happy Days, The Flintstones* and *The Brady Bunch,* and I can recite nearly every line from the movie *Stripes.* Yet, the only novel I can remember reading from start to finish is Ernest Hemingway's *Old Man and the Sea* (only because it was really short and about fishing). I've read a few nonfiction books, such as the former Montreal Canadiens goalie Dick Irvin's memoir, *In the Crease,* and *A Season on the Brink,* John Feinstein's journalistic account of spending the 1985–86 season with the Indiana State University basketball team. I have read a smattering of self-help books, my favorite being *All I Really Need to Know I Learned in Kindergarten.* But more robust, literary-caliber books intimidate me. The classics are for pointy heads, the pimply kids in the Gifted and Talented in my high school, whom my friends and I dubbed the "Gay and Talented." When my ninth-grade English teacher assigned *The Odyssey,* I stopped just a few pages into it out of stultifying boredom; then I bought the Cliff's notes. When it came time for the multiple-choice test on that phonebook-fat book, I made sure I sat next to the smartest girl in the class and copied her multiple-choice answers, being sure to write an incorrect answer every ten or so, just to make it believable to Mr. Tutuska, who, having had my older brothers in his class, knew I was about as scholarly as the bartender pouring fifty-cent drafts down the street at Callahan's.

My admission isn't a total sham. Besides expecting me to uphold the Red Raiders' fighting tradition, the university has placed one major condition on it. Due to an application essay in which I repeatedly misspelled *believe,* misused commas and semicolons and showed a tendency to repeatedly split my infinitives, the school makes me take a remedial writing class my freshman year—a course populated with football players, basketball players, hockey players, affirmative-action cases and turban-topped engineering majors from India. I like writing—heck, I've been pouring my thoughts and feelings into a diary since I was eleven—but the admissions officer tells me that my prose is "technically weak." I take his assessment to mean that, technically, I suck. I will spend most of my college career avoiding classes that require me to write a lot of academic papers; I end up majoring in geology, partly because I am genuinely interested in earth science, but mostly because the geology department doesn't make me write many essays about rocks.

Considering my lackluster credentials, not to mention my social and fashion faux pas, it's no surprise that Wilhelm Wundt's historic contribution to the field of psychology went unappreciated by me that first day of psych. True appreciation won't come for another twelve years, when, while rummaging through my closet, I find a notebook stuffed into the bottom of a cardboard box marked "college stuff." Handwritten on its red cardboard cover is "1988–89"—the diary of my first year of college.

I sit on my living room carpet, thumbing through the yellow pages, and stop at the entry for January 1, 1989, a couple weeks after the end of my first, 2.4–GPA semester at Colgate:

I sleep with a bear. A cute little stuffed bear named Rudy. Every night I lie down with this little guy. He gives me that extra security that I need on cold lonely nights (and warm ones too!). Ya know, it's not cool for a guy to sleep with a bear, but it's cute for a perfectly mature woman. I've always wondered why this was.

Heck, a few hormones here and there and men really aren't that different than women. I wish it were cool for me to sleep with a bear. And, ya know, I bet most guys feel the same way.

I can't stop rereading one sentence: *Heck, a few hormones here and there and men really aren't that different than women.* This, I realize many painful years later, is evidence that, indeed, man cannot solve his mental puzzles by introspection alone. Evidence that suggests why I ended up with a D+ in Psychology 101. Evidence of an inability to be aware of a growing gender ambiguity building inside of me. Most freshman guys don't want anything to do with stuffed bears, especially ones that their high school girlfriends gave them as a going-away present. While

I cower into college as a bear-hugging Joe Sensitive, most other guys are too busy getting drunk, pledging fraternities and, most enthusiastically, trying to get laid. I doubt any of them are sitting around pondering the unfairness of society not approving of adult males sleeping with stuffed animals. What the *fuck* is wrong with me?

Dad is right: I am different. I am not like the rest—of my family or of the world. And no matter how intense the peer pressure, I am determined to carve my own path however I want. At least I've tried to have sex. Okay, so it wasn't all it was cracked up to be. But sex has only gotten people I know into trouble, anyway. Kevin, my oldest brother, already has a kid, with a sixteen-year-old girl. And, well, I know that having sex with my mom stands as my father's grandest error, at least according to his woeful version of history.

"How's it goin', Kenny?" Dad, now a three-hour drive away, asks in one of our nightly phone conversations.

"Aside from a few spoiled brats here and there, I like it a lot. But I haven't met many hockey players yet. We'll see."

I don't tell Dad that I was so scared about leaving home that I cried on a bench in the quad after he dropped me off that first day of school. I don't tell him that I miss riding bikes with my little brother and playing catch at the park. I definitely don't tell him I miss Jenny, whom I can't even afford to call and so must write letters—at first, daily, now weekly.

"How's Kris doing?" I ask.

"Fine," Dad says plaintively. The more emotional my dad gets, the less talkative he gets. "He's at the playground shooting hoops. I'll tell him you called." And so the content-less conversations go on and on . . .

I'm not usually ultra-talkative because my roommate is eavesdropping from across my dorm room. He is a swimmer from San Diego named Kevin. He's the first person I have ever met from California, and here I am forced to sleep ten feet away from this surfer dude who wears sandals in November. I wonder if he and I are the subjects of one of those college social psychology experiments, with the two-way mirrors and video surveillance.

Kevin is tan; I am pale. Kevin listens to hip West Coast bands I've never heard of, like Oingo Boingo; meanwhile, I think Supertramp is cool. Kevin has well-to-do parents who have never been divorced and his dad is a square-jawed Navy captain; my mom is scraping to pay the rent, my father hasn't worked for the last two months and leaves the top button of his pants undone because (a) he is too fat for them and (b) he is too poor to afford new ones.

Fatter than ever, Dad nearly went into a diabetic coma a few weeks ago. In fact, up until the day before my first day of freshman orientation, I thought I was taking the bus to Colgate. Dad has lost a third of his eyesight because, thanks to neglecting to take his insulin pills, his insulin level plummeted toward zero. He now has to inject himself with insulin twice a day and is doing telemarketing for a roofing and siding company (the pitch: "Buffalo winters are the harshest in the nation. Ma'am, have you or your husband thought about installing vinyl siding to protect your home from the elements?") to pay the rent and to support my little brother Kris, who, since he's no longer speaking to Mom, is living with Dad in a two-bedroom duplex that abuts the railroad tracks.

The hardest thing about the day I left for Colgate was saying goodbye to my little bro'.

He was twelve, and for most of his life I had acted as something of a surrogate father to him. When Dad left home, Kris could rely on me. When he was ten and being taunted by his classmates for being the new kid in school, he would come home every afternoon crying his eyes out and begging Mom to let him go back to his old school. Whenever Dad fell ill and couldn't give Kris a ride or make him lunch, I did. When my dad, who had remarried a Bulgarian immigrant who badly wanted a green card, was worried that Kris would freak out about his third marriage, I was the one who broke the news to Kris, who had hated my dad's second wife, who in turn despised Kris, mostly because he wasn't hers.

Dad had been lonely and sick. I think he feared not having a woman around to take care of him. Who better than an Eastern European woman who would be indebted to him for his getting her citizenship?

This is how I informed Kris that Dad, who had been single for about a year after divorcing his second wife, planned on making the Bulgarian wife #3.

"Dad's getting married again," I said.

"You're kidding," Kris replied.

"No, Kris, I'm serious. Dad wanted me to tell you."

His face turned whiter than the blade of a snow plow and he sighed, "Here we go again."

I followed him outside.

"Don't you want to know who she is?"

"Fine. Who is she?"

"She's from Bulgaria."

"How does Dad know her?"

"I guess they went out on a date last night."

"What?"

"They went out last night."

"And now he wants to marry her?"

"I guess so. Or at least that's what he said."

"You're kidding."

"Nope."

"What an idiot."

"Yep."

I wish Dad is kidding when he calls me at Colgate occasionally and tells me the latest mischief that Kris, now sixteen, living alone with a sick, burned-out father and his Bulgarian wife, has gotten himself into.

Kris got caught stealing a cassette tape from the drug store today . . .

Kris got picked up by the cops this morning for mooning a bunch of old ladies at the library . . .

Kris's girlfriend might be pregnant . . .

I feel somewhat responsible for Kris's missteps. Mom and Dad might not have always been there for him—and Kyle, Keith and Kevin certainly were not—but I always was. Until now, that is. What kind of role model am I? I am so caught up in my college life and all my anxiety that I don't have time to call him. Maybe it has something to do with the fact that I am tired of carrying the weight of Dad's neglect.

My family becomes an ugly stepchild I don't like to talk about. I don't want anyone to know the whole sordid tale of the dysfunctional disaster that awaits me back home.

I can't tell any of my college friends; they won't understand. They seem to have perfect families, with fat-ass bank accounts and designer wardrobes and European vacations. They're probably just trust-fund babies who have had everything handed to them. Although I wouldn't mind the luxury they enjoy, I keep telling myself that at least I possess a scholarship, not to mention *character.*

In my first week of college, for example, I have witnessed things that Kiss Ass Kenny would never do: The guy down the hall who chugged a can of Milwaukee's Best while being dangled upside down by his ankles; some drunken girl who flashed her bare breasts for a free beer. And I saw someone snort coke.

Up until now, everything I've done in my life has been focused on living as squeaky-clean and disciplined a life as possible, in order to play for a Division I college hockey team and, with enough hard work, someday make it to the National Hockey League. I had assumed everyone—that is, except for the losers back in Hamburg—would do whatever they could to have a better life. Yet, most everyone around me, it seems, is doing everything they can to piss this golden opportunity away.

Except, much to my surprise, for my roommate, Kevin. It turns out that despite his neon beachwear and surfer-boy looks, despite his private-school background, Kevin the Californian also feels like something of a freak among Colgate's 2,700 students.

I conclude that Kevin's not so bad on one of the first Friday nights of the semester. It's around midnight and the entire fourth floor of our dorm is empty; most everyone is either at frat parties or in one of the pickup joints in downtown Hamilton. Having decided that if I don't start studying I will fail out of school before the first game of the season, I am lying in bed reading, as fate would have it, *The Odyssey*, required for my Roots of Western Civilization class.

Kevin blurts out from across the room, "That guy Tom is a total chump." Tom is one of our neighbors, a spiked-hair rich kid straight out of a northeastern prep school and the pretty-boy grandson of the founder of a famous frozen-food company who likes to strut naked down the hallway, probably just to show everyone how big his cock is.

"Yeah," I reply. "He's probably gay too."

"Probably?" Kevin asks. "I'd say *definitely*."

We spend the next few hours talking about how spoiled so many of the guys in our dorm are acting. I like his attitude; he's not one of *them*. It turns out that Kevin is as monkish in his dedication to swimming as I am to hockey. Although I've technically had sex, I'm not exactly Don Juan. Neither is Kevin; I suspect he's not very sexually experienced either. Like me, he's not a big drinker. I have never seen him barf from alcohol poisoning, which, judging from the behavior we've been observing around us the first couple of weeks of college, must be an admission requirement to Colgate. Kevin attended a private school in the coastal city of La Jolla. He has swum in the Pacific, has seen ocean sunsets I've seen only in pictures. Yet, I relate to him because he is not from a privileged northeastern prep school and is proud of it. "These chumps act like they're in Grade Thirteen or something," he sighs.

The following night, Kevin and I again are hanging out late in our dorm room. Kevin is practicing his Russian while listening to a mix tape of his favorite tunes. A short guy with short-cropped black hair pokes his head through the doorway.

"Good evening, boys," the little bespectacled guy says with almost British formality. He's wearing a pair of Bermuda shorts, flip-flops and a white tank top. "Hmm," he adds. "Looks like you two boys and I are the only ones studying tonight."

"You're from California, aren't you," Kevin says.

"East Los Angeles, actually," Sean admits, sipping from his (gourmet) coffee mug. "I'm Sean."

We shake hands. I get the feeling Sean is a normal guy too.

I've now made two friends at Colgate. They're both from California and, like me, not in the social mainstream.

If I could pick one word that sums up my first year at Colgate, it would be the nickname my teammates slap on me: "Pear," as in my body resembles a pear: round at the waist, narrow at the shoulders. I would prefer "Boom Boom" or "The Rocket" or "The Great One," but my underdeveloped physique precludes such macho monikers. As a result, from the very first time I stand naked in the team shower, my conspicuous midsection and sloping shoulders earn me this most unflattering nickname. There's "Boomer." Mike Bishop is "Bish." Scott Young is "Younger." Craig Woodcroft is "Woody." Dave Gagnon is "Davie" or "Gags." As for Ken Baker? Well, a few of the nicer guys, like Karl and Jeff from Buffalo, call me "Bakes." Yet, the majority of the Canadian upperclassmen prefer "Pear." This wasn't the Big Man on Campus treatment I had been told to expect, and I hate it.

Actually, in the first few months of my freshman year there are things about the Colgate hockey team I don't like very much . . .

Let's start with **Coach Slater**. . . .

No matter how well I play in practice, which is usually quite well—not to mention equal to or better than the team's other two goalies—Slater never plays me in a game or even lets me dress in my equipment, nor does he ever offer any explanation. Instead he ignores me and I spend the first few games sitting in the press box chewing pencils, and my fingers, as I watch Dave Gagnon become the starting goalie and all-around campus superstar while I am left to wonder why I fell for Slater's bullshit and came to this school in the first place. Even though Dad insists that I confront Slater about my bench-warming, I am too fearful that he will take away my scholarship if I dare rock the boat. As he screams in the locker room, he is "The General" and we are "the Good Soldiers." Finally, a couple months into the season, Slater puts me in the starting lineup and I back up Dave in a game against Princeton, another school that had recruited me and that, along with most every other college in our league, I'm thinking of defecting to if I don't start playing soon.

A year ago everyone thought I was the shit, a stud, a demigod in American junior hockey circles. I played all the big games on my team. In 1986, I had won a gold medal for my country, the first U.S. hockey victory in a world championships since the storied 1980 Olympics. Pro scouts came to see me play. Just a few months ago, in fact, the assistant coach of the Buffalo Sabres came to see me play. My dad made sure to introduce himself and talk his ear off about how great I was (which annoyed most parents to no end and probably didn't help my chances with the Sabres either). I was the subject of glowing feature stories in my local paper.

Now I'm in college and riding the pines, pulling splinters out of my ass while clinging to the hope that the first-string goalie will get hit in the balls and Slater will have no choice but to put me in. Then, as my plan goes, I will play unbelievably and take over the job.

Sadly, it doesn't happen—despite clearly outplaying and outhustling Dave in practice. And despite Dave being a partier.

In fact, Dave's frat-boy partying gets so out of hand that, by the second semester, Slater forces Dave, a native of western Ontario (of course he is Canadian), to move out of the Beta Theta Pi house and into a dorm, up on the hill, away from the shenanigans on Frat Row. By chance, and by the sick humor of fate's hand, Dave ends up moving into the single room next door to me and Kevin. From the start, his room becomes a fraternity annex, where his Beta brothers and his girlfriend, Laurie, come for nightly visits to party, smoke, screw and generally keep Kevin and me up all night.

Then there's the **Three Other Freshman Players**. . . .

Three of the four new recruits are Canadians. Jamie and Jason, from Toronto, and Dale, from Ottawa. They play in every game and, despite their rookie mistakes, Slater never benches them. I and Dave Doherty, a funny Irish guy from outside of *Bah*ston, are the Americans. Neither of us plays.

Dave calls me "Bakes," but the other three freshmen, while they are otherwise likeable chaps, sometimes call me Pear and rarely want to hang out with me because, seeing as I'm just a lowlife sub, I am not cool enough.

And, finally, there is the **Hazing Hell**. . . .

Not only must I face the daily humiliation of being called Pear, being ignored by most of my freshman teammates, and being relegated to the status of backup goalie, but the upperclassmen decide to make me miserable with a humiliating, homoerotic series of rituals that I must perform before I am accepted as a real member of the clan known as the Colgate Red Raiders.

It starts when the guys give me a choice: I can shave my head, or shave my entire body—from the armpits down to my toe hair. Not yet fully beaten into submission, I refuse to do either. Fine, they say. If I'm not willing to shave myself, they promise they will pin me down and shave me themselves. They give me a week to change my mind.

"Come on, Bakes," another freshman says a few days later. "Just do it. They're going to fuck with you even more if you don't shave. They just want you to be one of the guys. They had to go through this shit, and they just want you to do the same. It's not like they're asking us to do anything they haven't done themselves."

"Fuck 'em," I say. "That doesn't make it any more acceptable. If they force me to do anything, I'll just tell the administration."

"Yeah, then you'll be blackballed," he snarls. "You think it's hard now, if you nark on them, the guys will fuck with you until you quit."

"I don't care."

But, of course, I do.

Even so, a week passes, and while the other freshmen have taken a razor to their armpits, chest, ass, legs and balls, I haven't yet shaved an inch of my body. I'm the least hairy of all the guys, but it's not the hair, it's the principle.

I get to practice early, before anyone can see me naked; after practice, I stay out on the ice late. When it appears that everyone has left the arena, I head for the locker room, hoping to sneak out without anyone accosting me.

I'm in the shower rinsing soap off my face when I open my eyes and see a group of five or six upperclassmen surrounding me. One's holding a can of shaving cream; another is waving a Bic razor in front of me.

"Time to shave, Pear," one of them says.

I stand under the rushing water, feigning that I am not terrified.

"You're not leaving till you shave, you know."

"Listen," I say. "I'll do anything but shave my body. I just don't want—"

One of them pushes me against the tile wall and holds my wrists together over my head. When I squirm and slip onto the floor, they laugh.

"Okay, all right," I say, nearly in tears. "I'll fucking shave. Just leave me alone. I'll do it my fuckin' self."

The meatheads leave, except for one, who for the next fifteen minutes watches me shave almost every inch of my body. I hope he enjoyed himself . . . the asshole.

My initiation continues on our first bus trip to Boston. A long-standing Colgate hockey tradition is that on the team's first road trip every freshman must tell a joke to the rest of the guys. And if the joke isn't funny, you are forced to strip naked and locked in the bus's coffin-size bathroom until you come up with one that makes the cavemen howl.

On a Thursday afternoon in late October 1988, I climb aboard the team bus headed for Northeastern University. It is my inaugural road trip, as well as my formal initiation into a club that I am increasingly questioning whether I want to be part of.

I have about as much of a choice to not go through with the initiation rituals as do adolescent male members of the Amhara tribe, rural cultivators in Ethiopia who force their young men to endure whipping contests they call *buhe*. I recently read about them in my anthropology book. Evidently, the Amhara elders hold these ceremonies in which the boys are forced to stand amid a circle of older men cracking whips. If the bloodied youths (whose faces and bodies are cut with the lacerating whips) show any signs of meekness, such as crying, they are mercilessly mocked and taunted. Afterward, to prove their manliness, the young men are encouraged to burn long scars on their arms with hot embers.

You think these Ethiopians are vicious? Try the manhood rituals endured by young men in Melanesia, in the highlands of New Guinea, which anthropologist David D. Gilmore has so described:

> [*Boys*] *are torn from their mothers and forced to undergo a series of*
> *brutal masculinizing rituals. . . . These include whipping, flailing,*
> *beating, and other forms of terrorization by older men, which the*

boys must endure stoically and silently. As in Ethiopia, the flesh is scored and blood flows freely. These Highlanders believe that without such hazing, boys will never mature into men but will remain weak and childlike. Real men are made, they insist, not born.

So as I nervously try and memorize my jokes on the team bus that afternoon, I can be glad that at least I live in a society where hazing of young men is of the more humane variety. Or at least that is what I keep telling myself.

Since my teammates mostly enjoy racist and sexist humor, I have scribbled a few such jokes (which my Dad told me over the phone the night before) on a piece of paper crumpled in my pocket. It's about a four-hour drive to Boston, leaving plenty of time for them to commence their rolling production of *Lord of the Flies*. The only thing that keeps me from totally crapping my pants is the presence of Coach Slater in the front seat. No matter how much of a cold shoulder he has shown me, I doubt he will let things get too far out of hand.

Dave Doherty goes first, grabbing hold of the driver's microphone and delivering hilarious punch lines. The guys applaud with raucous approval. After a few more zingers, he heads back to his seat, fully clothed, the upperclassmen high-fiving him as he passes down the aisle. He has passed the test.

Then it is Dale's, Jason's and Jamie's turns to step up to the mike. One by one they all bomb. As promised, Boomer instructs all three to take off their clothes. They do. He then rustles them up like Canadian prairie cattle, shooing them into the tiny bathroom.

By now, my heart feels like it is going to burst through my breastbone. I make my way up the aisle and grab the mike, noticing out of the corner of my eye that Slater is staring out the front window with a smirk on his face, as if he is oblivious to the student-code–breaking hijinks being committed all around him.

Spotter shushes everyone, and I begin.

"What do you call a black hooker with braces?"

After a few seconds of silence, a player in the back of the bus shouts, "A Black & Decker pecker wrecker!"

Oh, shit. He just gave away the punch line. My face almost certainly turns whiter than a Buffalo blizzard. Flustered, I try and think quickly to cover up this most tragic turn of events.

"No," I say, still thinking, ". . . no, you mean an *expensive* Black & Decker pecker wrecker."

Their confused and disgusted faces tell me just how unfunny the joke is. A chorus of boos gives Boomer the green light to push me in the direction of the bathroom. "Back of the bus, Pear."

"But I have another joke," I plead. I hate having to resort to moron humor, but I feel as if I have no choice.

"Go ahead," he says, letting go of my shirt. "It better be funny."

I step back to the front. A few players throw wadded paper balls at me; many are still booing. I clear my throat.

"Why did the black guy say he wore a tuxedo to the hospital for an operation to get his balls chopped off?"

Before anyone can inject the punch line, I affect a stereotypical ghetto-black accent and reply, "'Cuz if I'ze gonna be im*po*tent, I wants to look im*po*tant."

A few guys chuckle, but Boomer has already decided I'm going into the shitter.

I open the door and see Jason, Jamie and Dale crammed into a bathroom made for one. Suddenly, I am overcome with dread.

"NO!" I growl, pushing away from the bathroom. "I'm not fucking getting in there."

"I have twenty guys here who think different," Boomer says.

He doesn't realize how serious I am. But I really do mean it. I am not squeezing into that bathroom. Uh-uh. No way. It's too small. A heaviness fills my lungs. My breath grows short. The mob is shouting at me. I wish Coach Slater would stand up and put an end to this craziness. But he doesn't.

Hazing is as much a part of college hockey tradition as horn-blaring bands and crowds taunting goalies. I had heard stories of freshmen head-shaving, of players being locked in closets until they drank a bucket of warm beer, of freshmen being forced to sit in a circle and jerk off into a Dixie cup. It's amazing that no player has ever died or that school officials let these things happen.

On the bus, I whisper into Boomer's ear that I'm claustrophobic, and he somehow finds whatever shred of compassion he has remaining and lets me sit outside of the bathroom. But just when I think I'm in the clear, he commands me to take off all my clothes, then ties them in knots with the other three bathroom-entombed freshmen's shirts and pants and underwear. He uses our socks for ropes, tying them snugly around the tangled mess.

I could think of more humane male-bonding rituals, but just as few men get to choose their culture's rites of male passage, few prisoners get to choose their captors or the gender of their captors. Either way, I doubt the female hockey players are getting their panties tied into a bunch. *Men are so fucked up.*

Boomer throws our clothes into the bathroom as if they are an unsolved Rubik's cube and he tugs on my lifeless arm. "Since you're too pussy to be in there," he says, "you have to run the gauntlet."

Figuring it's better than being locked in a bathroom, I comply.

As I run naked up the aisle, my teammates slap and kick me in my pale ass. One guy gives me a stab in the stomach. "Free shots!" Boomer announces gleefully. Everyone is laughing but me—and Slater. The bastard looks out the windshield with a blank stare.

Later that night, the bus rolls to a stop in front of the Marriott at Boston's Copley Square. Slater hands out room keys. Mine is on the thirty-third floor, and as I make my way to the elevator bank I realize there's no way I am stepping into that elevator, a box not too unlike that bus bathroom. I feel too claustrophobic. *What if it gets stuck, and I can't get out, and I start hyperventilating and get dizzy and pass out and die?*

After the other players ascend to their rooms, I find the stairwell and begin climbing all twenty-six floors with my forty-pound hockey equipment bag slung over my shoulder and a suitcase in my hand.

Ten minutes later, I enter the room, breathless, sweat soaked into my shirt. I drop my bags and immediately splash cold water on my face over the bathroom sink and see my Olympic and NHL dreams slipping through my fingers like the rushing water.

(PROLACTIN LEVEL: 450 NG/ML)

Upon returning to campus from Boston, I head straight for my fourth-floor dorm room in West Hall, of course taking the stairs instead of the elevator. Kevin, who along with Sean and a few other guys on our floor listened to the Northeastern game on the radio, eagerly asks how the trip went. "Fine," I mumble, ignoring him.

I stuff my textbooks into my backpack and trudge down the hill to the main library to camp out in my favorite study carrel tucked behind a row of books on the basement floor. Where no one can see me. There, I read my psych text, which says that claustrophobia, the irrational fear of closed-in spaces, can be brought on by anxiety in one's life; issues of feeling out of control or helpless may also manifest themselves in the form of claustrophobia. I am deathly afraid of elevators, and seeing as though I'll have to stay in a hotel every other weekend on hockey trips, if I don't get over it—fast—I'm going to be one miserable boy named Pear. My hockey career will cease.

A week after the Boston trip—I climbed the thirty-three flights of stairs seven times that weekend, rather than risk getting stuck in an elevator—I make an appointment with a staff psychologist at the student counseling center. My mother tried to get me to see her psychologist, James, after the divorce, so that I didn't have any "issues" later in life. But I refused. Psychologists were for the weak, I thought.

Needless to say, I don't tell Dad or Kevin or Sean or certainly anyone on the team that I am seeing a shrink.

I have set up an afternoon appointment, right before hockey practice, since the counseling center sits conveniently halfway down the hill on my walk to the rink. I don't wear my gray and maroon Colgate hockey jacket, lest anyone spot me. My picture is on the team schedules that are posted all around campus as well as the downtown restaurants and shops. Even though I'm not the starting goalie, seemingly everyone—hockey is *the* most popular sport at Colgate—knows who I am. Since this is such a small school, only 2,700 students, if one person finds out that I am fucked up mentally, then the fast-moving gossip mill will reveal it to everyone. A hockey coach once told me that goaltending is eighty percent mental. If I don't believe those watching me are under the illusion that I am invincible and confident, my powers of focus and puck-stopping hubris will be impaired. I need to get over this problem.

Twisting my head, I look back and make sure no one is watching as I make the left turn onto the path leading to the counseling center, which is purposely tucked behind a stand of trees.

The psychologist greets me at her office door. A plain, mousy lady with scarecrow-straight brown hair, she asks what she can do for me in a voice so timid I can barely hear her.

"I think I'm claustrophobic, and, well, I really don't want to be, so I want to fix it."

I tell her about the bus trip.

"Oh, I'm a big hockey fan," she says.

Great. Now I'll have to worry about her watching me from the stands, knowing that no matter how tough I look on the ice, I am just a neurotic little shit underneath all that equipment.

She says she's *so sorry* when I recall the whole hazing ritual. Then I tell her about my dad, and how he is sick all the time and how I am afraid he is going to die any day, and how Jenny is starting to hint that we should "see other people," due to the long distance. I tell her that I don't really fit in at Colgate, that I hate the drunken frat scene, and that the best grade I've received so far is a B-minus. And, of course, I tell her that I feel as if Terry Slater is basically destroying my hockey career and, thus, my life. I do *not,* however, mention my sexual performance anxiety. That's too personal. That's tucked away, behind sandbags. Another thing I don't tell her is that not only do they call me Pear, but the other day an upperclassman snuck up on me in the shower and started squeezing my breasts, chortling, "Nice titties, Bakes!" I hate my body.

Shrink asks if I ever have felt claustrophobic before, and I tell her I have, when my brothers would stuff me in closets. After a couple more of these Shrink sessions, I make a breakthrough: So many things in my life are out of my control. My father's health, my girlfriend, my academic experience, my hockey coach, the uninvited taunting from other players. Shrink says claustrophobia is just a symptom of all these so-called control issues.

It makes sense, but the bottom line is that I'm still horrified at the mere thought of stepping inside elevators. Shrink suggests I try a treatment called "progressive desensitization." Gradually, she says, I can make myself less anxious and fearful about riding elevators by stepping inside a larger-size one, then quickly stepping out; then by riding a smaller one for just a floor; then riding in one packed with other people. And so on and so on, until I am able to ride in any kind of elevator without feeling terror.

Shrink offers to accompany me. But this whole therapy thing is ego-crushing enough; the last thing I want Spotter to see is me walking around campus holding Shrink's hand. I tell her I can do it on my own, thank you.

I begin my self-treatment by finding a wider-than-average elevator in Lathrop Hall. Chemistry teachers use it for hauling laboratory equipment. Since it's not one of those phone-booth–sized ones, I can handle it. Every day, on my way to study at the science library, I press the call button. The first few times, the door slides open, and I only peek in. A few times later, my heart pounding on my chest like a little boy locked in a closet, I get in and ride it one floor down (going up is riskier, since it may get stuck between floors). In hotels when on hockey trips, I force myself to take the elevator (hoping that it's large or at least glass-encased, which isn't so scary) and I pray that it doesn't get stuck. It never does, although I remain tremendously nervous about riding in them. Call me a functional claustrophobic.

I learn how to manage my fear, but not how to eradicate my frustrations.

I don't play a single minute of hockey my entire freshman season, a fact that with the help of Shrink (whom I stopped seeing after four sessions because I figured I was now strong enough to handle it myself) I conclude is for reasons totally out of my control. Dave is older and playing well and Slater apparently will play him until he falters.

I opt to spend the rest of the season trying to focus on those things I *can* control. I work hard in practice and lift weights afterward in order to make myself a stronger and faster goalie, hoping that a more muscular body will earn me a new nickname. While sitting on the bench during games, I play entire games mentally, pretending that I am Dave, the starting the goalie. In these imaginary games, I usually let in fewer goals than Dave does. This way, I stay mentally sharp, the part of my game that, more so than my reflexes, is my single most valuable goaltending skill. I was phenomenal that day in 1983 against the Rochester Americans because of my ability to block out distractions (in that case, my parents' divorce), not because I was the fastest or biggest goalie. I could, however, control my mind.

One evening in the library, where I start spending more time than the ice rink, I come upon a philosophy book. I don't remember the title, but I remember not being able to put it down until I finished it. Its central thesis is that the universe is in a constant state of entropy—disorder, chaos, whatever you want to call it—yet, humans only have the illusion of control. That's it! Fate is my master—not Slater, not how much I beat myself up about not playing. Certainly not Dad, who in so many words has communicated to me that my freshman year has been a major disappointment to him. So silly are we humans to think we actually have control over anything. Life, sports—it is all so random.

That book reminded me of my first Olympic team development camp in 1985, when a group of sports psychologists from Michigan State University led a series of seminars on how to master the mental part of the game. They suggested we read a book titled *The Inner Game of Tennis,* which I did. Its author, W. Timothy Gallwey, divided every game into two essential parts: the inner game and the outer game. Gallwey argued that a solid inner game (self-confidence, concentration, focus, calmness) allows one's outer game to flourish.

In goaltending, the outer game consists of executing skills such as skate saves, stick saves, pad saves, glove saves, two-pad stacks and the controlling of rebounds. I was confounded that sometimes I could make every save with strength and confidence and other times clumsily let in goals because I lacked confidence in my abilities. Gallwey wrote that a negative inner game is the single greatest impediment to a positive outer game. In other words, if you think you suck, you will. Gallwey's philosophy, essentially a westernized application of Zen Buddhism to sports, was to "let things happen" instead of trying to "make things happen." Let your racquet strike the ball, let the action flow as free as a river. To do this, he wrote, one must "still the mind" and practice a "nonjudgmental awareness" of his athletic performance that doesn't judge an action as either good or bad, but merely an opportunity for observation. Translated into hockey terms, I determined this to mean I could unlock the great goalie inside of me by not *trying* to be better than Dave, not *trying* to convince Slater I was the best goalie; rather, I needed to simply *let* myself play to my greatest potential and *let* the chips fall where they may.

I figured I could do the same off the ice as well.

In my diary, I start referring to myself as "Zen Ken" as if I were chronicling the inner game of my life. Dad wants to smoke himself to death? *Fine. Nothing I can do about it. Just let him be.* My psych professor gives me a D+? *Well, I just have to do the best I can and let the grade point average fall where it may.* Jenny, who two months into the school year wants to break up and date guys at her college, is having doubts about our future? *Go right ahead and do whatyagottado, babe.* Guys on the hockey team want to put me down and call me a homo behind my back because I don't scam on all the hockey groupies? *Whatever, dudes. Think what you will. I'm well practiced in being true to myself despite outside pressure to be different—case in point: my KAK-calling brothers abusing me.* Those same teammates want to corner me in the shower after practice holding a disposable shaver and force me to shave my freshman body from the neck down? *If that's what will get them off my back, whatever.*

I've recently discovered a new song that I like very much, a laid-back reggae tune that exhorts all to "Don't worry, be happy."

I don't remember exactly when I first realized I might be able to do something productive with my life besides playing hockey, but it was probably in spring of 1989, near the end of my freshman year. That's when my academic writing assignments no longer intimidate me, and when the academic dean no longer makes me take a remedial writing course.

The instructor of that class compliments me on my improved grammar, my sentence structure and my "strong voice," which I've realized is the voice that I've been scrawling into the pages of my diary (back then, I called it a "log" because a diary was a pink book in which Marcia Brady wrote about boys) since age eleven and was writing about snowy days, my hockey dreams and my favorite TV shows.

I have become an all-around better student and more comfortable with my anti-partying social life. I become just as comfortable studying in a carrel in the library as stopping pucks in front of a net. I read every book on my class reading lists, front to back (often on the team bus while other players listen to CDs and chew tobacco). My teammates, many of whom attend classes just so they are eligible to play, consider me bookish, and, well, I am. I even carry a hardback Webster's Collegiate Dictionary in my backpack everywhere I go, so, whenever I come across a word I don't know (a frequent occurrence), I find it in my dictionary, highlight it and memorize its meaning.

I especially enjoy the reading assignments in philosophy class: Kant, Buber, Nietzsche, Matthew, Mark, Luke and John. I devour *The Rules of Attraction* by Bret Easton Ellis, a novel mostly about sex and debauchery on a fictional New England college campus, circa the late-1980's. I am struck—make that, disgusted—by the similarities between real-life Colgate undergrads and the hedonistic students at Ellis's Camden College, so much so that I write a paper indicting young men and women I deem unscrupulous, dehumanizing, soulless Darwinian sexual predators:

> *The Dressed to Get Screwed parties that the students have in the novel are not that much different than an average fraternity party or a Friday night at The Jug. Go to any fraternity party and you will find plenty of girls "dressed to get screwed." Some of the clothing, or lack of clothing for that matter, can make even the most sexually serene man's heart rate increase. Unlike in the novel, not everyone is at these parties to get screwed, but the similarities between their organized sexual extravaganzas and our (Colgate's) social functions are quite striking. If examined closely one will see that Colgate University and Camden College have more in common than just being drinking resorts for rich kids.*
>
> *Being a male, I obviously view the mating situation here from a male's perspective, which is exactly how I am going to describe the status of the social scene here at Colgate.*
>
> *Women are viewed as sex objects, objects that will satisfy the*

men's sexual wants and desires. Not all women are used to satisfy the men's lust; only those who make it through an extensive judging process are given the illustrious opportunity to be used. The cattle-auction—like process has occurred at every party I have been to while at Colgate. The process begins as soon as the piece of ass, I mean girl, comes into the guy's view. First her general appearance is re-marked upon, such as "She's kinda cute." Followed by a more specific observation like "And a nice set of tits too!" If the girl makes it this far into the screening process, she is subjected to the most crucial judgment of them all: whether he'd fuck her or not. If the guy con-cludes, "Yeah, I'd fuck her," then he'll move in on her. If he concludes conversely, then he will not pursue the venture any further. Why should he waste time hanging out with a girl he would never fuck anyway? The entire process is termed "scamming." . . .

One might blame their having sex so often as being the main problem facing the characters in the story. Their sex is unimagina-tive, fake and too frequent. But sex is not the problem—fucking is the problem. When one has sexual intercourse, one is either making love or fucking. Sex between two people involved in an authenti-cally mutual relationship in which love is present is termed love-making. Whereas sex done only to satisfy the wants and desires of people who do not truly love one another is referred to as fucking. I'm not saying that fucking is always wrong and that making love is al-ways right, but I do believe that making love is more meaningful than fucking. Fucking only gives one a feeling of emptiness.

Colgate's ever-popular Spring Party Weekend is the manifes-tation of an entire year's worth of scamming and fucking crammed into one weekend. I personally spent three hours during this past rain-drenched Saturday afternoon drinking beverages and listen-ing to a discussion about some of the "easier" women on campus and how, when and where the men participating in the discussion had sex with these women. I was even ridiculed for not having had a sexual encounter with one of these highly acclaimed women, be-

cause, "everyone on the hockey team does this girl." Something very
wrong is going on here. . . .

I was right. Something *very wrong* was going on. While I was taking the moral high road, I really wanted to be part of the predominant,
low-road crowd. What really was wrong wasn't the eighteen-to-
twenty-two-year olds around me exploring their sexuality; rather, the
problem resided at the base of the brain of this very frustrated
nineteen-year-old student-athlete with an undiagnosed lump of ab-
normal cell tissue that had been strangulating his hormonal functioning for the last several years. As my college career was just starting, I
found myself on the outside of all the fun. I coped by telling myself that
there is more to being a man than having fun and having sex. It was an
attitude that I wouldn't truly feel proud about having until my body
permitted me to make the same choices as one of those typical males
I so dreaded in college.

I was handicapped, but all I knew then was that my reflexes would be
even faster with less fat. So I went home for the summer with the goal
of getting stronger, faster and losing weight. I went on starvation diets,
ran five miles a day, did five hundred sit-ups a night. My body trimmed
down a little, but it stayed relatively flabby. I blamed my genetics:
Heck, my dad and older brothers were all overweight. Maybe this was
my curse and I had to *let* my body be whatever it was. Turns out, of
course, that my muscle-building efforts were tantamount to inflating
a pinpricked balloon. I was nineteen and couldn't remember the last
time I had had a spontaneous erection.

At least I had my newfound Zen-inspired philosophy of life to
keep me from thinking too much about my disappointment and frustration. I read the stuff constantly. One passage, by the late Zen master D. T. Suzuki, stands out; he wrote, "Man is a thinking reed but his
great works are done when he is not calculating and thinking. 'Child-

likeness' has to be restored with long years of training in self-forgetfulness."

When my freshman year ends, I return to Buffalo, return to living with Kris, Dad and hanging with Jenny. I am looking forward to being "childlike" and forgetting about Colgate for a few months. But like seemingly everything in my life lately, it doesn't exactly work out as planned.

(PROLACTIN LEVEL: 600 NG/ML)

On my birthday, I receive an envelope in the mail. It's from Dad. Inside is a Happy Birthday card. Instead of containing the usual twenty-dollar bill, there's an empty, crumpled pack of Pall Malls. Flakes of tobacco fall out of the card as I read his handwritten note: *This is my last pack of cigarettes. I am quitting. Happy Birthday, Kenny!*

A few months ago he asked me what I wanted for my birthday: "A case of beer? . . . A subscription to *Playboy?*"

"No, Dad. I want you to quit smoking."

He was up to three packs a day. He had been smoking since he was twelve years old, and I feared that if he didn't quit soon, he would die before I made it into the NHL, before I truly made him proud of me.

Since I was two hundred miles away, I had no way of knowing whether he was keeping his promise. In fact, as the school year progressed, I spoke to Dad less and less, from every day to about once a week. Part of the reason is that he only wanted to talk about hockey (which I was sick of rehashing over and over again), and that he was always bellyaching about his problems.

Nine out of every ten phone conversations began with him telling me how weak and tired he is all the time. He also began grumbling about a faint but constant aching in his toes and fingers. He had recently been diagnosed with a diabetes-induced disease called neuropathy, in which the nerves in the extremities die. It started with a tingling sensation and has since digressed into a sensation he describes as someone poking him with hundreds of tiny needles. It's driving him crazy, he says, and he can't sleep. Valium eases the pain, but it also starts him on a drug-addicted descent.

Not too long ago, he quit his job selling printing—due to the pain, he tells me. His income now consists of a thousand-dollar monthly Social Security disability check and whatever money he can weasel from people by selling vinyl siding to them over the phone (he never calls it "telemarketing," but that's what it really is).

The first thing he tells me when I return from school is that he is "maxed out" in the financial department. Rent on his two-bedroom yellow duplex (Kris calls it "urine-colored," compared to our old Harwood duplex, which was "shit-brown colored") in a scrappy lower-middle-class neighborhood called Blasdell runs him about $350 bucks a month; surviving on a fixed government income of under a thousand a month, he is strapped for cash. He says he owes medical bills he will never pay, and, as such, he will never again step foot in a hospital. When the collection agency letters arrive in the mail, he tosses them in the garbage without even opening them.

I would move in with Mom and Norm, but the house they're renting in Hamburg, right next door to a fire station with a siren so loud that you have to stop talking during its thirty-second wail, is not big enough. To placate Dad's worries that he will have to support me for the summer, I tell him I'll be working for the town, mowing baseball diamonds and weed-eating ditches. Mom got me the job. I'll be making close to five bucks an hour.

It's only a few months after my "present," but the first day I am back I learn that Dad is still smoking, although he is trying to eat healthier and regularly giving himself insulin injections (unless he needs me to poke him in the rear because the scar tissue on his arm makes it difficult to break the skin). His diabetes makes him more prone to infection, though, and in the sticky peak of summer he is struck by yet another flare-up of epididymitis.

He's running a 102-degree fever and his right testicle balloons to tennis-ball size. He stays flat on his back for a week, but, despite the dozen aspirins a day, the infection persists and the swelling won't go down. His doctor calls to advise him to check into the hospital. Dad says that his insurance won't cover all costs; a few days in the hospital, recovering from a draining abscess on his sperm duct, would put him into even more debt.

He insists on toughing it out.

So we wait. But days pass and the swelling only magnifies.

"Ohhhh . . . ohhhh . . . ," he wails, quavering like a grieving mother over her child's grave. The curtains dampen the afternoon light. Dad's humanity amounts to a moaning lump of blanket.

I bring him a glass of water and five Bayers, as he requested, although aspirin, which thins the blood, probably won't help stop the bleeding. My mind's too cluttered—I'm too scared—to think straight, so I give him the aspirins anyway.

He's on his back, his giving-birth legs spread, wearing nothing but a bathrobe; the pillow is a sponge for his sweat.

I leave the water on his nightstand and tell him I'll be in the living room with Kris, if he needs anything.

We have been through this at least three or four times before, but the swelling usually went down after forty-eight hours. This time the fluid has been accumulating for over a week and the red bulge between his legs is only getting bigger. He reveals the abscess and I feel vomit curdling in my esophagus.

Running a fever fueled by the more than 90-degree temperature outside, he cries, "Get me a knife, Kenny."

"A what?" I ask.

"A knife. I'm gonna poke it, to relieve the pressure."

"No way. You'll bleed to death, man. I'm calling the doctor right now."

"I have to, Kenny. I can't take it anymore. I need to drain it—real bad."

I tell him the *smart* thing to do is to call an ambulance.

"If this doesn't work," he sheepishly reasons, "then you can call the ambulance. Now, please, Kenny, just go get me a knife."

"Kris, just go back to the living room," I tell my brother, who is standing behind me in the hallway. *No son should see his father so pathetic.*

Hands trembling, I pull a four-inch steak knife from a kitchen drawer and rinse it under a stream of hot water. I then rub it dry with a clean towel, a crude method of sterilization.

I hand him the knife and a couple of feminine napkins I bought at the corner store earlier that morning to soak up the blood.

"Here," I say. "Be careful."

He squirms up off his damp pillow to sitting to get a better angle on his groin.

I wish I was on Cape Cod right now, soaking up rays and drifting away in Margaritaville with my Colgate friends, rather than soaking up pus from my dad's balls.

"Should I stay?"

"No," he says, sipping his water. "Just leave me alone for now."

I leave the room, cracking the door open, and join my little brother on the couch where he lies stone-stiff, curled into a fetal ball and watching television. Kris is now too old to distract with a shadowy game of war. So I turn down the volume and big-brother rub his back.

"Don't worry, little dude. He's going to be fine."

It takes fifteen minutes of tentative poking before Dad works up the nerve to gently slice the abscess.

A grunt . . . a shriek . . . a cry: "Oooooooooh, JESUS!"

I cover Kris's ears.

A few hours later, the swelling recedes and Dad sleeps for the first time in days. And I breathe.

• • •

Throughout the summer, Jenny and I see each other almost every day. We watch TV, go see movies at the mall and hang out with my dad as he tries to get his health back. But the passion between us is not there—mostly from her. We have sex once in three months. Whenever I start talking about where we might live together when I graduate in three years, she stops me. "I'm just living in the moment," she asserts. By the end of the summer, she confesses to having kissed another guy at school that spring. An accident. She was drunk. Stupid move. She feels bad. So do I, and we vow to be more honest with each other.

A few months into my sophomore year, Jenny informs me over the phone that she will be leaving Upstate New York to attend graduate school in California. And, in keeping with our full disclosure pact, she wants to break up, explaining, "You need to experience other people before you know for sure that I am the one."

I tell her I don't want to see other people. We're Jack and Diane. Two peas in a pod. Birds of a feather.

It doesn't matter. She has made up her mind. We've grown apart, she insists, and she's leaving for LA. "It's just the way it's gotta be," she says.

It's not that I *want* her back, that I crave her presence. I'm just afraid that without her as my sexual security blanket I will have to go out and meet other girls, expose my insecurities and sexual hang-ups to someone who might not accept me for the different kind of guy that I am. Either that, or I will be a lonely loser.

Dad is right: Girls will ruin your life.

Coach Slater calls me into his office after practice one day to tell me not to worry, that he knows that in practices I have been outperforming the other two goalies, Dave and Greg.

"But I have to play Davey as long as we are winning," he explains.

The team is ranked number two in the national polls behind powerhouse Wisconsin. It's the winningest season in Colgate hockey history. I understand the situation. Sports coaching is a profession rife with clichés, and among the most prevalent is "If it ain't broke, don't fix it." The team does not need me.

But that doesn't make not playing a single minute of college since joining the program any easier to swallow. If I practiced voodoo, I would be poking needles into a Dave doll before every game. Since I am a Catholic boy from Buffalo, however, I just keep working hard and hope for a break.

Finally, I get one.

Two months before the NCAA Final Four Championships in Detroit's Joe Louis Arena, where we eventually will lose in the finals to Wisconsin on ESPN, Dave strains his knee. He can't even walk, let alone twist his knee ligaments like the joints on a rubber stretch doll, which is what we goalies often must do to stop the puck.

The next game, against Harvard, Slater puts in Greg, who is a year ahead of me. Although we win 6 to 1, I can sense that I soon will get my shot.

A week later, on February 16, 1990, Greg starts against Brown University. Our team has lost only three games out of the last twenty-six, all but one played by Dave Gagnon. Brown, however, has lost more games than they have won. We should crush them. But Greg lets in seven stinkers, and we are losing. I'm where I always am during games: at the end of the bench, cheering on my team, like a good soldier, but secretly thinking, *I shouldn't be sitting on my ass, I should be in the NHL!*

When Greg lets in another atrocious goal with twelve minutes and fifty-two seconds left in the game, Slater stomps in his black "good-luck" sneakers over to my end of the bench. He slaps my shoulder pad and bends over to me.

"Kenny," Slater says, so close I can smell his coffee breath, "get in there."

I react with a Who-me? gaze.

"I said get in there!" he says, smiling.

Before he can change his mind, I slide my mask over my head, grab my goalie stick and skate swiftly to the goal crease, where Greg stands with his shoulders slumped. He doesn't see me until I stop right in front of him, and when he does he shakes his head disgustedly. *I've waited too long for this chance, pal. Move the fuck over.*

"What the fuck's going on?" he says.

I point at Slater, who is motioning for Greg to come to the bench. *Sit down, Waldo.*

Greg slinks back to the bench.

The crowd, about three thousand of them packed to the rafters in their flannels and fleece and mittens and maroon Red Raiders caps, sits silently, probably wondering, *Who's this guy . . . this Ken Who? . . . Who's this guy nervously stretching out and doing deep-knee bends like he's in a 1950's Army recruiting film?*

I block them out. *Zen Ken . . . This is my moment. . . . The inner game . . . Let it happen.*

I try to not think about how bowel-emptying nervous I am to be finally getting my chance. The fans thumb frantically through their programs. . . .

#2 Ken Baker, Sophomore, Goalie, 5-11, 180, Blasdell, New York

YEAR	GP	MINS	GAA	SAVES PCT.	W–L–T
1988–89	*no statistics*				
1989–90	*no statistics*				

. . . undoubtedly prompting the more optimistic fans to turn to their neighbors and say, "Well, at least he's got a perfect record."

A half hour later I do.

I stop ten out of ten shots. A perfect performance. Still, we lose 7 to 6.

After the game, as I'm skating toward the locker room, Slater pulls me aside and says, "You're starting tomorrow. Get a good night's sleep."

In the locker room, Boomer comes over to my stall. "You've earned it, Bakes."

I call Dad from a pay phone in the lobby. *I'm starting!* I don't tell him Boomer finally called me Bakes, rather than Pear, because I am too ashamed to ever tell him that I had been nicknamed after a female-shaped fruit.

To keep his ticker from seizing up like an un-oiled engine, the doctor prescribed him a tiny glass bottle filled with nitroglycerin tablets, which he is supposed to place under his tongue whenever he feels the tightness building, the panting, the light-headedness, the . . . heart . . . attack . . . coming. He pops them at least once a week, usually when carrying grocery bags from the car to the kitchen or climbing a flight of stairs. He's not even fifty years old; it's a sad sight.

"I wouldn't miss your first game if I had to stick an oxygen tube into my nose," he says. "We'll see ya tomorrow."

I'm so amped up, I don't sleep a wink. I have had enough dress rehearsals. It's time for the show.

I have seen our team's pre-game routine so many times—either from the bench or the press box (where, out of boredom, I have occasionally done color commentary on the student radio station)—that I could start this game with my eyes closed.

Forty minutes before the game, the team—the goalie always goes first—leads the players out to the ice for a fifteen-minute warm-up. Players fire pucks at the goalie—at first slowly, then they slap them rocket fast—till he breaks a sweat. Then the team heads back to the locker room for a pep talk by Slater.

As the crowd fills the bleachers, the Zamboni floods the ice, turning the snowy surface into a icy pond so smooth you want to lick it like a Popsicle.

The referees, then the visiting team, take to the ice, to a chorus of boos from the Starr Rink faithful.

Inside the sweaty locker room, Slater sermonizes to the players, a variation on the same strategic and motivational themes. *Dump and chase the puck. Work the boards. Play the man. Use your legs. Shoot, then go for the net.* After a season and a half, I've heard just about every different permutation of the Terry Slater Pep Talk.

When the team manager gives the nod that the enemy has taken the ice, Slater usually barks, "Let's go, Dave!"—only this time, he says *"Kenny."* The moment I charge onto the ice, the pep-band musicians rise to their feet and—THE PLACE GETS ELECTRIC—a brassy cacophony of tubas, snare drums, bass drums, trumpets, clarinets, cymbals, explode into a pounding rendition of the Colgate Fight Song. Frenzied students, most drunk off their ass, wave maroon-and-white banners and sing along to the marching-band melody:

> *Fight, fight, fight for dear old Colgate!*
> *With heart and hand now we'll win for thee*
> *Oh, we will fight, fight, fight for Alma Mater*
> *On to victory, we're marching*
> *Foes shall bend their knee before us*
> *And pay homage to pow'r so great*
> *And so let us send out a cheer and banish all fear*
> *While we are fighting hard for Old Colgaaaate*
> *Fight!*

The collegiate partisanship and pageantry gives me goose bumps every time. This is *war,* after all. Not the type Kris and I used to play with toy soldiers. This is for real, acting out my most primitive of human instincts—*fight for alma mater!*—and Darwinian impulses—*fight, fight, fight!*—for the next two and half hours. I will never feel so alive as when I am playing hockey, never so much of a man.

The game starts. The action is faster than any of the hundreds of practices I have endured over the last two years. Not having started in an actual hockey game for nearly two years, I am rusty. And nervous. I've sweated so much that in between the first and second periods I have to change into a dry T-shirt. But by the second period the butterflies have left, my heart rate is steady, and I drop into the ever elusive Zen state—*no distractions, no one in my way, free of negative thoughts, fears, insecurities*—of goaltending, existing somewhere between unconsciousness and total self-awareness. I feel the energy of three thousand bodies of humanity, three thousand fans staring down at me through the Plexiglas. Their shouting isn't a distraction; it's fuel. The puck is metal; my body, a magnet.

During a stoppage in play I glance up to the stands and see Kris and Dad watching my every move—just like old times. There's nearly three thousand people in the building, but I only care about two. I love them, and their attendance is an expression of love; my playing my heart out for them is mine. In my family, no one says "I love you," no one gives hugs or kisses. My father doesn't *tell* me he loves me; Kris doesn't *say* he's proud of me. It's an unspoken rule—show me; don't tell me—that my family has always lived by.

After the game, Kris tells me Dad popped half a nitroglycerin tablet in the third period, during a particularly hectic five-on-four power play in which I had to kick out a flurry of six or seven shots. We won 7 to 5.

I start the last two games of the season, losing to RPI 6 to 2 and beating Vermont 5 to 4. I'm not exactly Jim Craig in the 1980 Olympics, but, hey, at least I have a winning record.

Dave returns for the playoffs, and he is back to his goaltending acrobatics. The heart of the team and an All-American, Dave is both the man I despise and the man I want to be. I'm just the team's margarine, a mere substitute for the real thing; yet, I have just earned my stripes in a way that no funny joke or body shaving ever did.

(PROLACTIN LEVEL: 850 NG/ML)

Dave Gagnon, my pothole in the freeway to the big leagues, drops out of school near the end of his junior year. After carrying the team to the NCAA finals, Dave signs with the Detroit Red Wings. Finally, as a junior, I have a realistic chance to shine.

With Dave gone, Slater and the players treat me differently, with more respect. All of them call me "Bakes" now (it helps that I have lost about ten pounds, mostly through a regime of running and starvation). And the season has started smashingly. I have beaten Cornell, Princeton and Yale—shut those bastards down. I was even voted the MVP goalie at Yale's annual Thanksgiving tournament. I'm starting to feel again like that that boy from Buffalo with big dreams and big glove saves in the final minute of overtime.

Dad drives to Hamilton for every home game, even though he is high on Valium most of the time, complaining that the pain in his arms and legs from the diabetic neuropathy is driving him mad.

Townies, previously ambivalent about my existence as a bench-warmer, want to know me; kids beg for my autograph; the postmaster from a nearby town asks me if I want to take his seventeen-year-old daughter out on a date. Local charities ask me to appear at their fund-raisers. The old lady who makes sandwiches at the Annex always of-fers me free grilled turkey subs and french fries. Students chant my name at the games; a few even fashion signs out of the sides of cardboard boxes (GO BAKER!). Pretty girls, just like the ones in my freshman psych class, approach me at parties, wetting their lips and flashing flirtatious eyes. Even though I don't have a girlfriend, I don't flirt back or try to "do" them, as my teammates tell me to. I ignore the girls. Instead of admitting to myself that I am afraid of them, I tell myself that I don't want to fuck up my hockey focus by getting distracted.

I have changed. I am no longer the bitter class warrior that I was when I arrived at Colgate. I don't despise anyone just because they are rich; instead, I first give them the benefit of the doubt. If they are snooty and annoying, I just try to ignore them. This happens rarely, however. I may not be as into partying as most of the other students, and I may not be as studly with the girls as I'd like to be, but I can't blame my feelings of inadequacies on the other students. That's my own deal.

Above all, though, the puck is my focus. I split time with Greg Menges, now a senior. I start a game, then he starts the next. With Dave gone, Slater is running a two-goalie system. I'd rather be the team's sole number-one guy, but it's better than not playing at all.

Then Slater altogether stops playing me. He gives no explanation. And I return to riding the pines. In fact, even the freshman goalie, Shawn Murray, an NHL draftee from Minnesota, is dressing in my place as I watch from the press box, disgusted but glad that I at least will have a real career to fall back on now that I have over a 3.0 GPA every semester and now that I have learned to love the written word as much as the slapped puck.

It's time I start thinking about Plan B, and that plan is journalism. My English professor, Don Snyder, suggests that (a) I read as much journalism as possible, and (b) do an internship at a local newspaper before I graduate. I heed his advice, devouring every periodical at the library; for the first time in my life I read *The New York Times*—every day. Just as I used to learn from watching the goaltending acrobatics of Tom Barrasso, Patrick Roy, Tony Esposito, Mike Palmateer, I start dissecting the style and structure of Maureen Dowd, Rick Bragg, John Tierney, Chris Hedges and any other writer who is getting paid to do what I think I may like to someday: tell other people's stories. *The Syracuse New Times* generously publishes my amateurish attempts at feature writing about the life of a wheelchair-bound man, the gambling controversy on an Iroquois Indian reservation and an ambitious but misguided businessman who wants to build a *Wizard of Oz* theme park on a remote farm in central New York.

Growing up in a place like Buffalo, closer to Cleveland than Manhattan, you feel like you are in the middle of the country, away from the places where life *really* happens. Or at least that is how I always felt. I didn't live in the United States; rather, I lived in Fly Over Country, where I would lie on my back in the front yard, staring up at the jets scraping chalk lines across the sky, passing over peons like me to more exciting people and places. The media—mostly MTV and *The Buffalo News*—offered me a window into those more important places. The news fertilized my imagination and brought me to places I otherwise couldn't afford to visit in person. So it's no surprise that I end up aspiring to write the news.

But all that journalism stuff is still a backup plan. Right now, though, I am continuing to work on Plan A, and I desperately want to know why Slater has cut me down at the knees after teasing me with the thought that maybe he doesn't hate me after all.

"You should disguise your voice and call in to his radio show," Dad jokes one night on the phone, "and ask him why Baker isn't playing anymore because he did so well at the start of the season."

"I have a better idea," I say. "I'll get Friberg to do it for me."

John Friberg is my new roommate, and my best friend. He is a normal guy like my other closest friends at Colgate—polite Sean from East LA (who, it turns out, is gay), John Marrin (a computer-gaming addict and English major from Manhattan) and Kevin (my freshman-year roommate, who, alas, has transferred to Berkeley, because it has a better swim team). Friberg is an excellent student, but not exactly in the school's mainstream "hip" social crowd of jocks and fratboys. But the goofball New Hampshire native is willing to do anything for the sake of a good laugh.

Slater takes phone calls from fans on his *Coach's Corner* radio show every Monday night. Friberg chugs a Heineken at the kitchen counter, perhaps to take the edge off, and dials in to interrogate Slater. I lie on my bed, listening to my clock radio.

> **Skip Barlow (the host):** "Okay, this is *Coach's Corner* with Colgate's hockey coach, Terry Slater. We're going right to the phones tonight. Hello, you're on with Coach Slater."
>
> **Friberg (in fake, deep voice):** "Hello. Um, I know that Coach Slater said that he has three good goaltenders and, uh, and that's certainly true. We've seen a lot of Menges and Murray recently. But what about Ken Baker? I saw him at Cornell, against a tough Big Red squad, and I was very impressed with that. The home games against Princeton and Brown he looked good in as well. Why haven't we seen him in some time? I think it has been since the Syracuse Invitational?
>
> [Awkward pause.]
>
> **Slater (in unsteady voice):** "My feeling right now is that, uh, Kenny is playing just as well at practice as, uh, Murray and Menges. Um, if we would have played the, uh, the game against Mercyhurst College last week, Kenny was due to play in that game to get him back in action and he would have saw some pucks, and saw a little bit of game pressure because they've got a pretty good hockey team, and then probably I would have either used him this weekend or used him the coming next weekend coming up. So the rotation would have gone with the three goaltenders.
>
> **Friberg:** So you are rotating the three of them, sort of on a semi-regular basis? Or do you have any long-term plan for the three of them?

Slater: I'd rotate them. Uh . . . uh . . . my theory of looking at the goaltenders is to look at them all week in practice and who I think is hot that week, by Thursday, I judge the number of shots they've had—I keep a record of it—and if I feel that one goaltender is stronger than another, usually he will get the nod on Friday night. The long-term range is that Menges is a senior and we've got Kenny and Murray, who are both good Division I goaltenders, so both of them will see a lot of action.

Friberg: Ok, thank you very much, Coach Slater.

Yeah, thanks, Coach Slater. Thanks for stating what I had surmised over the last three years: No matter how hard I work in practice, no matter my being the "hot" goalie in any particularly week, you don't think I am worthy of the starting nod. Thank you, very much.

As much as I hate to admit it, Slater may be right. Maybe I'm just not worthy. I work harder than any player on the team; I work harder than I did when I was a teenage prodigy, when I would improve a thousand percent from one season to the next just by putting in my time. What the hell has gone wrong? Is it because I don't see enough game action (which is faster and more challenging than practice), or is it because I have lost my killer instinct, my drive, the motivation that always carried me to the next level? What the fuck is wrong with me? I lift weights three days a week; yet, I don't see any results of my hard work. Instead of turning fat into muscle, I turn fat into hard fat. Some athlete. Colgate pays me over twenty grand a year in tuition and room-and-board fees for me to build this inadequate body?

I am an upperclassman, a campus celebrity. I'm invited to fraternity and sorority parties every weekend, but I rarely go. I must have received a dozen valentines last year, half of them from girls who I'd imagine any guy would dream of dating. So, then, why am I still single? Why don't I ever make the move? Why have I never gone on a date? Why am I so afraid that my dick isn't going to work, like that night in Toronto with Jenny that still haunts me some four years later?

The team locker room is a perverted confessional, where my teammates boast of their sexual adventures from the night before. Meanwhile, I never have my own conquests to boast about. I grow most uncomfortable whenever one of the guys admits he was too drunk to even get a hard-on, an affliction they jokingly call "whiskey dick." I doubt they would joke about it so much if, like me, their dick malfunctioned even without the disabling powers of Jack Daniel's.

I usually just sit at my locker stall, put on my equipment and let out a manly chortle at the appropriate moments while the kiss-and-tellers have their fun. I am the team's anti-stud, the intellectually inclined, pasty-white goalie from Buffalo. Even though I haven't had the most distinguished career, the players do respect me for sticking it out and giving it my all—day in and day out—throughout the season.

My senior year, the athletic department honchos give me the Rob Ries Award, a plaque anointing me "the varsity hockey player who best demonstrates qualities of leadership to his fellow players." I'm also inducted as a member of Colgate's senior honor society—the first hockey player to do so—for keeping my GPA above a 3.0 and volunteering in local charities like the village of Hamilton Big Brother/Big Sister program.

I appreciate all the recognition, and it's heartening to know that I probably won't have to return to Buffalo and eke out a depressing postgraduate existence, but what the hell is wrong with my body? It's not as fast as it used to be. But, then again, the pucks come at me faster now than they did in high school. I don't know. But I do know that I feel sluggish—constantly. I don't even bother scheduling classes before ten in the morning because I can never drag my sallow ass out of bed that early. And what's with the dark, Goth-like, half-moon circles under my eyes? *Man, I look like shit.*

In high school, when I'd complain about my sorrowful abs and flabby butt, my dad called it "baby fat" and assured me it would go away as I grew taller. But it hasn't. At five feet eleven inches and 175 pounds, my dimensions—on paper, at least—seem solidly athletic. But I hate the person reflected in my mirror: his spare tire, the womanly saddlebags hanging just below his butt, the Play-Doh–soft biceps. Pear.

I might have once possessed what Olympic team coaches called "lightning-quick reflexes," but that was when everyone else had a prepubescent musculature. Now I am competing against the big boys, despite my adolescent physicality, and they have thighs like tree trunks and forearms thicker than my calves.

They don't realize how lucky they are. If they like a girl, just about the only thing stopping them from being with her is the girl. I also have to contend with myself. I used to think that I was better than everyone else, that my thoughtfulness and respect toward women was a gift, but more and more I feel like I am a fraud—tough and manly by image only. I even let a girlfriend cheat on me and get away with it. I let teammates tool on me and coaches treat me like shit. And I do nothing about it. Where's my *oomph*?

I don't know what's causing this hormonal misfiring. I don't want to know. I can beat this malaise. I *will* beat this malaise. And that's what it is: a mental condition that I will overcome with hard work and dedication to my sport and to life.

As for sex, I don't need to practice abstinence; I already practice avoidance, which is a whole lot better than experiencing main-engine shutdown when a girl is priming me for launch.

I can just see it: I'd take a girl home, one of those fresh-faced fans, kiss her and let her touch me. She'd rub my crotch, but my dough wouldn't rise. She'd slide down my pants and use her mouth, but, still, my dick would stay as squishy as the foam finger ("Go Raiders!") she was waving in the arena stands a just few hours earlier. *Ohmigod! Ken Baker—the goalie!—is impotent!* She'd tell her sorority sisters, who would tell their boyfriends, who would then tell my teammates, an insensitive lot who invariably would razz me, tell me I'm for sure a homo, a FUCKING FAGGOT! Indeed, impotence, or at least the fear of it, has kept me celibate throughout most of my college career. Other guys, it seems, have a sex drive emanating from an inner need and desire for pleasure, while I act more out of obligation than titillation. I fear that if I don't pursue girls, my friends will think the worst. On a hockey team, homosexuality is equivalent to leprosy.

Throughout my freshman year, Jenny occasionally paid me weekend visits. Jenny was always neurotic about sex, even after my devirginizing debacle in Toronto, often insisting that I wear two rubbers so she wouldn't get pregnant, which, she'd remind me repeatedly, would ruin her life, prevent her from getting her doctorate in psychology, rendering her nothing but a white-trash young mother with a bastard child, blah blah blah.

My most memorable college sexual encounters are with Amy, a long-legged varsity athlete whom I met at a friend's lakeside cabin in Maine the summer between my junior and senior year.

Throughout my senior year Amy drunkenly stumbles into my off-campus apartment nearly every Saturday night, typically following hockey games, during which she sits in the bleachers, amid a pack of her friends, chanting my name—*KEN-nee! KEN-nee!*—and waves banners and, basically, looks primped and pretty.

Topped with long brown hair she likes to pull back into a ponytail or pigtails, Amy is as undeniably beautiful as she is easy to spot in a crowd, which I do during breaks in the on-ice action.

My friends lust after her more intensely than I do, actually. John can't understand why I have not yet capitalized on her puppy-dog eyes and "tight little package" and deflowered her. I don't know what to tell him. I also consider Amy attractive, but I don't burn with desire to do anything sexual with her. It is more of an intellectual attraction: In my mind I want to, and I know nature has wired me to, but my penis remains apathetic. I never stop to think that I may have a physical problem—I mean, I am a varsity athlete, for Christ's sake!

But, still, my male ego won't allow me to totally resist her come-ons; I psych myself up to want to get in her pants, to get some of that "pussy" I have been promised from Day One. I don't want love; I'm not searching for a soul mate here. I just desperately want to be, sexually, *the man.*

During Amy's frequent late-night visits to the apartment that John, who now has a girlfriend, and I moved into near downtown, we kiss or pet playfully on my living-room couch. One winter night she shows up unannounced in my bedroom, reeking of vodka.

I find Amy splayed on my bed in a black cotton miniskirt and a tight-fitting white top; her heels dangle off the edge of my mattress.

"Hi, there," she giggles.

Okay, okay, relax. Play it cool. I will do it—the nasty. I will stick my "cock" into her "pussy"—just like my teammates. Yeah, that's the ticket. Then I'll boast about my bedroom shenanigans the next day at practice. Yeah, I fucked her. She's got a fire bush, man. Maybe then I'll gain access into their studly club.

"This sure is a surprise. How'd you get in?"

"The door," she says.

Uh-oh. Here we go. . . . Oh, God, please make my dick work this time.

I plop down on the bed next to where she has fallen horizontal and she nestles beside me, wrapping her arms around my lower back and stroking my bare legs. Her drunkenness relaxes me—a little because it inhibits her from realizing how nervous I am.

"I like your boxers," she says, stroking the silk. "They're cute."

Some nine years later, the haunting images of what follows flash, frame by vivid frame, over and over with tragic repetition—my personal Zapruder film, reminding me of my biological imprisonment. The moist meeting of our lips . . . her gentle stroke moving up my thigh to my crotch . . . our wrestling tongues . . . the pressing of our naked bodies . . . her repeatedly squeezing and pulling on my flaccid penis . . . the failure . . . yanking her hand away . . . her pleading, "Is it me?" . . . me telling her to "Just go home."

The morning after, Amy calls and leaves a message: *Is everything okay? Are you mad at me? If I did something wrong, I'm sorry. Call me.*

I never call her back. My inability to get hard embarrasses me too much, and I figure I have nothing to say. I was just nervous, is all. Nothing is wrong with me. I was just psyched out or something. You know, uncomfortable. I feel badly that I've upset Amy. She deserves better. She deserves a guy who can be normal, make her feel good, be goofy. With me, she's left wondering what her defect is—whether she isn't pretty, smart or vivacious enough because I don't respond to her advances. I'm too afraid even to begin trying to explain why I can't have sex with her. It's easier to just avoid her, not return her calls and anxiously wait for my college career to end, like a white-knuckle passenger on a turbulent flight who's praying for it all to end. Perhaps when I escape this collegiate pressure cooker, steaming with hypersexual students and rabid hockey fans, I will be comfortable in my skin.

To an impotent man, sex becomes all about the act; it has nothing to do with emotional investment or romantic love. Sex becomes an enemy to fight—*fight, fight, fight!*

If romantic love is nature's way of bonding men and women who mate so that they will jointly care for their offspring, then impotence biologically handicaps a man's capability for romantic love, since sex and romantic love are inextricably linked. A severely impotent man will thus quash his hunger for that ultimate bond with a woman because it is an emotion that frustrates him as a forty-yard dash might a quadriplegic. Since emotions—love being the most treasured of them all—are what most differentiates humans from the rest of the animal kingdom, an impotent man very easily can feel less than human. If the bottom-line biological reason for a male's existence is to pass on his genes via ejaculated sperm, when his mating desire and his ability to achieve the erection needed to deliver this life force is impaired, he is made to feel as if he inhabits a gender netherworld—neither male nor female, gay nor straight, man nor woman. He feels androgynous, uncomfortably so. He can either fight, seek an escape from that netherworld, or he can peacefully accept his middle place amid the sexual spectrum.

This is me as I near college graduation. I am tired of fighting against my own body, sick of it not behaving as I want it to. But I am not the kind of person to throw my stick down and skate away, and, thanks to my father's dubious example, I'm definitely not quick to admit weakness.

Instead of retreating, I begin flirting with girls more than ever. I may be a wet firecracker, but maybe I can light my wick if I strike enough matches. I will compensate by being as sexually predatory as I have been retreating. Then, I hope, I will find my comfort zone.

I start my quest for mating normalcy with a not-so-pretty but famously promiscuous senior who is notorious around the locker room for her desire to screw a hockey player before she graduates. She has cornered me countless times around campus, focusing her crazy blue eyes on me like a libidinous laser. *What are you doing Friday, Ken?* . . . *We should do dinner some night.* . . . I always had plans, but with my college career nearing completion I finally relent.

We go to the movies a few times, heading to The Jug afterward and making out in a shadowy booth. But when Horny Girl invites me over to her place, I decline—in a cool-guy way that suggests I have better things to do, not in a way that reveals my fear that she will find out that my dick isn't as strong as she has fantasized. I simply don't want to get too close, too vulnerable. The same avoidance happens with other women—Laura, Sarah, Christina—from whom I run away when our relationship progresses to the point where I either have to get naked or suddenly get up and leave the bedroom.

If I go through four years of college without getting laid, my attempt at having a social life will be a colossal failure. Only a month remains in my college career, and the prospect of graduating without having had sex looms. I should partake in some of that decadent sexual behavior that, I have been led to believe, is the birthright of collegiate males of America. Enough of this "lovemaking is more meaningful" bullshit that I used to write in philosophy-class papers. Where has this ascetic lifestyle gotten me? I am more miserable and more of a lonely monk than ever before. I'm sick of being the good son, tired of being Kiss Ass Kenny and doing all the right things. I'm sick of being celibate. All I want is to please myself—not just my misogynistic dad, not just my ambitious hockey-goalie ego. I am lonely and pleasure-deprived. I just want to be whole.

Throughout the final month of the school year, there are plenty of opportunities to prove to myself that I can be a sexual creature. Twice a week, the senior class council throws parties at one of the several downtown bars, sexually charged shindigs that I religiously attend with my friend—let's call him Joe Cool—a fellow hockey player. Joe, six feet of *GQ,* has a reputation around campus for being, well, a male slut. Canadian and cocky, he relishes the reputation and does everything he can to live up to it. In fact, when Boomer graduated, Joe Cool took over the role as team sexist. I consider him a worthy mentor for my late-college sexual quest.

I head over to his apartment before these parties, invariably finding him coifing his heavily moussed hair in front of the mirror. Which is exactly where I find him on this Wednesday night.

"Hey, Bakes," he says, not even glancing away from his reflection.

"Bakes, we gotta get you laid tonight, man."

"Dude, you're so preaching to the choir," I reply. "I have the feeling tonight's the night."

"That's the attitude," Cool says, finishing buttoning his oxford, the veritable uniform for Colgate guys, including myself.

Cool thinks I've been having sex with all those groupie girls who hang around me. I'm too embarrassed to admit I can't confirm the color of their pubic hair. So I lie.

We walk across the street to a hole-in-the-wall bar that is the site of the, as the flyer advertised it, "Senior Pukefest." Beer is only a dollar a pitcher. Cool and I sit down at a table and order four beers, hoping a couple of upstanding and horny ladies will saddle up between us.

Five minutes later one does: a curly-haired party girl named Annie. Short, about five foot two, Annie's most conspicuous feature is her set of plump breasts, which, being too large for her petite body, distinguishes her in the eyes of many Colgate men, including Cool. Annie tells us she has dated the same guy her entire college career—until now. She is free. Single. Good to go! Judging by the way she keeps stroking our thighs, she has a lot of pent-up energy to release.

Two pitchers later, all Annie wants to discuss is sex, her bra size (34D) and the size of our dicks (longer, we boast, than that beer glass over there).

When Annie broke up with her boyfriend earlier this year, she must have made it her mission to bed a hockey player, because just a few weeks ago she managed to make out with celibate little me (we got as far as under her sheets, but I—drunk—told her I had to get home and finish a paper before she started pulling down my pants or something as terrifying as that).

Annie reveals that she and Cool have had sex about a dozen times, evoking an aw-shucks grin from Cool.

"It's such a pity *we* never did it," she adds, shaking her head.

"Yeah, well, I was saving myself," I reply.

"For when?"

"For tonight."

My beer-buoyed, Cool-inspired cockiness elicits a smile that stretches her mouth from one freckled cheek to the other. Cool high-fives me like I have just scored a winning goal. Annie's clearly enjoying our fraternal banter.

"Then let's go," she says, abruptly standing.

Cool stands up too. "Not without me."

Peer pressure weighs on me; alcohol lifts my inhibitions; several years of sexual frustration boils inside me.

"Okay." I spring from my chair. "Let's go."

Annie squeezes my ass like a roll of Charmin, causing me to spill my cup of beer all over my jeans. The three of us then gallop across the street and up the stairs to Cool's sloppy love nest. Ol' Boomer would be proud.

"Bakes, I can't believe this happening," Cool whispers as Annie pees in the bathroom. "She wants it soooo bad, man." He combs back his mane of hair with his fingers and adds, "Just don't touch me, man." He punches me in the arm; I give him a friendly shove to the shoulder. "Don't worry," I say. "I'll have plenty of other stuff to touch."

If I were sober, I would leave the apartment right now, claiming I have a moral problem with the very idea of a ménage à trois or that I forgot my wallet at the bar; if I were as horny as Cool, I probably would already have my pants off. Neither being the case, I plop down on Cool's ratty couch and chug the remnants of my beer, numbing myself.

Annie returns and snuggles next to me, sucking on my neck like a vampire. Inserting a U2 CD into his stereo, Cool stares back at us and feigns jealousy. "Hey, guys, don't start without me."

Too late. Annie straddles me, locking her hands behind my neck and pulling my face to hers. Cool hunches behind her and starts unbuttoning her shirt and caressing her breasts as she grinds against me to the rhythm of the music.

It's one love / We get to share it
It leaves you baby / If you don't care for it

We're all naked, a panting maze of smooth skin and hands and tongues. Cool may as well be invisible. My eyes are on the pale, supple female skin. I feel her wetness as she tugs at our penises. "Oh, guys" she coos. "I'm so loving this."

I am getting hard, blood is filling my penis. At last, freedom. Reckless abandon! Fucking!

I kneel beside the couch and start kissing her. Neck. Cheek. Lips. Nipples. Big red nipples! Cool hands me a condom, and I tear open the foil packaging. Inexperienced with rubbers, I fumble in the dim light with the slippery sheath. *Fuckin' thing. Is it inside-out or something?*

"C'mon, Ken," she says. "Come into me."

By the time I slide the condom on, the blood has left my dick.

I frantically jerk myself.

My heart is racing.

I keep jerking.

Panic!

I jerk harder.

It's no use. The condom sags over my limp organ like a Ziploc bag around a Ball Park frank. Hoping I can revive my boner, I try forcing my penis into her vagina, but it crumples like an accordion.

"What's wrong?" she asks, peering down at my flaccidity.

"Aw, just this stupid thing—it's all fucked up," I say, ripping off the condom and standing up. "I'll be right back."

Cool immediately hops onto her and they fall to the floor. I slide on my jeans and head for the bathroom.

You ask me to enter / But then you make me crawl . . .

I sit on the toilet, looking at myself in the mirror, disgusted, my hands trembling. My face is sallow. Bags the size of Samsonites sag below my eyes. *You ugly fucker. Sad, ugly, pathetic freak.*

Through the wall, I hear the music stop and their bodies slapping against each other. Her moaning; his grunting. They're dancing a biological ballet that I neither can perform nor can understand. I feel less-than-human; I am a pseudo male.

I start yanking at my hair until the pain draws out tears. I pick up a ceramic soap dish and chuck it at the pathetic image in the mirror. Grabbing an angular shard of glass from the tile, I press it against my wrist. But I can't slice my own skin, can't put myself out of this misery. *You don't even have the guts to kill yourself.*

Spring has brought life to the oak and willow trees and lured students out of their winter hibernation. I take walks alone around the village of Hamilton, appreciating the bucolic beauty of central New York State in springtime: mooing cows, cottonball puffs of clouds floating above the greening hills and valleys, rivers rushing with the melted remnants of the winter snowpack. Up on campus, the mood is hopeful, as the Class of '92 graduation is just a month away. While the frat boys sit on couches on their porches and girls don skirts and cutoff shorts and tank tops that give the frat boys eye candy, I mostly walk alone and ponder.

I try not to think about that night with Annie and Cool. After they finished sex, I came out of the bathroom and Annie offered herself to me.

"Nah," I replied. "I'm too drunk."

"That's okay," she said. "So am I."

It's all in my head, I tell myself. Maybe I am a sexophobe. As I take long walks in the Upstate New York countryside, I think that maybe all my madness will soon pass. I think about how I actually have a lot to be proud of, mainly that I will walk away from here with an eighty-thousand-dollar bachelor's degree that, thanks to ice hockey, cost me nothing. While here, I became a better student, a more learned person. Now I know there is more to life than hockey. But even knowing this is not enough to lift the cloud of mourning that I can't shake, for as much as this time of my life is supposed to be about a new beginning, I'm painfully aware that it marks an end that had begun about a month ago at Starr Rink.

We had just lost to Yale, ending our season. I sat at my stall in the silent locker room that had become my second home over the last four years. Like a death row inmate in his final moments, I went through a familiar postgame ritual. Only this time it was different.

I leaned my Sher-Wood goalie stick against the cinderblock wall, lifted my mask off my head, peeled my white Colgate hockey jersey from my body and wiggled out of my sweaty chest protector. As I had since I was eight years old, I undid the leather straps on my leg pads, stepped out of my bulky maroon padded pants and unlaced my skates. The sweet smell of wet leather. My pale skin coated with a slick layer of sweat. My gray athletic department T-shirt so sweat-soaked I could have just been swimming.

Now crying, I hung my skates on two metal hooks screwed into my locker, glanced above at the plastic nameplate—BAKER #2—and the tears streamed down my cheeks. At age twenty-one, when most athletes are just starting to reach their prime, I had just retired.

AWAKENING

When I wake again, the first thing I hear is the hissing. It sounds like a tire being inflated and deflated every five seconds. Or maybe it's a ventilator forcing oxygen into my lifeless lungs because I'm paralyzed. For all I know, my neurosurgeon may have severed one of the dozens of delicate veins and arteries crisscrossing the base of my brain, perhaps causing a stroke or bleeding or damaging the part of my brain that controls speech and language. And maybe the part that regulates my breathing.

I don't know. Whatever happened—seeing that I am, presumably, alive—the operation must be over. But I am groggy, too exhausted from five hours of anesthetized surgery to wonder whether Dr. Shahinian, my brain mechanic, actually got the tumor out, to even open my eyes a twitching slit, to talk, to move my arms, which someone—a nurse?—has aligned beside me corpselike on the sterile-white hospital blanket. An IV and a few other tubes pierce my right wrist and forearm. All I can think is, Where the hell am I? *I can't moan, can't even move a single muscle. Then everything goes black.*

In a blink, or what seems like a second but just as easily could have been several unconscious hours, I separate my crusty eyelids and see the blurry images of two people standing silently at my bedside; they're solemn and rigid, much like myself as I stood beside my grandmother's casket. At least I'm not dead. An oxygen mask is cupped over my mouth like a barnacle, enlivening me with oxygen. My nostrils are stuffed with cotton; I can only suck the mask's dry air through my mouth, being careful not to choke on the fluid—mucus, blood?—that's oozing down the back of my throat.

A minute later, the bedside images sharpen into a more defined haze: blond hair, a young woman; dark hair, a short man. I squint into focus, and I recognize them: my girlfriend and my friend Sean, who is wiping tears from his eyes and gently stroking the back of my limp right hand, careful not to touch the IV needle stuck into one of my veins. I curl my fingers around his forefinger, and I hold on.

But what's that noise? That hissing that won't stop? It sounds like it's coming from around my legs. I slide my hand under the blanket and can feel something wrapped around my thighs. It's hollow, the texture of those plastic floaties my mom made me wear around my three-year-old arms while swimming. Inflatable pants? What the . . . ? No one told me about these. I wiggle my toes and bend my knees a smidgen. Okay, good; I can move. At least it's not a breathing machine, at least I'm not paralyzed.

All I can do now is stare at the ceiling and wait for the discomfort to subside. God, I hope that I not only will survive but that, once I recover from this postoperative trauma, I also will be able to live as a fully functioning man who someday will be capable of excelling in sports, dating women, having sex, fathering children—all the things that a chestnut-size tumor at the base of my brain has prevented me from enjoying for nearly all of my adult life. I'm trying to think positive, but I can't help but ponder the hormonal assault that I most certainly will suffer—again—should Dr. Shahinian have failed to excise the tumorous demon that has been pumping the female hormone prolactin into every cell of my body for longer than any male should ever have to endure.

As I count the steady bleeps of my heart monitor, I can't help but remember the demise that preceded my date with a brain surgeon and how I once wanted to die rather than live another womanized day masquerading as a normal man.

But I don't want to think about this now. I just want to breathe. I just want the pain to go away. I just want everything to go black.

A week after graduation, I pack up all my possessions in three boxes and a suitcase and drive my matchbox-size Ford Festiva back to where it all started, Buffalo. Back to sixteen pizza-and-sub shops per square mile. Back to blizzards in March. Back to Friday-night bowling in smoky alleys. Back to my brothers—two (Kyle and Keith) are bong-carrying Deadheads, one (Kevin) is in the Ozarks studying to be a Pentecostal preacher, and poor little Kris, who is in high school and living with Dad, with whom I will be living too.

Dad and his Bulgarian wife—whom we call "Green Card"—have moved everyone into a new three-bedroom duplex. But space is tight; four people already live in the vinyl-sided eyesore. There's one bedroom for Green Card and Dad, whom I recently have taken to affectionately calling "L.B." (for Larry Baker) because "Dad" seems a tad too little-kiddy for a mature college grad such as myself; there's a room for Green Card's two-hundred-pound teenage daughter; and one for Kris, who immediately volunteers to move into the basement, thus making space for me. At first, I think Kris is just being a good little bro', but I soon learn there are forces propelling him to live underground.

I may have a room to crash in (at least until I get a real job), but the household's family dynamics are as dysfunctional as ever:

- Kris hates Green Card.
- Green Card hates Kris.
- Green Card's daughter—let's call her "Olga"—hates her mom, but she desperately wants Dad and Kris to like her.
- Nevertheless, Kris can't stand Olga because she eats all of his coveted high-schooler junk food, especially his Doritos, and Dad can't stand Olga because she is so fat and complains that—between his monthly government check and Green Card's paltry teacher's salary—he can't afford to feed the Old World monstrosity.

With their thick Eastern European accents, Olga and her mom call Dad *Leeery* and say things like "I veel be goingz to zee store, *Leeery*." I'm actually impressed with their grasp of the language, but their immigrant English aggravates L.B., who's not the most politically correct guy in the world, seeing as though he still calls blacks "niggers," Asians "chinks" and Latinos "spics." Dad also complains about the omnipresent garlic stench that their Balkan cooking has brought to the duplex. The ever-annoyed diabetic calls his stocky stepdaughter "Mount Olga" and tries not to talk to his third wife enough to need to call her anything. You'd think that after three wives he would have learned something about how to achieve a state of normal, healthy husbandry.

And you'd think that Loverboy Larry, someone who spent years harping on me about how evil women can be, would have exercised better judgment before marrying a woman who barely spoke English and who wanted passage into America more than the loving glance of a bankrupt Buffalonian. *I've listened to this guy's bullshit all these years? Where did it get me? NOWHERE.*

Just a few months ago, I had hoped that I—fresh off the collegiate ivy—would, at minimum, weasel my way into an entry-level journalism job in New York or Washington and live the 9-to-5 yuppie lifestyle, free of the pressure of hockey, free of my sexually inexperienced self-consciousness, free from Dad's expectations that I make him proud. Instead, I have landed smack in the middle of this *Brady Bunch* gone bad, constantly hoping that I will get that newsdesk assistant job at the ABC News bureau in Washington, DC, where I had interviewed during spring break rather than road-tripping to Florida to drink beer and ogle breasts with my Colgate buddies.

Day after day, I pray for the ABC News bureau chief to call and transform me into a bonafide, college-educated workingman. But the call never comes.

"Kenny," Dad begins one night during a particularly bombastic episode of *Crossfire* where Pat Buchanan and Michael Kingsley are, per the usual theatrics, debating some absurdly sensationalized, politically polarizing issue.

"Why don't you try out for one of those minor-pro teams that keep sending you letters?" he says. "I bet you could make it."

Oh, no. Here he goes again. . . .

I know he means well, but for months I've had to listen to him pestering me about how I should not have quit hockey, how I am as good as any goalie in the NHL, how I easily could get back in shape and try out for an East Coast Hockey League team, toiling three notches below the big leagues. Yes, a few teams, such as the Raleigh Ice Caps and the Nashville Knights, have contacted me, having gotten my name from a list of just-graduated goalies—certainly not from seeing my less-than-illustrious play last season.

I'm not sure I would play even if the Buffalo Sabres wanted me. Frankly, I'm sick of the mental grind, sick of feeling like I have to prove myself every time I take to the ice, sick of the pressure from teammates, coaches, fans, L.B. and, most of all, myself. I am sick of constantly fighting—*fight, fight, fight!*—to keep my body in shape: the weight-lifting that only keeps me from getting flabbier, the (useless) sit-ups, the sprints that most goalies never do but that I must to keep my legs strong. Most of all, I am sick of being immersed in a macho jock culture when I feel neither macho nor much like a jock.

• • •

Late at night, as Dad lies in his nightly Valium-induced coma to escape the pain of the dying nerves in his arms and legs (and, recently, his neck), I channel surf into the wee hours until my index finger cramps, passing over the soft-core porn on cable (why would I want to be reminded of what I cannot do?) and occasionally stopping at the ads promoting 1-900 numbers for phone sex with voluptuous women in bikinis talking into the phone. Judging by the cheesy guys pictured from the shoulders up talking on the phone, this T&A idiocy apparently is targeted at lonely, unemployed young men who are up late at night for lack of a warm body awaiting them in bed and who have nothing productive to wake up for in the morning—a demographic of which I am clearly a member. But I find those female bodies about as erotic as a hockey puck. *Come to think of it, when's the last time I even masturbated, let alone ejaculated in the presence of a woman?*

I click the remote and happen upon the "Abs of Steel" infomercial, featuring mannequinlike men with six-pack abs that make my abdominals look like abs of oatmeal. TV is not the place to look for inspiration.

One day, while walking around downtown Hamburg, pondering the meaning of it all, I stop outside the U.S. Army recruiting office. When I was a hotshot senior high school hockey recruit, uniformed coaches from the U.S. Military Academy at West Point practically begged me to enlist at West Point. They guaranteed me admission; they promised me a starting slot. I turned down the offer, though, because, after graduating from the academy, I would have to serve at least five years in the Army, which was unacceptable to me. I planned on playing in the NHL right out of college, not commanding troops. Now look at me: I am out of college, unemployed and retired from hockey. That recruiting poster in the window—*It's not just a job, it's an adventure!*—looks quite appealing at the moment.

I'm greeted inside by a Sgt. So-and-so, a stocky guy with a buzz cut and the stiffest-looking green shirt and pleated pants I've ever seen. He reminds me of that professional wrestler Sgt. Slaughter who I've been watching on late-night episodes of the World Wrestling Federation. When Sarge hears that I'm a Colgate grad, and a hockey player to boot, his eyes light up.

"You ever wanna fly choppers?" he patters like a tommy gun. "We could get a guy such as yourself into officers training school right-quick."

Sarge then leads me back to his office and sits me down in front of a TV screen. "This could be you," he says, pressing Play on the VCR.

On pops a video of strapping young men in tight shorts and ARMY T-shirts running through an obstacle course, doing sit-ups, manning the controls of a Huey helicopter. Heretofore, my knowledge of the Army consists of nonstop CNN coverage of the Persian Gulf War, and what I've seen of Bill Murray in the movie *Stripes*. And now, I suppose, this Army video.

"Being a hockey player, I'd imagine you like to kick a little ass every now and then," Sarge says when the video ends with an aerial shot of a helicopter firing a missile into a tank or something hard-core like that.

"Uh, actually . . ." I stammer.

". . . and I bet you know what it takes to be a winner," he continues.

At this point, I decide to just shut up and let him vomit his cock-swinging spiel.

"You ever fire a gun?"

I have to think hard about that one. "Yeah, uh, one time I went deer-hunting with my hockey coach. But that was a while ago."

"Doesn't matter," he says. "We can teach you how to fire weapons, how to fly helos, you name it and we can teach it to you. You're a smart guy, pilot material, and you're obviously athletic. You, my friend, are a dream officer candidate."

Of all the bullshit that comes spewing out of Sarge's mouth for the next five minutes, the one thing that stands out is the part about the military pay scale. If you've got a bachelor's degree, it actually ain't so bad. As an officer, I could make a decent living, pay off my couple thousand in credit card debt I racked up last semester after my scholarship money ran out, and still be able to tuck some away in savings for a house and college for my kids so they don't have to live in ratty duplexes and athletically whore themselves to a university athletic department. Join the Army, and maybe I won't end up broke and pensionless, like L.B. All I'd have to do is get the *cojones* to kill other people for a living. It only takes a few seconds of consideration for me to conclude that I don't have the balls to stomach that, no matter how great the financial rewards. I never even liked to participate in bench-clearing brawls on the ice, let alone hand-to-hand combat. Leave violence for other guys. I'm simply not wired for battle. Nature may arm some men with warmongering testosterone, but I feel as if God gave me a low supply: Despite the sexual slump I'm in, I don't mind being a pacifist.

Sarge hands me a propaganda folder, and once out on the sidewalk I toss it in the garbage can and head home to do . . . well, I don't really have anything to do. Except, that is, to feel sorry for my sorry ass.

Considering my general malaise, dwindling self esteem and vocational desperation, the last thing I feel like enduring is L.B.'s Buchanan-like grilling of me while I'm just trying to relax in front of CNN. But that is what I get, anyway.

He means well, but, vintage L.B., he won't shut up.

"I think you should play at least *one* season of pro, Kenny. You've worked so hard all your life. You should at least get paid to play, then quit knowing you gave it your best shot. Then you know that all the hard work you've put in over the years has been worth the effort."

"I would do exactly that, Dad," I snap. "If I actually still *wanted* to play hockey. If you haven't noticed, I'm trying to move on with my life."

"I was only making a suggestion," he says, chuckling as Michael Kingsley, the liberal *Crossfire* host, takes a blow from the right. "And, by the way," he adds with his eyes on the tube, "you don't *have* to move on. You've got a lot of unfinished business to take care of with hockey.

You have your whole life ahead of you. If I were your age, I wouldn't be in such a hurry to get a real job when you could be getting paid to play hockey."

"I know, I know," I say, annoyed. "Believe me, I wish I wanted to play hockey, but it's just time to let it go and start a new career. There's more to life than hockey, you know. I have a degree and stuff."

Like Buchanan, who's ranting now, L.B. feels he must win every argument. Not this time; not this one, he won't.

"Don't worry, L.B.," I quip. "I know I'll get a job, something in journalism."

"Like what?"

"Like that ABC job. Man, I'll even sharpen pencils at *The Buffalo News.* I don't know. I'll do anything to get my foot in the door."

A few days later, unfortunately, I land the Anything job: installing drainage pipe (a.k.a. "digging ditches") for the town of Hamburg's Highway Department.

A week before I'm to start my ditch-digging job, which I only got because my mom is the assistant to the Highway Department superintendent, I call Jenny, who's now living in Los Angeles, where she always dreamed of moving after college and has been going to grad school for the last two years. I haven't spoken to her in several months; and I haven't seen her in over a year. Before I move on to the next stage in my life, before I really start honing in on a potential wife and finding the romantic love I desperately want, I need to find out if Jenny and I will ever get back together. Moreover, I need to conduct a test of my temperamental genitals, because, you see, I've made a preliminary self-diagnosis: My inability to achieve and maintain hard erections, as well as my fear and loathing of women in general, are a product of my not yet being "over" Jenny. In other words, I think I still love her and posit that I can't have sex with anyone else until I figure out where my emotions stand with her.

Our conversation, pathetically, goes like this:

"Hi . . . Jenny?"

"Ummm . . . yeah, this is Jenny."

"It's Ken."

(Stone-cold telephonic silence.)

"Ohmigod!"

"Long time no hear, huh?" I say, all cheery. "How've you been?"

"Oh, just real crazy-busy lately, you know, with school and work and—"

"Me too."

I know Dad can't afford this long-distance call. So I get right to the point. "I have some free time before I start my new job, and I thought it might be nice to come and visit you."

"See *me*?" she says.

"Yeah, you."

"I kinda thought you hated me or something."

"Oh, no, no, no. I don't hate you, Jenny. I've always loved you."

(Silence.)

"So . . . is it all right if I come out and see you . . ."

(More silence.)

". . . you know, for just a few days . . . ?"

(More silence.)

"I've never really seen L.A., and, you know, I would like to see you."

Whoa there, Chachi. Back down. You're starting to scare the girl.

"Don't worry," I interject, before she can. "There's also this guy— this Colgate alum who's a correspondent at ABC News in LA—who I want to meet while I'm out there too. So it's not like I'm just going out there to see you." This is a 99-percent lie because I could talk to my ABC contact, Brian Rooney (a Colgate grad), over the phone.

"You mean you might get a job out here by me?"

Hmmm . . . "Out here by me" . . . That sounds so possessive, so you're-invading-my-territory of her to say.

"I don't know," I reply, suddenly flush with embarrassment that I've even called her.

The truth is that I would move to LA—if she wanted me to. I am desperate and sex-deprived. Not only I am unemployed, but, judging by my physiological performance amongst the co-ed crowd, it appears that I am physically incapable of having sex with anyone other than Jenny, and that was a couple years ago. I need to see her, if only to determine whether my sexual hang-ups are a product of my being in love with her, and her only.

"Why do you ask?" I add with faux nonchalance.

"I just thought you hated LA is all."

"I do . . . uh, I mean, judging from what I hear about the smog and traffic and all that. But I'm open to moving just about anywhere. So should I go ahead and get tickets?"

(More silence.)

"Ken, why don't I call you back later? Like tomorrow or something? I'm in the middle of something right now. I'm a little distracted. I'm sorry."

We hang up and I chew my nails for the next twenty-four hours. The next night, on a Tuesday, she calls me back.

"I have to work Thursday and Friday, but I think it would be great to see you."

With a phone call to the United Airlines reservations number, I extinguish my entire life savings ($500) and buy a round-trip plane ticket to Los Angeles to test my genitals.

When I exit the jetway into the terminal, Jenny greets me with the kind of stiff, asexual hug my grandmother gives me. She still has the same microcar that carried me to Toronto over four virginal years ago. Everything else about her, though, is as alien as the smog layer I noticed hovering over the LA basin as my plane descended through the slop.

For our first stop Jenny skirts around South Central, home to the riots just a few months earlier, and takes me to a decidedly nicer part of town: Beverly Hills. I remind her that this is where she used to dream of someday opening up a private practice. "That was a looong time ago," she sighs, turning onto Rodeo Drive.

The bland, stucco storefronts strike me as cheesy and superficial. Later, when we spot the guy who plays Doogie Howser sitting in cool-guy shades at Johnny Rockets on Melrose, I'm even less impressed with Jenny's La-La Land.

After dinner, we get back into her Escort and head to her apartment. Somewhere around downtown LA, she drops the bomb.

"Just so you know, I've been dating people," she says, obviously waiting for me to react, which I don't, except for a conspicuous nonre action. "Are *you* seeing anyone?"

"No, not really," I say. "But I've been dating too."

Dating. What is dating, anyway? I've been wondering lately what that entails, and why people do it. The whole ritual seems like such a colossal waste of time. I mean, isn't the whole idea of coupling to find a person you want to marry? Dating. I've seen The Dating Game, *where young, attractive, supertan superhumans exchange sexual innuendo in order to get a date. But that's just television, right? Women wear those skimpy dresses, with their boobs billowing out from beneath the Lycra, just for show. It's not some Darwinian mating behavior, because, well, if it is, it's not attractive to me. I just want a girl who makes me feel comfortable in my own skin, who makes me calm enough to have an erection.*

"It's been so nice just to be free out here, meeting people and everything," she continues.

"Any one special guy?" I ask.

"Well, yeah, his name is Rob. But"—she interrupts herself—"it's not a very emotional thing with him—not like it is with us, I mean, like it *was* with us."

I bite. "What do you mean?

"I don't know," she sighs. "With Rob, it's just about great sex. There's no deep connection."

I don't feel upset by what she has said. Not jealous, not envious. Or at least this is what I am trying to delude myself into thinking. I am as neutral as Switzerland and as cool as Lake Erie in January. How can I be jealous of this phenomenon she has described—hot-and-heavy, *great* monkey sex—when I virtually know nothing about it and am afraid to engage in it myself? Plus, we aren't even dating. I feel bitterness, perhaps, but certainly not jealousy. Romantic jealousy stems from possessive, hormonally passionate urges. Jealousy, in my book, is Dad shouting at Mom for having lunch with a male coworker. Jealousy is an emotion felt by human beings in an obsessive, muddle-minded mating mode—not by human beings in a state of sexual apathy and ambiguity such as me. Jealousy, I tell myself, is an emotion for the weak and vulnerable, not members of the strong male elite, such as myself. Under this logic, I'm *too* much of a man to feel jealousy.

Stop the bullshit. I am so hurt! Admit it: I am bitter AND jealous. I just want someone to love. I don't need this immature, wild-sex-all-night singlehood annoyance that seems to be the hobby of most people my age. My hobby? I have fantasies about being married . . .

About being some vague older age, around thirty . . .

Living in a nice home just outside of a city that is not Buffalo—the freshly mowed green lawn, the plastic patio furniture (with musty seat cushions), the shady trees to climb with my two kids, a son and daughter.

And there's my wife: Just look at her in her tight-fitting blue jeans and a sweat shirt. . . . She's a fit, pretty woman (but not too pretty, of course; then they use their beauty as a weapon against you) with a goofy sense of humor, a woman who appreciates just hanging out and enjoying life, not playing mind games, not making sex a high-pressure activity that makes me feel as though every encounter is a test of my virility. She's a woman I can play catch with. Oh, man, look at us—happy husband and wife—laughing! Hahahahahah . . . all the time, nonstop. We talk, we kiss each other good night and good morning. I will do this because I am NOT Larry Baker. I know how to love—and how to show it. We go on long walks, holding hands and laughing . . . best friends, who, only because that is what society expects two opposite-gendered best friends to do, happen to have sex with each other too. Sex is incidental to everything else: seeing movies, cuddling on the couch, holding hands. Honestly, except for the vaguest of mental images, I don't really envision us having sex, but that's because I know that we are placidly together—bonded, committed!—so I've got peace of mind knowing that sex isn't so important or high-pressured, like it was in college, or like it is now.

My fantasy, however, is being shattered on this freeway like Reginald Denny's skull at the corner of Florence and Normandie.

As I stare out the car window at the blurry graffiti and squat East LA bungalows, I'm thinking that maybe love isn't all about my fantasy, that there are elements to the mating equation that I have not yet realized. I mean, I am a pretty good-looking guy—honest, fun, intelligent, athletic, motivated, romantic. Plus, I stopped sleeping with a bear a long time ago.

So I wonder: Why is it that I have no sexual charisma? Granted, I'm not exactly out trolling for girls. If I don't alienate them by refusing to kiss or have sex, I always end up being their "friend." That five-letter word haunts harmless, husbandlike guys like me while the dickheads and the two-timers with the cocky swagger and wandering eyes get laid easier than a millionaire in a whorehouse. There's no doubt that Jenny would want me if I had been more of a sex machine when we went out. Then she wouldn't be having "great sex" with "Rob."

I picture these thought bubbles, comic-strip–like rising from my right temple and out the car window, floating into the smoggy freeway air. They are struck by speeding hunks of plastic and metal and glass, slicing through them like a blender mashing a suicidal hand. Pulverized into tiny pieces, flimsy remnants of love, thrashing above the concrete, above the people in their glamorous cars.

Gazing over at Jenny, I try and find a shred of raw sexuality for me to be drawn to. I notice she's got on a tight cotton tank top—which is too tight—pushing up her small breasts; they remind me of a set of butt cheeks, which is not very attractive. *I used to be attracted to her. But this is The Girl, the only woman with whom I have ever had sexual inter-*

course. As awkward as this is, I have to force myself to do it. As experiments go, this should be a reliable control variable, considering that if I can't have sex with Jenny, I can't do it with anyone.

Once inside her apartment, she walks into her bedroom, and I watch her undress from across the living room. She slips into nothing but a T-shirt and underwear.... *Nothing yet. No boner. No hint of wood, actually.* ... Yawning, she pulls out the futon in the living room and spreads a sheet and blanket over the cushion for me, wishes me good night and heads for her bed. I'm relieved; I really didn't want to do this anyway.

The next day we sight-see around LA, or at least check out whatever mildly interesting things there are to see amid the seemingly endless urban sprawl—kitschy water rides at Universal Studios, the decrepit HOLLYWOOD sign, the hardbodies nearly naked on rollerblades at the beach. I stay for only three days, although I'm supposed to stay for five. It's enough time to conclude that we're hardly even friends, let alone lovers.

At the airport, we hug. I know this will be the last time I'll ever see her. Even the summer heat of the San Fernando Valley couldn't rekindle the desire I once felt for Jenny, or that she once felt for me. I guess I needed to know that. I keep telling myself that it's not me that's broken; it is Us. And that Us is now over. I need a new beginning.

A month after I return to Buffalo, a month after reading *The New York Times* front to back ten times a day, every day, in between my ditch-digging duties, a month after hearing a cretinous coworker recite his daily list of things he'd fuck ("I'd fuck that chick in the shorts." ... "I'd fuck that mom over there pushing the stroller." ... "Man, I'm so horny I'd fuck that pipe"), I finally get the call of my dreams: ABC News offers me a job as a newsdesk assistant at their Washington, DC bureau.

(PROLACTIN LEVEL: 900 NG/ML)

Looking back, there were so many times when I wish I could have possessed the self-knowledge to stop and realize my body was lacking the
normal amount of male hormones and was grossly saturated with a female one. I can't help but wonder, What if? Would I have been a wom-
anizer, or would I have been a respectful young man who only made
love to the woman he was in love with? What if prolactin had not
been mellowing my demeanor? Would I have reacted more aggres-
sively when, during my first week of work at ABC News, I answered
the phone on the newsdesk and was verbally assaulted?

"ABC News, this is Ken."

"Gimme Cullen."

"Excuse me?"

"Pat Cullen! Put him on!"

"May I ask who's calling?"

" 'May I ask who's calling?' " the apparently insane man mimics
back.

"What I mean, sir, is can I have your name?"

"DONALDSON!" the man growls.

I instantly realize it is Sam Donaldson.

Not soon thereafter, I conclude that (a) most network news

beasts—even the telegenic women—suffer from testosterone-poisoning, and (b) if I wanted to avoid getting my ass reamed every day by the man who perfected the art of abusing American presidents, I better learn to recognize Sam's voice.

But I don't conclude that I am sick. I am simply behaving how I have for as long as I have been an adult.

I am a twenty-two-year-old single man who has had sex less than ten times in his life. Breasts don't mesmerize me. Buns don't blow me away. Whether a fit young woman is wearing a tight, short skirt or baggy jeans, I don't really notice the difference in her degree of sexual attractiveness. It's not like I don't love women. I do. It's just that I first see them as actual fellow human beings, rather than as a potential moist home for my penis, a fact that even the nicest guys I know admit guides most of their male-to-female behavior. So while it may seem like I'm just a gentle, intelligent guy who isn't controlled by his base sexual instincts, and therefore I would be a real catch in the eyes of women, the opposite is true. Being so uncharacteristically, unstereo-typically male, I feel as if my male clothes are so ill-fitting that I need a new, more attractive wardrobe.

As for sports, I don't really give a shit about sports anymore. Occasionally, I'm dragged to one of those *Monday Night Football* nights at a bar in Georgetown where lobotomy cases drink pitchers and suck grease off chicken wings (the DC bars call them "Buffalo wings," but, being a Buffalonian, I am qualified to say the Capital's deep-fried poultry pales in comparison to the real deal) and shout at their big-screen TVs, not to mention ogle every young lady who ambles by their stool. At times like these, I am ashamed of my gender. Yet, a part of me also envies how confident and comfortable they are with themselves. I watch in both awe and disgust.

. . .

At the ABC bureau, just a few blocks north of Clinton's White House, I work even harder at becoming a famous newsman than I did at becoming a famous hockey player. Within a few months, I am the newsdesk assistant whom the producers and correspondents will call upon when they need a rewritten script run to their desk, the first helper Carole Simpson looks for when she needs a cup of water right before the weekend evening news. Even DONALDSON!, who at first seemed like a tyrannical talking head, doesn't treat me like the TV rookie that I am. Occasionally, a few minutes before *PrimeTime Live* is about to go live at ten o'clock East Coast time, Sam will hand me a script that he has just banged out (it's usually an on-camera intro to an exposé on one of Sam's favorite topics of journalistic inquiry: "waste, fraud and abuse") and he'll ask me what I think of it. Although he apparently likes me, I'm not quite a member of "Sam's Angels," a gaggle of assistants and interns whom Sam enjoys taking out to dinner on show nights. Yet, I do earn the occasional invitation from him to a post-show round of drinks at the lobby bar of the Hotel Washington.

Sam's a gut guy. His gut tells him within a matter of seconds after meeting someone (or grilling them, if they are a politician) whether or not he likes and trusts that person. If he doesn't like you, watch out. If he does, he's your greatest ally. I like Sam because he possesses an aggressive, alpha male side of his personality that I am severely lacking. I begin to think that maybe if I hang around Sam long enough, I will become more like him.

At ABC, I'm a glorified secretary, a news grunt, but I learn the ropes of television journalism very quickly. Soon, I start producing "bumpers" (the five-second teasers promoting pending stories before every commercial break), as well as voice-over clips of various international and national news stories.

The war in Bosnia is at its peak of daily massacres. On weekends, I plop down in the video suite at the bureau at five in the morning to record satellite feeds of the carnage beamed to us from the war zone.

ABC has a correspondent with a British accent who is covering the conflict. The scenes he describes day after day in his voice-overs are horrific: *The shelling began early in the hills overlooking Sarajevo. This bread line was struck by a series of missiles. Five were killed; dozens wounded.* . . . The massacres often bring tears to my eyes, while the coffee-addicted techies twisting dials around me seem emotionally immune to the bloodshed. One of the guys calls Bosnia-Herzegovina "Bosnia Hurts-a-Vagina." He's the same guy who, in trying to convince me to ask a busty producer out on a date, informed me that ABC stands for "All Boners Come." Sexist cretins like him are as plentiful as the scent of hair spray around the anchor desk. For me, though, it's all about the work.

A few months into my job, I'm put in charge of putting up all the names printed on the screen of guests and hosts on *This Week With David Brinkley,* a task that requires me to sit in a dark room behind the *Brinkley* soundstage, commanding a techie at the controls. As the pundits yap away, the director barks into our headsets which talent to identify with a "super" (graphic lettering that identifies them by name and title at the bottom of the screen). The show appears live on the East Coast, which means there's no fucking up, a rule which the show's taskmaster executive producer has lectured me on every day for months. I've heard stories about production assistants getting canned for one misspelled word. He's put me in charge because someone told him I was smart. So I really don't want to fuck this up.

The show starts, and I put the supers on the screen as the director requests them . . .

George Will
Sam Donaldson
Cokie Roberts
David Brinkley
George Stephanopoulous

Oh, no! I spelled it fucking wrong.

"Pull the super," I yell to my assistant the second I see that I have misspelled the then Clinton adviser's name.

"Why?" she asks.

"Because we have one TOO MANY U's IN STEPHANOPOU-LOS!"

Just then, the red phone at my desk—the so-called Bat Phone linked to the control room—rings. It's the show's ball-busting executive producer—"Get that off the fucking screen RIGHT NOW!" He is not a happy camper.

The phone rings again.

"Stephanopoulos is spelled—" someone says.

"I know," I bark.

The phone rings again, and I pick it up.

"I KNOW!"

Panicking, Betty's tapping buttons like a *Star Trek* technician on the bridge of the *Enterprise*.

It rings again.

Before another know-it-all caller can reprimand me, I hold the phone an arm's length away and shout into the receiver, "I KNOW." Then I slam it down and unplug it.

Man, you'd think my finger was on the ICBM launch button at NORAD.

Betty deletes the second U and, the next time the director wants to ID Stephanopoulos, we put it up on the screen and peace is restored to the bowels of the *Brinkley* set. Or so I think.

"What happened today is just unacceptable, Ken," a producer harangues me in the hall after the show. "One more fuckup like that and I'll have to let you go."

My feelings are so hurt I leave the building and wander the city, in and out of tears as I stroll hangdog along The Mall, past the Lincoln Memorial, along the reflecting pond. It's all so fucking melodramatic.

I used to be a tough-nosed goalie, just like my dad had taught me, but now I'm a drama queen. *What has happened to me?*

I'm not longing to be some Neanderthal knucklehead who barrels through life without feelings. I just want to be . . . strong. Instead, *I'm soooo tiiiiired.* Emotionally and physically. The reason I butchered Stephawhatever's name is that I am just plain exhausted, all the time, 24/7. No one would understand even if I tried to fully describe to them the depth of my fatigue, how damn hard it is for me to drag my ass out of bed in the morning before the sun is up, and walk down Connecticut Avenue, half asleep, like a zombie into the news bureau. And it doesn't matter how much sleep I get, my legs sometimes feel as if they're dragging twenty-pound ankle weights. And the headaches. No matter how much allergy medication and Advil I swallow, I have head pain, as if someone is constantly twisting the loose tissue just under the skin on my temples. Lying on the couch is my best pain reliever. Problem is, it's depressing to veg out all day while the city people bustle on the sidewalk below my window.

The best thing about my life right now, I suppose, is my roommates. Steve, Kelly, Dan, George, Jim, Peter. They're all Colgate grads and smart dudes. Although I didn't know them very well, they took me in when I arrived in DC, a homeless yuppie needing a place to sleep. The guys are not at all like the hockey players I've been around all my life. They aspire to more than chugging Molson and doing chicks. They work for law firms, for lobbyists on Capitol Hill, for think tanks. They *think* for a living. They're good role models for me—socially and professionally. I can't tell Dad these things; he wouldn't understand, and, if he did, he would be jealous.

I am a little envious of their normalcy, actually. When they go out and party, either with their girlfriends or out looking for one, I usually have to stay home and hit the sack early so I don't fall asleep in the darkened video edit suites in the morning, which, alas, usually happens anyway, which, alas, is probably why I misspelled that damn name.

Let you go, the producer said. I've heard that one before: Slater held that over my head, and Jenny has let me go. I can't fuck this up, because I have nothing to fall back on but a five-dollar-an-hour job digging ditches in Hamburg, living in a house for loonies and the terminally ill.

Hockey is over. My equipment sits in a box in Mom's attic, gathering dust, filled with the stench of wet leather and the memories of the glory days past.

Exercise, now that's what I need to jump-start my life. I've been so busy working fifty to sixty hours a week at ABC, taking care of other people—fetching copy for Donaldson and Koppel, ripping the news wires for Brinkley—that I have forgotten to take care of myself, namely my body. That must be my problem! That explains why my body feels ten times the force of gravity, why I feel so goddamn sloth ful most of the time . . . especially in the morning. Maybe that explains why I come home after work, make a bowl of pasta, and veg out on the couch, then almost always immediately fall asleep, the emptied bowl still in my lap and its starchy carbohydrates turning immediately into fat cells on my hips and chest. About my chest . . . I must not be doing enough push-ups or something, because the other day, while brushing my teeth in front of the mirror, I noticed what used to be my right pec jiggling like a Jell-O mold. Gross.

In order to combat my low energy and high adiposity (and despite my headaches), I decide to train for the Marine Corps Marathon, which is held in DC every year. I've got two months to prepare. *No problem. Ken Baker is back. He is ready to fight, fight, fight! As he always has.*

Luckily, Kelly and Dan are athletic and willing to join in on my twenty-six-mile footrace. Kelly is a natural runner, lean and short. Dan's got a runner's build as well. The other guys in the apartment offer their moral support.

In the evenings, after work, the three of us jog down the bike path in Rock Creek Park, past the Watergate complex, looping around the Lincoln Memorial, and then back again. Kelly and Dan are slightly faster than me, which is good, because they push me harder. We average close to seven-minute miles, a respectable pace. I need a good kick in the ass, what with me sitting around feeling sorry for myself and whining like a little girl every time my feelings are hurt or when I look in the mirror and don't like the body that I see in it.

The four-days-a-week running regime helps. I feel like I have more energy, and that spare tire around my waist gets a little less rubbery. I don't stop there, though. I join the YMCA down the street from the ABC offices. I lift weights two or three days a week, obsessively trying to construct a male physique like the ones I saw carved into marble at that exhibit of classical Greek sculpture at the Smithsonian, the Kouros boy with the broad shoulders and firm buttocks, the male body ideal, the ancient predecessors of Calvin Klein underwear models, the male form that I long to embody.

This middle-aged guy named Fred works out at the YMCA at lunchtime with me. He often spots me during my bench press and overhead lifts. He's a political junkie and a journalist. He's a nice enough guy, if a little pudgy around the middle and a little bald up top, physical qualities that are as prominent in wonky DC as fake boobs are in LA. I grow to like Fred. I don't feel pressured to act like a foolish macho man around him, as I always have around most guys my age in weight rooms. Fred and I talk about Newt Gingrich and Sandra Day O'Connor, rather than whatever hot chick may happen to amble by at any given moment. We also talk about my father's illness. The day LB had another heart attack and I had to rush home to see him, Fred called ABC for me and let them know I would be out that day.

The sexist blather at the bureau is really starting to bug me, though. I think I'll puke if I have to watch another producer call the busty news desk assistant Eileen into the control room just so they can look at her boobs. I swear I will also barf if I have to witness another slimeball producer (who is probably married) rush up to his office with the makeup girl to do whatever it is that they do that causes their hair to turn frizzy while they are away. When Peter Jennings came down from New York for the presidential election coverage, and I had to see him

KEN BAKER

flirt with every be-skirted little assistant within his eyesight, I almost popped my button-down collar with disgust. One of the female desk assistants was so unnerved by his heavy flirting that she refused to ride alone in an elevator with him.

At least guys like Fred keep me from feeling like a complete male mutant. Fred is an avid golfer, and since the biomechanics of hitting a golf ball aren't all that different from shooting a hockey puck, Fred convinces me that I will be pretty proficient at the sport. Turns out, he's right.

Whenever I'm working the late shift, or on my days off, which are usually in the middle of the week, Fred picks me up in the morning at my Dupont Circle apartment and we drive over to DC's public course just south of the Jefferson Memorial. He knows I'm not the richest guy in the world, so he usually insists on paying my greens fee (and a soda afterward). I haven't had this much fun just hanging out with an older guy since Dad and I would pal around at the ice rink, before I left for college, before his diabetes starting killing him slowly.

Because I'm fond of Fred, I think nothing of taking him up on his offer to go swimming in the rooftop pool of his apartment building after a particularly muggy day on the links.

"Here, try these on," he says, tossing me a pair of swim trunks from his dresser drawer.

I step into the bathroom and slip them on.

"They're a little baggy, but they'll do," I shout out to him.

When I return, Fred is sitting naked on his bed, sliding his socks off his hairy legs. Having grown up in locker rooms all my life, I've seen plenty of naked guys; as such, I'm unfazed by his nudity. Yet, as I fold my clothes into a pile next to his bed I notice out of the corner of my eye that Fred is not putting clothes on.

I glance over and see that his dick looks—doh!—hardening. He smiles at me.

Oh, I get it. Fred must be gay. That picture on his dresser of him and that guy—"a friend," he said—is of him and a lover. Oh, shit.

I pretend not to notice his dick and leave the room. "See you up at the pool," I say, my heart racing.

Does he think I'm a homo? Why the fuck else would he do something like that? Do I emit gayness or something? Just because I'm not into checking out girls and devoting all my spare time to try to get laid, this guy thinks I am a fairy? This is not good. . . . What if I am gay? What then? Oh . . . my . . . fucking . . . god. Maybe this explains why I can't get hard when I'm with girls! I could be gay. Maybe that's why I feel overly sensitive when the boss criticizes me or when my friends leave me behind when they go out at night. Maybe that's why girls have always described me as a "different" kind of guy.

As I'm about to head up to the pool, I turn around and walk back toward his bedroom. Luckily, Fred has put a pair of shorts on, albeit Speedos.

"Hey, man," I stammer. "I forgot that I have to go into work early this afternoon, so, uh, so I can't go swimming today." I step halfway out the door. "Sorry, Fred. But you can go ahead without me. I gotta get going."

And as I do, I'm angry. Not with Fred. I am mad at myself. For being so frustrated about not relating to women sexually while spending most of my free time with a man who is attracted to me. I'm ashamed. I'm embarrassed too. Embarrassed that I am emitting such a non-heterosexual vibe that even a homosexual man can't detect my sexual orientation. Still, I haven't a clue that my behavior may have something to do with a hormonal imbalance, that my gender identity is in some way being shaped by a malfunctioning pituitary gland.

It doesn't even occur to me that I am sick when that fall, somewhere amid the twenty-six miles of the Marine Corps marathon, my nipples start aching. Pulsing, actually. They feel like pink balloons designed to hold an ounce of water but that are filled with ten gallons. They literally feel like they are going to . . . fucking explode. I press my palms against the swollen tips, trying to push back in whatever's trying to get out. After a few more miles—at around Mile 20—my body is so numb I don't even care anymore, and so I just keep running.

Nearly four and a half hours after I started running amid the thousands of other bodies, I limp across the finish line, where I'm met by a volunteer who places a bronze medal around my neck. I stumble to a patch of grass nearby. I take off my sweat-soaked T-shirt and fall back to the ground. My nipples, again, start killing me. . . . I glance down and see blood dripping from my nipples. Looking closer, I see a whitish fluid oozing out as well. I pinch my right nipple, sending close to a teaspoon of the milky stuff seeping out through the center of my nipple. *My breasts are leaking milk.* I wipe my sticky hand on the grass and hope no one notices.

Like that incident with Fred, like all the times when my penis has failed me, like all my insecurities about not being macho enough, I know I will never tell anyone about this. I am starting to keep secrets.

As a teenager, the path to manhood seemed straightforward. As I interpreted the man-making process, since I had a girlfriend in high school, became a hotshot hockey goalie and finally got laid, I thought I had become a man. I was wrong.

While in DC I go on my first date as a post-collegiate man. Her name is Claudia. I'm determined to use her as proof of my virility.

My roommate Steve introduces me to her at a party at a friend's Dupont Circle apartment. I learn that she, too, has recently left college life behind. She, too, has brown eyes. She, too, is single. We begin talking, about everything from merits of George Bush versus Bill Clinton to the racial segregation in Washington's neighborhoods. My sexual mojo may be lacking, but at least I'm a good conversationalist.

As I have witnessed the frat boys and hockey meatheads do for the last four years, I smile and nod and inject funny little comments at the right moments. I also walk to the keg and pour Claudia beer after beer all night long. *If I get her drunk, then maybe I won't feel so nervous. I will be in control.*

I boast that I ran a marathon (*girls like strong men*) and that I'm a TV journalist (*girls like ambitious guys with high earning potential*), although I modestly call myself "a boy from Buffalo" (*girls like the vague image of machismo that Buffalo evokes*). With this kind of rap, Darwin might have deemed me worthy of propagating my genes.

"Can I be blunt?" Claudia asks me while wiping Budweiser foam from her pink-lipsticked upper lip.

"Please do."

"You aren't like most guys, Ken."

"I'll take that as being a good thing."

"Oh, yeah, definitely." She gently taps my arm and locks on to my eyes. "It is a *really* good thing. Most men I meet act so cheesy and hit on me so blatantly. It's a real turnoff. It's so annoying. It's refreshing to just have a nice conversation with a guy for a change. Most guys just want to get in my pants."

Wait. I thought I was hitting on her, doing all the flirtatious things a man does in order to lure a woman into his domain. Shake it off, hockey boy. Just keep being funny.

"But you're not wearing pants," I reply.

"Touché," Claudia says, before excusing herself for a bathroom break.

Admiring her high-heel gait across the hardwood floor, I notice that extending from her knee-length black cotton dress are long, muscular, runway-model legs that she is using not only to locomote but to arouse every man in the crowded hallway. Claudia continues her cat walk past a line of men waiting in line for the bathroom and makes them twist their necks so far sideways you'd think they were dogs being jerked by choke collars.

It's getting late, and, although I'm eager to embark on my post-college love life, I'm not quite ready to take the penile plunge so suddenly. Frankly, I am scared. I'm not ready to deal with my failure tonight. So when she returns from the potty, I inform her that I—*yaaaawn*—have to get up in four hours for work.

Before we leave, Steve and I get them to agree to go on a double movie-date the next day.

. . .

All day long at work, in between answering phones, running scripts, recording video of Bosnian carnage and making copies, I can't stop thinking about my date, about Claudia's olive-skinned loveliness, about how within a matter of hours I may—*gulp*—have sexual intercourse. My coworker Neki, one of ABC's only African-American desk assistants and my best female friend, senses something's up.

"Hey, Baker," she says. "Why you so smiley today?"

"I'm going to the movies tonight," I say smugly.

"With who?"

"A girl."

"Oh-heee-heee," she explodes. "Call the AP! Now, that's news if I ever heard it. It's about time, honey. You could use a little lovin'."

I'm always talking about girls with Neki, mainly about how I don't understand them. She is my enemy informant, my intelligence source from the "other" side who can make sense out of the seemingly senseless behavior of young women. When I lament how most women my age don't appreciate nice guys like me, Neki says not to worry, that in a couple years the same girls who are chasing hardbodied and hard-drinking fools will start lusting for the kind of guys who will make a good father to their kids, and before I know it I will be surrounded by a harem of female admirers. Neki's assurances make me feel like less of a freak, as if I am the normal one and everyone else is a hormonally driven lunatic. She gives me the kind of advice I imagine I would receive from a sister, if I had one. Neki browses the *Washington Post* movie listings and advises me to take Claudia to a "chick flick." Professor Neki then suggests *Singles*, a film about a group of twentysomething yuppies looking for love on the streets of ultra-hip Seattle. Matt Dillon and Winona Ryder star. *That's us! Me and Claudia, who, come to think of it, looks an awful lot like Winona.*

On the way to the theater, I set a goal: I will hold her hand during the movie. But that's it. No sex just yet. I need to ease into this.

The movie is just what Dr. Neki ordered. Lots of kissing scenes, lots of young, attractive white people and plenty of hip grunge music on the soundtrack: Pearl Jam. Smashing Pumpkins. Alice in Chains. At one particularly romantic moment, the Paul Westerberg song "Dyslexic Heart" bursts over the Dolby, and I place my hand on Claudia's thigh. She opens her legs. I'm so tense you could stick a piece of coal up my ass and I'd shit out a diamond. I'm twenty-two, but this is the first time I've ever made such a bold advance. Forget about the Associated Press; I should have Neki call *The Guinness Book of World Records*.

After the movie, we drive back to my apartment, where Claudia and I make out on my front stoop, oblivious to the pedestrians strolling up on down P Street. She's wearing a short skirt, but I leave the mysterious anatomy hidden beneath for another night, although I know that if we keep seeing each other, if we keep falling in love like this, if I don't let my fear of failure win out over my desire to prove that I am normal, I soon won't be able to put off the inevitable sexual collision that nature has in store for us.

Romeo and Juliet is a tragedy. A lot of people forget that.

People like to focus on the part of the play dealing with two star-crossed lovers so attracted to each other that they risk death to be together. People like to focus on lines such as the ones uttered by Romeo when he spots Juliet standing on her balcony from the courtyard of the Capulet mansion and intones, "But soft, what light through yonder window breaks? It is the east, and Juliet is the sun."

Looking down from the window of my third floor apartment, I spot Claudia walking up my steps on this, my only day off from work. My Juliet inspires not an eloquent monologue but rather an abiding sense of dread that I am about to confront the most beautiful yet the most dangerous creature on Earth. My reaction to the sight of her is felt not so much as a flutter in the heart as a knot in my stomach. *She's so sexy.*

Entering the living room, Claudia greets my dry mouth with a wet kiss.

Relax, man, relax. You can do this.

It's a warm summer day. "Rather than be all cooped up in here," I say, "why don't we go for a walk to Georgetown."

"I've got a better idea," she says, latching her hands around the small of my back. "Let's fuck."

We start kissing. Out of the corner of my eye I notice that the row of panel windows behind Claudia is wide open, exposing us to full view of the Tunisian Embassy directly across the street. It's the perfect excuse for me to pull away from her without seeming frigid.

"We're gonna get the Tunisians all riled up over there," I say, peeling her hands off my body and fussing with the curtains.

Before I close the last curtain, though, Claudia is sitting on the couch topless and wiggling out of her shorts. *A perfect body. A perfect woman. A perfect chance.*

More dutiful than lustful, I kneel in front of her and kiss her body all over. With my lower body out of her reach, the couch serves as a barrier between her and my penis, which, despite this most lovely display of naked femininity, remains as soft as sushi roll.

She gropes for my zipper.

Uh-oh. Now what do I do?

"No," I protest with a whisper.

"What's wrong?"

"Nothing. Just keep your eyes shut."

I know I can get hard. At least once a week I masturbate, just to make sure I'm still able to get it up. It sometimes takes a few minutes to stimulate blood flow, but it usually works—with enough help from the manual cavalry, that is. I will do whatever it takes to not blow this chance. I will use my hand.

Still kneeling before the couch, as I unzip my pants and start rubbing myself, I guide her hand down to her swollen clitoris.

"What are you doing?" she asks, smiling. "Why can't I look?"

I start kissing her down below, one aspect of sexual relations I gained experience in during college while avoiding doing the real thing.

"Just keep touching yourself," I instruct her, placing her T-shirt around her head like a blindfold.

No pressure. Her eyes aren't on me. Just keep yanking like I do when I'm alone.

"I've never done anything like this before," she coos. A minute later, she cuts off her orgiastic moaning and asks, "Do you have a rubber?"

There is NO WAY in hell I can get hard wearing a rubber. Fucking impossible. My bare shaft is dead enough to the world without a condom enveloping it like a sensory deprivation glove.

"Don't worry," I whisper. "I'll pull out in time."

My hand doesn't exactly make my dick rock hard, but it gets rigid enough. I slide it into Claudia—who, meanwhile, has digitally worked herself into a frenzy—before it gets any softer.

Now that I'm in, the pressure of getting hard abated, I tear the blindfold from her and let her watch as I rapidly pump in and out of her. Not even two minutes later, I am done—and relieved that I have passed my first test of post-college manhood. *I can do it. I can have sex!*

Although the bondage behavior is a far cry from sweet kisses and longing glances in *Romeo and Juliet*, our fledgling sexual relationship does have one thing in common with the Shakespearean play: It soon will become a tragedy.

"ABC News, this is Ken."

"I'm laying in bed naked, watching you."

"Oh, *reeeally*."

It's Claudia and it's almost the end of the Sunday evening news. I'm in the ABC newsroom, sitting at a computer terminal located about twenty feet behind the anchor, Carole Simpson. I'm pretending to be busily working as the credits roll on TV screens across the country. My girlfriend is getting off on the idea of millions of people seeing me, all cute and professional in my shirt and tie while she plays with herself.

"I want you to come over here right now," kinky Claudia says. "I have some ropes."

"Okay, settle down, Monster. I'll be there in fifteen minutes."

Monster. I have given her the nickname Monster. I should have identified that as an omen. I don't remember exactly when or why I started calling her Monster, but it seems to fit her perfectly. The nickname may have as much to do with how I regard women in general as it does with our relationship, which is about as sexually dysfunctional as they get (anytime someone needs ropes, blindfolds and their right hand to have sex, that's a firm sign of dysfunctional sexuality). Too busy trying hide my insecurity, I never think that maybe a girl whose behavior toward you earns her the name Monster (because she often scares you) is not a good girl to date. But, then again, my attitude toward women, as well as life, is about fighting. *Fight, fight fight!* I must constantly fight against my own self in order to be the man I want to be.

My sexual self-esteem is so low, I'm convinced I'll never find another woman who will put up with my disabled penis and the odd things—the refusing to have sex nine out of every ten times she asks, the bondage, the clunky preintercourse masturbation, my saggy breasts that I have to pinch the milk out of before she comes over—that I have to do because the useless piece of meat that is my penis otherwise will not rise to the occasion.

Perhaps what also obfuscates a more objective view of Claudia is that she can be such an exciting, sexy woman. First of all, she's a scientist with the federal government who got a nearly perfect score on the SAT. She can quote Einstein, the Torah and Stephen Hawking in one breath. Furthermore, when she wants to be she is sweeter than pie, making me sushi rolls, bringing me takeout Chinese when I am stuck at the bureau late at night. But our relationship has more ups and downs than Sam Donaldson's moods on show night.

Though an intellectual giant, she sometimes can act like an eight-year-old girl. She recently has started threatening at least once a week to break up with me and "see other people." One day she's convinced I'm cheating on her with Neki (although I've never had a single sexual thought about her); the next day she's telling me how sweet and kind and devoted and "special" I am and insists she never wants to ever lose me.

Whenever I'm in her doghouse, though, I beg her not to leave me—I grovel, actually. I tell her how I have never loved anyone as much as I do her (she doesn't know that she is only the second girl I've ever had sex with). I promise I will love her forever. After a few months, I get the impression she enjoys my pleading.

Of course, I'm not thinking about how awful this all is when I hang up from her come-fuck-me-right-now phone call. Instead, I'm focusing on the positive, trying to be Zen about it, going with the flow.

I've come to view the act of sexual intercourse sort of as a game of Hit the Gopher, a carnival game in which you hold a padded hammer and smash a mechanical gopher every time he pokes his head out of one of the five or six holes in a wood console. Likewise, bad thoughts—about my impotence, about the pressure and awkwardness I feel about sex—are gophers that I strike down with a dose of denial and repression and Zen-like meditative breathing. During hockey games, I would combat negative thoughts with positive ones. Similarly, I employ a complementary, yin-yang combat plan with my insecure sexual conscience:

(–) Thought	(+) Thought
My dick is weak as balsa wood.	My dick is strong as steel.
I'm a pathetic excuse for a man.	I'm a special kind of man.
I'm gonna go limp again tonight.	I'm gonna pump her like a piston.

As soon the evening news ends and the stage manager clears the set, I hang up on Claudia, clean off my desk and immediately jog up Connecticut Avenue to her apartment, where she has left the front door unlocked. I find her in her bedroom. As promised, Monster's got ropes.

Unlike most of our sexual encounters, though, this time Claudia wants to tie *me* up. She gives me a riot cop's shove onto her bed.

"You said fifteen minutes," she says. "It's been half an hour, boy. You've been very bad, Kenny."

Either she really is mad at me, or she's a great actress. It's hard to tell with Claudia.

She tells me to lie on my back. That's a no-no—that is, if she expects to have sex. I never lie on my back when we attempt to do it, because what little blood usually fills my penis just seems to fall back into my body instead of filling the tissue. When you're suffering from erectile dysfunction, lovemaking becomes more of an exercise in manipulating gravity than a lustful act of passion.

"Don't move," she grunts, wrapping the twine around my wrists and looping it around the bedpost. She folds a bandana and ties it around my face. "I'm going to rape you."

Just relax. My problem is that I think too much about sex. I've lost all concept of the inner game of sex. I have to stop my mind from getting in the way of my body. Zen Ken.

Claudia tries everything in her playbook—along with nearly every part of her anatomy—in an effort to get me hard enough to stick me inside of her and get off.

Nothing works.

The ensuing verbal lashing she inflicts on me hurts more than the twine burning the skin on my wrists:

"You're fucked up." . . . "It's like your wires are crossed or something." . . . "Aren't you attracted to me?" . . . "Seek help." . . . "Maybe you are gay."

I do need help.

I want to wield wood, but all I can muster is the physiological equivalent of a wilted flower. And the more erotic the situation, the less hard my dick seems to get.

She curls into the fetal position and starts sobbing.

"Why can't you have sex with me like I'm a normal person?" she whines like a little girl whose Betty Crocker bakery set has just broken.

"I wish I knew," I sigh. "I wish I knew."

We lay beside each other in silence, staring at the ceiling. Suicide crosses my mind. "There *must* be something wrong with you physically," she says.

But I've just run a marathon. I was a Division I hockey goalie. I run twenty miles a week. I lift weights at the gym. The last thing I'm about to consider is being physically ill. Plus, I went to the DC Public Library last week and read up on impotence. One medical book said the most common causes of impotence were high blood pressure, diabetes, poor circulation—old-guy ailments. In fact, it said that men over age sixty are most likely to suffer from erectile dysfunction. I'm twenty-two fucking years old!

"It can't be physical," I reply, sounding a lot like Larry Baker did when he would refuse to see a doctor even when a kidney stone had prevented him from peeing for four straight days. Like father, like son.

But wait! I did read that perhaps as many as twenty percent of cases of erectile dysfunction are caused by psychological problems, such as stress, anxiety or insecurity of some kind. That's it!

I'm feeling obligated to offer Claudia an explanation, especially now that she's groaning on and on about how my sexual inadequacy is probably all her fault.

I blurt, "It's my dad's fault."

"What does your dad have to do with your dick?" she scoffs.

"Really. No kidding. I really think my father has made me feel so bad about having sex that I am afraid to do it. I must have a mental block or something. I mean, my dad used to tell me shit like 'Girls are evil' and 'Women will fuck up your life' and all this other crap. It must have fucked me up somewhere along the way. I don't know why else I would be like this." I don't say the *I* word; I'm not ready to admit I'm impotent.

"You really think that's why?" she asks, rolling to face me. "You sure it's not me?"

"Positive," I say, running my fingers through her hair.

Lying naked beside Claudia, I start rhapsodizing a fully intellectualized explanation for my inability to achieve and maintain a normal erection. I devise what could be called the Unified Theory of Penile Anxiety (UTOPA), which, instead of confronting any physical causes of my illness, I will use to solve the riddle of my sexual angst for the next five years. The UTOPA equation looks something like this:

$$\text{I (impotence)} = \text{D (Dad's misogynist propaganda)} + \text{N (my nervous inexperience)} + \text{S (my "special" manliness)}$$

It make sense when you think about it. Hey, at least she has stopped crying. At least I'm starting to figure out my problem.

Nevertheless, a few weeks later, even my clever mathematical justifications can't keep Claudia from dumping me. Although I am convinced otherwise, she claims it's not because of our sex life, not because of me and my neuroses. Rather, she says, it's about her being too young to "settle down." She needs to "play the field" and "see what else is out there."

I don't even bother to put up a fight. I don't deserve a smart and beautiful woman like her anyway. I really can't blame her. After all, I'm an insignificant player in the evolutionary mating game. With scores of able-bodied young men out there lacking complications stemming from afflictions such as I=D+N+S who are just waiting to replace me, she *should* dump me. *I* would.

Alhough I feel completely deserving, it doesn't make my mental state any more stable or me any less obsessed about my emasculinity.

In an effort to try and forget, I go running. Every day after work I jog along the Potomac River. If I'm feeling weak or jittery or if my nipples start aching, I ignore it *like a man*. I force myself to run.

I run across the Arlington Memorial Bridge into Virginia, veering over to Roosevelt Island, a refuge of wetlands and dirt paths where I can just be alone, by the river. I run along the shady trails, beside the geese, running to forget and running to find peace, to solve the riddle that has become my existence.

Emerging from a stand of trees, I jog upon the gray granite slabs of the island's Teddy Roosevelt Memorial.

I stop. Catching my breath, I read Roosevelt's words etched into a towering vertical slab of rock:

MANHOOD

A MAN'S USEFULNESS
DEPENDS UPON HIS LIVING UP TO
HIS IDEALS
IN SO FAR AS HE CAN

IT IS HARD TO FAIL. BUT IT IS WORSE
NEVER TO HAVE TRIED TO SUCCEED

ALL DARING & COURAGE
ALL IRON ENDURANCE OF MISFORTUNE
MAKE FOR A FINER & NOBLER TYPE OF
MANHOOD

ONLY THOSE ARE FIT TO LIVE
WHO DO NOT FEAR TO DIE
AND NONE ARE FIT TO DIE
WHO HAVE SHRUNK FROM THE
JOY OF LIFE
AND THE
DUTY OF LIFE

As I run back across the bridge to the District, I see in the distance the stark white obelisk that is the Washington Monument, and I start crying harder than a year ago, when I had hung up my ice skates for the last time, ending the only true joyful display of manhood I have ever known. Through my tear-blurred eyes I stare at the erect Monument piercing the afternoon sky in the distance. My first thought is that the phallic symbol is just another reminder of my impotence, my male inadequacy. I shake out the bad thought and instead think about Roosevelt's words. *I will be better for all this misfortune. It will make me a better man.*

I run faster.

Finer and nobler. Finer and nobler. Finer and nobler. That's it. All this pain and confusion is making me finer and nobler. My failure, in the end, you see, will make me a better, stronger man.

I run back up along the Potomac, past the Watergate, into Rock Creek Park. The running doesn't stop for many more years to come. Looking back, I wish I could have run straight to the Georgetown Medical Center. I wish I could have realized I was running an unwinnable race against a biological opponent whose insidious power was widening the chasm between me and my sexuality, my manhood and the rest of the hormonally healthy world. But I didn't.

Instead, I just kept running.

Television journalism often emphasizes image and bravado over sub-stance and context. It is a profession staffed largely by a team of ener-getic young men and women running around on adrenaline highs behind the scenes, producing words and images narrated by talking heads. Print journalism is about interviewing people one-on-one, in private or over the phone, then returning to your keyboard and writ-ing a story in relative solitude. Television is visceral; print is cerebral. It takes less than a year at ABC for me to conclude that I'm not a TV guy.

Eight months into my job at ABC, I apply to the Columbia Uni-versity Graduate School of Journalism in order to become a print guy. Although I never quite attain his level of journalistic testoster-mania, I have impressed Sam Donaldson enough to convince him to write me a letter of recommendation ("Ken is a smart, hard-working jour-nalist . . ."). It must have helped, as in the spring of 1993, I am accepted into perhaps the most respected journalism program in the world. From now on, I have decided, I will measure my personal success by my journalistic achievements in the newsroom, not my athletic or sexual ones.

Although I kept telling myself that the reason I miss Claudia is be-cause I love her so much, and I believe that I always will, it helps that

I am getting away from her. In our last conversation, I asked her under what conditions she would take me back. "When you get your head screwed on straight," she told me. That hasn't happened yet, though.

Upon my arrival at Columbia, I vow to stop thinking about my inept ways with women, to make a new start, to carve out my place in the journalism world by getting a master's degree from this respected school. A six-class course load—plus my job doing research for a *New York Times* reporter—provides me a convenient excuse for not having a social life. A few weeks into the program, my academic adviser informs me that I have to decide soon what my master's project is going to be. The only restriction, he says, is that it be a work of long-form journalism focused on a single subject.

While walking through the student center one afternoon, I see tacked on a bulletin board a flyer from an after-school youth program called Ice Hockey in Harlem; it says the program is seeking dedicated volunteer teachers and coaches for the upcoming season. There's an informational meeting next week. Not only do I immediately plan to attend, but I'm relieved because I think I might have found the subject of my master's project.

I have been living in Manhattan alone in a dank studio apartment on the extreme Upper West Side for about a month. My sunlight-deprived box of residential isolation has all of two windows, both of which have a latticework of thick metal bars over them, offering an already uninspiring view of a six-foot-wide alley. The place is so small I can practically touch all four walls while lying on my mattress, which, when plopped onto the floor, covers three quarters of the entire floorspace. I'm not complaining, though. I've slept in worse places (our duplex on Harwood Avenue comes to mind); plus, hey, rent is only six hundred bucks a month, which is all I can afford on my student loan.

As rough as I think I have it, however, at least I'm not a kid living in a Harlem tenement. I may even be a role model for such underprivileged kids. I'm excited about the prospect of helping inner-city kids learn hockey. The sport got me out of Buffalo; who's to say it won't get one of them out of East Harlem? Besides, in the process maybe I'll boost my self-esteem and stop feeling so fucking sorry for myself. I doubt that Teddy Roosevelt held self-pity parties.

In addition to my Fly Over Country–bred curiosity, maybe part of what attracts me to journalism—not to mention to Ice Hockey in Harlem—is that it will require me to turn my gaze to other people. I can probe them, question them, alleviate the pressure on me. I needn't sit around and worry about my pathetic gender insecurities and dysfunctional sexual practices. After all, journalism involves documenting the lives of *other* people—not the lives of the documentarian himself.

Besides, introspection, the center of a so-called thinking life, has kept me from living life. While the unexamined life is indeed a life not worth living, I think I have gone overboard. Self-examination has blocked me from being "autonomic," Claudia's word for the kind of guys she had always dated (and is now back to dating) before stumbling upon my unique version of guyhood. Like a lot of the words she used, I had to look up its definition:

autonomic — *occurring involuntarily, automatically; of or controlled by the autonomic nervous system*

autonomic nervous system — *the part of the nervous system that is responsible for control and regulation of the involuntary bodily functions.*

Then I started realizing what she meant.

"Do you think something's wrong with my autonomic nervous system," I asked Claudia, a trained scientist. "I may have a nervous-system condition?"

"No," she said. "I'm just saying you're impotent."

After having Claudia, mid-breakup, turn the impotence mirror back on me, I decided to start spending a lot of my free time away from ABC at the grimy DC Public Library, reading up on impotence alongside the homeless guys snoozing between the air-conditioned rows of books. There, I hoped, I might find out what the fuck was preventing Private Dick from standing at attention.

I didn't know much about impotence. For example, until I educated myself on the subject, I didn't know that emotional or psychological factors (presumably, the cause of my affliction) account for less than twenty percent of impotence cases. I didn't know that in another twenty percent or so of the cases there is a neurological, vascular or hormonal problem to blame. I'd rather not hear or read anything about "erectile dysfunction," as the literature called it. It wasn't like I *never* got erections; it was just that it seemed like every other time I tried, my dick didn't cooperate. But while my erectability was impaired, my innate, preprogrammed, Darwinian knowledge that I inhabit this planet in order to have sex haunted me. How fucking frustrating! Imagine being hungry, famished, and someone places a slice of pizza in front of you. Now imagine your hands handcuffed and your mouth gagged, unable to eat the pizza, and that's, basically, how I felt about sex: tortured.

Even reading about it hasn't helped. Only vigorous masturbation gets a rise out of me—and even that process is as slow as leavening bread.

This is why now, even as a twenty-three-year-old grad school student, I am bitter about the concept of introspection, which apparently has only made me more impotent; while allowing me to devise intellectual equations (I=D+N+S), it has created more problems than it has solved.

Exhibit A: A phone conversation the other day with Fred from DC, who called and invited me to join him next weekend (paid for by him) on a golf trip to Palm Springs, California. I politely declined, telling him I was swamped with writing assignments, but neglecting to tell him I'M NOT A HOMOSEXUAL. An asexual, maybe, but I am not gay. Gays have a sex drive; I don't even have that.

. . .

I commit myself to try and do for Harlem's young hockey players what my dad has been trying to do to me my whole life: turn boys into men.

Armed with an idealistic, do-gooder spirit (and, of course, my self-denial), I attend the program's first teachers' meeting at a building in Central Park, where Ice Hockey in Harlem's practices and games are held on an outdoor rink.

"Don't feel as though you're obligated to be involved simply because you're here," says Debbie, the program's sassy twenty-nine-year-old volunteer coordinator. "This is not for everyone. I gotta be honest with you. Many of the kids will have behavior problems. You should think hard about whether you want to make the commitment."

Debbie says that each kid is required to attend a class, taught by volunteers like us, at an East Harlem public school once a week. The kids take classes such as Hockey Math and Hockey Geography, in which they learn about these school subjects in the context of hockey. (Example: *Wayne Gretzky plays for the Los Angeles Kings. In what state is Los Angeles located?*) The oldest kids must also enroll in IHIH's Community Service class, she says; Debbie hopes one of us will volunteer to teach a new communications class for the fourteen- and fifteen-year-olds. "If a kid skips class during the week," Debbie explains, "he won't be allowed to play hockey on the weekends."

As Debbie, who is white, gives us the straight dope, I look around the room at the other volunteers, noticing that only two of them are black (the rest of us are white). That's too bad, I think, because nearly all the kids are black or Hispanic.

Debbie goes around the room and asks each of us to introduce ourselves. I learn that the two black men are Ron, a thirty-two-year-old former Army infantryman who grew up in Harlem, and Myron Kellogg, a *New York Times* executive. Both have volunteered to teach the Community Service class. Being a journalist-in-the-making, I offer to teach the new Communications class.

Then Ron, a muscular six feet tall, stands and addresses the group in his staccato drill-sergeant cadence. He suggests we run our classes "like a little boot camp." "Many of these boys don't have fathers in their lives and are hungry for male attention," he says. "They need someone to tell them what to do, where to go, how to do it, because many of them don't get it from home."

Afterward, I share a cab uptown to Harlem with Ron. I admit that I am nervous about my ability to handle a bunch of black and Hispanic kids not even ten years younger than me.

"Don't worry, man," he says. "First of all, you're not as different as you think you are. If you just talk your language—not theirs—to them you will be fine, because what you speak is caring."

The cab turns left at the Apollo Theater and Ron asks the driver to stop in front of his brick apartment building. Before he gets out, he pats my back and says, "You'll be okay. Before they see you as being white, they'll first see you as a man showing them positive attention."

Two weeks pass. Two weeks of reporting and writing and reading and more reporting and writing. I usually stay up till three or four in the morning writing stories on my computer, late-night talk-radio hosts keeping me company.

After a long day of class at the J-School, I take the bus across town to 104th Street and Lexington Avenue to P.S. 72, in the heart of East Harlem, for my first night of class. The first thing I notice is that every volunteer—except for me—is black or Hispanic. When I ask Debbie what happened to all the volunteers from the meeting, she tells me all the whites have chickened out and quit.

Debbie briefs me on the backgrounds of a few of my twelve students: Tyrone's father died when he was three. Jimmy's mother recently died from a "drug-related" cause and his father is a former drug dealer living in California. José hasn't been the same since a gang of kids put a gun to his head last summer. Jonathan, she says, is functionally illiterate.

Her backgrounder, however, does nothing to alleviate my fears that these kids are going to eat my suburban ass for dinner.

Realizing the greatest thing we have in common is hockey, I introduce myself to the class as "a former Division One college hockey player." Judging by the sudden attention-giving gazes from beneath their backward-turned baseball caps, my introduction seems to get their attention. "Hey, you look like Wayne Gretzky." . . . "Where's Colgate?" . . . "Did you ever play in Madison Square Garden?"

They don't care about *no* Columbia University. They tell me so with their blank stares and idle chatter. These kids live two miles from the university; yet, most of them have never stepped foot on the campus. Their campuses are the drab brick high-rise housing projects that dominate the East Harlem skyline.

East Harlem — or "Spanish Harlem"—takes up a 2.2-square-mile patch of Manhattan's extreme Upper East Side. Nearly half its residents are on some form of welfare or public assistance; forty percent live below the poverty line; and children who grow up in a home without a father outnumber those who do. Although some of the richest, most famous residents of New York City, and the world, walk their poodles and get pedicures in the shadows of glitzy high-rise apartment buildings just thirty blocks to the south, East Harlem is a landscape dominated by scrappy sidewalk bodegas, garbage-strewn vacant lots and block after block of run-down tenements that make my old "Harwood Hell" look like Trump Tower.

Theirs is a violent world that bears testament to why over ninety percent of violent crimes are committed by males. I hope to do something to teach these boys that there is more to being a man than living by the lead of testosterone and the priority the powerful hormone places on sexual gratification, physical assertiveness and competitiveness. Through my example, they may learn that being more sensitive isn't tantamount to being less strong. I give them their first writing assignment: to write a paragraph on why they think they are a leader. Only four of the twelve kids can think of a reason.

• • •

For New Year's Eve, Claudia comes to visit me in New York. We've been exchanging E-mail for the past several weeks, and we've decided it would be nice to see each other. Neither of us admits it, but I think we want to see if there's still a spark between us. She writes, "I fear that I will never find another guy as sweet, kind and loving as you. You are a special boy with a special 'problem.' Now you just need to become a man. I love you, Ken." I reckon it's mostly because of that last line that she hops the bus to New York. I also reckon another reason is that neither of us wants to be alone on New Year's Eve.

We meet on the windy afternoon of December thirty-first at the base of the granite steps of Columbia's library. I haven't seen her in over four months; she is even prettier than in the photo of her I have tacked onto my wall. All of her life, Claudia has been told she could be a model, and seeing the way the soft skin of her chin brushes against her scarf I wonder why someone so beautiful would be attracted to someone as unbeautiful as me.

We walk over to my tiny apartment just south of campus, on 113th Street, and we put on our sneakers. Like two long-lost *platonic* friends, we walk eighty blocks down Broadway, talking about everything and nothing at the same time. Wanting to show her my favorite view of the Manhattan skyline, we walk across the Brooklyn Bridge and sit on a bench overlooking the East River, a perch from which we stare at the glassy fortress that is lower Gotham. Moms and dads pass by, pushing strollers. Lovers amble by hand in hand. Norman Mailer, the writer who lives in the neighborhood, shuffles past us looking scraggly and lonely.

"I don't ever want to be old and lonely," I say. "That would be so depressing."

Claudia stares across the cold, black river. No talk of sex. No talk of my penis and how she and I silently hate its meddling third-party disruption of our relationship. *I wonder if Mailer's dick works. If my dick is this lifeless in my twenties, what will happen when I'm in my seventies?*

Maybe I will end up an old and lonely guy ambling around Brooklyn by my-self on New Year's Eve.

Sometime before midnight, we meet up with Claudia's friends, a guy and a girl. Claudia suggests we ring in the new year at Times Square, so we cram into a mass of bodies a few blocks block from the bedlam at One Times Square. From our vantage point we can see half of the world-famous giant white ball that sits atop a pole. The human warmth tempers the chill of the steady pelting of rain. We squeeze our way to the front of the crowd, closer to the ball. Every few minutes or so, an ABC cameraman pans the crowd, prompting our drunken neighbors to wave cardboard signs at Dick Clark, clink champagne glasses, celebrate a new year in their lives with smiles and levity I can only fake.

Over the course of an hour, the crowd grows bigger and bigger. Packs of revelers are emerging from the nearby subway exit, hundreds of them, squeezing into the roped-off viewing area. Burly NYPD of-ficers—some holding riot shields and nightsticks, others on horse-back—guard the area just in front of the first row. Helmeted officers are pressing their batons against the front-liners whenever they heave forward.

By a quarter to midnight, the crowd has grown even bigger and starts pushing forward, more steadily, more drunkenly. People are pop-ping champagne corks; a brass band is blaring "New York, New York," which I can barely hear over the buzzing chorus of ten-cent kazoos. Three shirtless frat boys with painted torsos—spelling **A B C**—whoop whenever the camera lights shine down on them. Couples are kissing.

Where's Claudia?

Amid the ruckus, I have somehow separated from her. Suddenly, the crowd—at least a thousand strong now—surges forward. A girl next to me lets out a scream right out of a horror movie. People who were happy-go-lucky a second ago are now either scared or extremely pissed off; members of the latter group start pushing back. Their shoving throws me off balance and I topple forward, slamming my nose into the shoulder of the guy in front of me. When he steps aside, I'm sent crashing face-first onto the pavement.

I look up as the crowd swallows the air above me. A boot steps on my hand. A kick to the face.

"Let me up!" I shout into the muffled mass of winter coats and umbrellas. No one seems to hear. "Let me up!"

I am in a claustrophobic panic worse than the thought of any stuck elevator ever incited.

Grabbing onto jackets, pants, whatever I can get a hold of, I claw to standing and wriggle through a half dozen or so bodies until I reach the wooden blue police barricade corralling the herd. I drop to all fours and start crawling underneath the barrier—until a baton is thrust into my collar bone.

"Sir, you can't cross this line," the cop shouts over the noise.

Tears are streaming down my face. "But I can't breathe!"

More annoyed than compassionate, the cop yanks me beneath the barricade and points to the roped-off sidewalk: "Go!"

I sprint to the sidewalk, collapsing against a lightpost. I slide down to my butt and suck in the cold air as the wind dries my tears and the crowd counts down in unison.

10, 9, 8, 7 . . .

I stand up and desperately scan the crowd for Claudia . . .

6, 5, 4 . . .

Still standing bewildered on the sidewalk, I spot her, amidst the revelers, jumping up and down. Her perfect, smiling row of teeth stands out like a cottonball in a pile of coal. Ebullient, glowing, just as she should be. Young and beautiful with so much to offer. A woman filled with verve and potential and joy and life. She's a good woman who deserves a good man.

3, 2, 1 . . .

1994!

A blizzard of confetti, corks, hats and plastic cups jettisons skyward and swirls in the Midtown wind. Claudia kisses and hugs her friends. She's swiveling around, looking for me. I can see her, but, appropriately, she can't see me. No one can; I feel so neutered—sexually and emotionally—that I might as well be an invisible man. I don't matter.

An hour later, we're back at my apartment. Knowing that I will be taking off my shirt in front of her, I go straight to the bathroom and lift my shirt, pinching each of my nipples until the gross, milky fluid stops seeping out from them. Once I have squeezed in the new year, I dab my nipples with a piece of toilet paper and flush them down the toilet, ready to return to Claudia as a normal man, not the freak that I am.

This is a new year. A chance to turn over a new leaf. A chance to just relax and have sex. Relax and do it.

Claudia is sloshed and dizzy, a nonstop giggle machine. She unbuttons her blue jeans and begs me to take them off her. Reluctantly, I start to and we fall down to my mattress and kiss tenderly as she climbs atop my naked body, pressing her body against mine. "I've missed you so much," she whispers.

After a couple minutes she reaches down and finds that, as was the case a few months ago, my penis isn't doing what we want it to do. She leans forward and presses her deflated cheek against my chest.

I pound my fist against the mattress.

She wraps her arms around me. "Shhh . . . shhhh . . . it's okay . . . shhhh . . ." It is the last time we touch.

With the first week of January comes a much-needed week off from school. Lacking the money to go anywhere else, I take the eight-hour bus ride across the state to Buffalo to see my family.

Dad complains that Kevin, who once was a budding rock star and now is an evangelical church pastor, visits once every couple months, if that. Keith, who lives in a trailer just outside of Rochester, is busy raising three kids and working constantly. Kyle has gone back to college.

Kris lives in the basement of Dad's duplex, and when he isn't fighting with Green Card or blowing off Mom (she lives three miles away with Norm), he is arguing with Dad.

Dad is dying. He aches nonstop from his neuropathy. The pain he feels—in his hands, his legs, his neck, his arms—is the sensation of his nerves dying one by one. He calls it torture. The army of brown plastic pill bottles lined on the kitchen counter are his only weapon in this battle that he, unable to work for the last two years, is clearly losing.

Most days he wakes up around 6 A.M., when the Valium wears off. Clad in a pair of baggy Fruit of the Looms and a dress shirt he wore to work before he started spending his life on the couch, he slowly sits up. After a minute of eye rubbing, the flabby fifty-year-old battles gravity and, with his feet barely lifting off the worn shag carpet, labors toward the kitchen.

His hair is a messy thatch of black and gray and his skin looks yellowish under the fluorescent overhead light as he fumbles with the pill bottles. It is a morning ritual he has perfected: twist, dump in palm, swallow; twist, dump in palm, swallow. For the past few years he has methodically repeated this routine eight times every morning.

Names such as Procardia, Vicodin, Lasix and, for a short time, Prozac, have entered the household vocabulary over the years. Of all the pills, however, he concedes that it is "the little green ones"—the Valium—that are absolutely necessary these days.

Just a few years ago he could sleep without them. But when nightmares and burning pain in his swollen arms and legs kept him up all night, he gave in.

His brain issued the first warning while driving home from work one night. Obese and unaware of his extremely high blood sugar level, he broke down and wept on the shoulder of the New York State Thruway. Diabetes—the genetic curse he had ignored his entire life— finally caught up to him. His three brothers all had "sugar problems," as they call it, but ice cream, cookies, soda, and chocolate were Dad's weaknesses. So was his ability to deny the fact that a five-foot eight-inch, three-hundred-pound man with a family history of diabetes would eventually self-destruct. Tears cascaded down his face as his hands trembled uncontrollably over the steering wheel. He was going into diabetic shock. He was confused. "I can't see," he screamed, pulling to the side of the road.

Dad suffered irreversible nerve damage that night. The tingling in his toes and fingers eventually turned to pain. He looks forward to total numbness, depressing because it means the nerves are dead, but encouraging because it means the pain is over. The doctors say he is a lucky diabetic because he hasn't gone blind and he hasn't had to have an arm or leg amputated.

"Lucky" diagnoses for him have become more common as his heart has grown weaker and his nerves have slowly deteriorated. "He's lucky he was near a phone when the chest pains started." . . . "He's lucky only two toes got frostbite."

Dad doesn't feel fortunate; most of the time he just feels sorry for himself.

He could have gone to a psychologist to help him cope with the effects of the insidious disease: the phobias, the impotence, the fits of depression, the constant pain from neuropathy, a degenerative disease common in diabetics in which your extremities feel like they are being pricked by needles. But he says "shrinks" can't understand his misery. For him to admit pain—especially of the emotional variety—is effeminate behavior, just not the manly thing to do.

"I'm as rock 'n' roll and apple pie as you get," he likes to say. The 1950's, for Dad, was the best time to grow up in America. Elvis was the King, father always knew best, cars were fast, cigarette smoking was cool and, most importantly, the American dream dangled before him. Two heart attacks, five kids, a kidney operation and two failed marriages later, idealism now seems as foreign to Larry as 45's are to the CD generation.

When Orbison's classic "Pretty Woman" comes on the radio, he orders Kris or me to turn up the volume. "Damn it, Roy's on!" No matter how intense the pain, he will sit up, close his big brown eyes and tap his foot to the backbeat rhythms of his rock hero's melodies.

But when the tape ends and the music fades, the grim reality that his heart flutters at forty percent of its capacity haunts him. He still smokes two packs a day. He wants to care but doesn't, because his body—and his destructive treatment of it—gives him little reason to hope.

He reached the nadir of his physical health last month, shortly before Christmas, when he was rushed to the hospital after collapsing at the mall.

The doctors said "memory loss and drug-induced confusion" caused him to mistakenly overdose on insulin, which drastically lowered his blood sugar level. His heart, weakened by an attack three months earlier, nearly ceased.

He had been depressed for months because for the first time he couldn't afford to buy Christmas gifts for his family. He won't admit it to me, or to any of my brothers, but he tells Green Card that he feels guilty for all the mistakes he made raising us. He is sorry that he all but ignored Kyle, that he beat Kevin black and blue, that he let his bond with most of his sons break when his marriage did.

Lately, the holiday season has only reminded him of past years, before the illness, when he had money, when life was about working hard, making deals, playing catch with his kids, cheering on his son at hockey games, having sex. But now his body is shot and doctor bills, of which many will never be paid, are siphoning most of his monthly Social Security checks. "The government," he tells me one day, "pays for some of my dying bills and none of my living bills."

Two months after his depressing Christmas, Green Card leaves a message on my answering machine in New York. She's whispering, and it sounds like she's crying. "Ken-eee. Larry not good. Bad things happen. Pleeze call me soon."

When I call, she breaks me the news: Dad has lung cancer. It has spread. The doctor has given him a year to live.

When the specter of my dad's death prevents me from being able to attend classes, let alone write a news story, I open the phone book and find an affordable psychologist. By our second session the talk has turned away from my dad and to my sexual frustrations.

"You know, Ken," Frank, my Upper West Side shrink, suggests midway through one of our sixty-dollar-an-hour sessions. "Maybe you should just try and not think about sex so much."

Having made zero progress in two months, Frank, a balding man in his sixties, has actually advised that I practice denial in order to get over my so-called erectile dysfunction and feelings of insecurity. He has already tried the conquer-your-problem-by-figuring-out-your-problem approach by giving me a reading list, notably the book *Sons and Fathers* by D.H. Lawrence. The theory Frank was floating was that I was unable to have sex because I had become codependent with my father and his problems. In other words, Dad's illnesses have become my illnesses. My father is depressed; so am I. My diabetic father is impotent; so am I. Or at least that was his theory. He figured that, being an Ivy Leaguer, I would make an intellectual breakthrough by reading Lawrence. But the book only depressed me.

Now he is promoting the same sort of Zen—*just be*—approach that I have been attempting for years.

Early on in our therapy, Frank asked me if my penis problems could be physical. "No way," I insisted. "I'm in great shape. I haven't had to see a doctor for anything since I was a little kid." The only physical problems I have been having are headaches, which come and go and are probably the result of stress or allergies. My problem, I insist, is in my head.

"You have spent your entire life trying to control everything—your dad's opinion of you, your hockey ability, even the cleanliness of your messy childhood home. Now that your penis is out of your control, you don't know what to do. The last time you felt so out of control of things, back at Colgate, you developed a phobia over not being able to control whether elevators would get stuck. And now you have a phobia about your inability to have sex. But it's irrational, Ken. You are a healthy young man. You just need to let go."

He makes sense. I have just been emotionally traumatized by a lover, I am uptight about successfully completing graduate school and now my father is dying of cancer. Even so, all of the Zen meditation and psychoanalysis in the world doesn't seem to be helping me overcome my problem. I don't even masturbate anymore; I don't want to be reminded that I even have a penis, let alone that it doesn't work.

At my wit's end, Frank then recommends I stop thinking about my father, stop thinking about Claudia, stop fearing performance anxiety and, for the first time in my life, just go out to a bar, pick up a girl and have sex with her. He clearly is trying to light a fire under my ass. "Maybe you just have to prove to yourself that you can have sex," the Ph.D. says. "You just need to learn how to enjoy your body."

Yeah, maybe, Doc. But I am never going to set myself up for a sexual fall ever again. Never again.

I write him a sixty-dollar check and never return.

I am in journalism school, learning the art of interviewing, the craft of probing, of figuring out people that aren't Ken Baker. Some of the best interviewers in the news business—Dan Rather, Terry Anderson, Tom Brokaw, Terry Gross—make the pilgrimage up Broadway to the journalism school and impart their wisdom. I soak it up, loving every minute. It's nice to experience joy, even though it's not of the sexual variety. Journalism is my feel-good tonic, and I am good at it. I may even be better at it than I was at hockey.

I even start feeling more confident when dealing with the brazen teens at Ice Hockey in Harlem. When they start talking over me in class, I sternly tell them to "shut the fuck up." I am not afraid to kick kids out of class and suspend them from playing hockey that week if they don't do their assignments. Whenever I need to use what Dad used to call "tough love," I just pretend I am my father, circa 1982, when he kicked Kevin out of our house every other night for doing drugs. Deep down, though, I know that I am only acting the part of the tough guy, but my "sensitive guy" approach is outdone by the freight train that is their hormonal might.

The Monday-night classes at P.S. 72 also remind me that, no matter how tough I had it as a kid, no matter how distressing my petty little insecurities, these kids *really* have it rough. And there are times when I see sensitive cracks in the hardened armor of their male egos.

My student Lydell, for example, can't remember ever meeting his father.

One night after class I ask Lydell, who was acting uncharacteristically glum, how his father died.

"My mother don't want to tell me," he says.

"Why not?" I ask.

"I guess it's bad. He had a disease or somethin'. I don't know."

"Do you ever miss him?"

His brown eyes glisten with tears as he mumbles, "I don't know."

For the first few weeks after he was diagnosed with cancer, Dad was too depressed, and drugged up, to talk on the phone. Eventually, though, he emerged from his haze and now he wants to chat all the time.

The diagnosis has changed him. Unlike his past illnesses, which he has always blown off with a joke and halfhearted promises to his doctor that he will do better, this one has shaken him. It's terminal, and he knows it. So do I, which is why I return to my dank apartment and call him once a day.

Most often, our conversations are his bitch sessions. He bitches about how Green Card is an asshole. He bitches about the hospice nurses who insist he keep an oxygen tank in the living room. He complains that he doesn't like to be touched because it hurts too much. Even when someone gently rubs his leg, the pain is unbearable. For the first time in his life, he has begun being honest with his feelings.

"I was an awful father," he tells me near the end of one of our conversations. If he is crying, he's masking it over the phone. "There were so many things I would do differently if I had the chance."

"Well, for what it's worth, I think you were a damn good father," I say. "Nobody's perfect. I wouldn't want anyone else as a father. I mean that."

I interpret his silence as acknowledgment.

When he laments how not working and having grown kids makes him feel useless, I ask him for advice. I don't let on to my confusion and pain over Claudia, but I do tell him I'm bummed out about not having a girlfriend, to which he replies, "Don't worry about the broads. They'll always be there. For now, you just need to focus on your career. All that stuff will take care of itself."

Although he has never uttered the three-word phrase, I tell him over the phone, "I love you, Dad."

"I know," he says abruptly.

Following graduation from my one-year master's program, I say goodbye to my tiny apartment and to my Harlem kids and move back to Buffalo for a three-month paid internship as a city reporter for the newspaper I delivered as a kid, *The Buffalo News*. My plan is to gather some much-needed experience and clips that I can send out at the end of the summer to newspapers looking for new reporters. I also want to spend as much time with L.B. as I can.

He undergoes several chemo treatments, although he knows deep down that it isn't going to cure him. After work I sit in the backyard on a lawn chair, telling him about the stories I covered that day: the fires, the murders, the train wreck story on the front page. For the first time since I quit hockey, Dad can relate to what I'm doing. Whenever my byline appears, he calls all my brothers, and their wives and girlfriends, to alert them. He cuts out the articles with scissors, not always very well due to his rapidly deteriorating muscle strength.

In August, I land a feature-writing job at *The Daily Press,* a small but respected newspaper in Newport News, Virginia. They need someone to cover the local church community and to write general-interest feature stories. Every week, I cut out my stories and send them to Dad in a manila envelope with a little note. Kris tells me that, besides his monthly Social Security disability check, it is only thing in the mail that makes him happy.

The happy moments are rarer and rarer. The cancer has spread to his stomach and the tumor in his chest is pressing against his aorta, sapping his heart of the blood it needs to pump. The doctors say he isn't strong enough to survive surgery. A twenty-yard walk from the car to the pharmacy counter puts him out of breath.

In reply to my weekly mailings, he scribbles me notes. It's obvious from the almost illegible handwriting that he is quickly losing control of his hands, which are now so numb he says he could stick a pin in his palm and not feel it.

10-24-94

Hi Kenny—

I've been worse lately. Pain + shortness of breath is beginning to be critical. I have a call in to my doctor for Rx to help me breathe. Last night was the worst I've had. I don't want to suffer. Make sure that Marcia takes care of Kris. Without me he will feel lost and alone.

See ya
Dad

At my request, the American Cancer Society sends me reams of information on chemotherapy, which Dad has ceased undergoing because it made him so sick. I want to confirm what I already suspect about his decision: It will kill him. On page thirteen of a pamphlet, it says, "Some people believe cancer treatment is worse than the disease itself. This is a very dangerous idea, since the cancer that is not treated places you in far more danger than a cancer that is treated. If you do not treat a tumor it will grow and hinder other body functions. It will be very hard to manage."

Down in Virginia, a day's drive from Buffalo, I focus on my newspaper writing and reporting. I attend church every Sunday. Ostensibly, my churchgoing is so I can meet the leaders of the church community as part of my duties as a religion writer. While there, I close my eyes and pray for a miracle.

By the time my plane lands in Buffalo, everyone has returned home from the hospital. Mom picks me up and drops me off at Dad's duplex. I run inside, down the stairs to the basement, and find Kris curled up on his bed crying.

"Tell me everything," I say.

"It all happened so quick, Kenny," Kris begins, sitting up. "I woke up around nine and went upstairs to take a shower and he was sitting in the living room sticking the oxygen tube into his mouth and freaking out. His eyes were popped open real wide. He was all disoriented and didn't know what was going on. He was trying to say things, but it was like he was too out of breath to get the words out. He was speaking like he had just run a mile. I don't know if he was hallucinating or what, but he didn't even know who I was. He kept turning his head and, like he was seeing people walk by that weren't there, he would say stuff like, 'Kenny, what are you doing here?' Then it was just gibberish. Nothing made sense. He was done, man. He was on his way out. It was like his organs were shutting down.

"I called the hospice nurse, then I called Kevin and Keith. That's when I called you, too, and said, 'You better fly home fast.'

"While I was calling everyone, he got up and walked to the bathroom, still holding the oxygen tube in his mouth, and he sat down to take a shit. He kept moaning and saying he had to take a shit real bad, so I told him to just do it and then go lay down. But he kept saying, 'I can't go, I can't go,' and all of a sudden he stood up and walked back to the living room with his pants around his ankles. I don't even think he realized his pants were down, man. He was just totally out of it.

"It was snowing, and it seemed like it took forever for everyone to get there. He didn't want to go to the hospital. We were trying to talk him into it, but he would just say NO. When the ambulance came, they gave him a shot of something and it settled him down. They put him on the stretcher and carried him outside. But it was so cold that they couldn't get the legs on the fucking stretcher to collapse. They had frozen stiff. Keith was yelling at the ambulance guy to put a blanket on Dad because he was trembling. Finally they got the stretcher to fold up and started pushing him into the ambulance. The last thing Dad said was 'Nooo!'

"He didn't want to go, Kenny. And I didn't want him to go. But the lady kept saying, 'He has to go. There's no choice.'

"We followed the ambulance to the hospital. We all sat there in his room with him for like an hour. His eyes were opened real wide, but he was barely breathing. His chest would just rise a little. He could hear us, though. When I would talk to him, tell him to hang in there and stuff, he would move his eyes from side to side. He knew what was going on. We agreed with the doctors to let him lay there without any machines, no oxygen mask or anything. It was no use.

"The priest came in a little while later and started reciting some prayers to him. The priest said something like, 'You are forgiven for all your sins, Larry,' and Keith was like, 'What sins? That's bullshit!' The priest calmed Keith down and told us, 'Tell him to go. He is holding on for you. He is waiting for you to tell him to go.' So we told him to go, and he went."

(PROLACTIN LEVEL: 1,300 NG/ML)

A father, I believe, is the single most important person in a male's life. Even to a guy who has never known his father, the absence of that male role model can define how he perceives his manhood.

For twenty-five years, I was lucky enough to have a father intimately involved in my life. He often didn't say or do the right things, but he always did what he thought was best for me, and now that he is gone forever, I realize that his trying was his most redeeming quality.

I miss him. Not a day passes when I don't feel the urge to pick up the phone and shoot the bull with him—about politics, the Bills, whatever. Since he was basically glued to the couch for the last few years, I could always count on him being home and wanting to chat. I suppose that his accessibility was the only good thing about his illness.

For so long I fretted over his dying and feared the moment when he would no longer be around. But now that he's gone, I actually feel more relief than grief. I no longer worry about him suffering all the time; the omnipresent reminder that, no matter how good I felt, my dad was dying a slow, torturous death has been lifted. I want to turn his death into an opportunity for me to move on, and I vow not to make the same mistakes he did. I don't want every woman I become involved with to become the embodiment of evil. I don't want my children to fear me so much that they end up disrespecting me when they get older. Mostly, I just don't want to die sick and broke at age fifty-one.

Perhaps his death will free me to lead a healthy, normal sexual life too. Maybe Frank was right in observing that, out of some twisted form of codependent empathy, I had started taking on my father's impotence as my own illness. With him gone, I should be liberated from that mental bondage. And I just want to have fun for a change.

Two days after his funeral I am back in Hampton, Virginia, where I have been renting an upper apartment in a Cape Cod–style house two blocks from the Chesapeake Bay and a ten-minute drive in my Ford Festiva from the *Daily Press* newsroom. The southern pace and the weather of Hampton suits me better than the harshness of Buffalo. It rarely snows down here, just north of the North Carolina border, and there's something about a Southern drawl, which I have affected slightly to fit in, that makes the people seem nicer than Northerners. The local history alone (founded in 1610, it is the oldest continuously English-speaking settlement) is more appealing than Buffalo's blue-collar industrial historical backdrop. In Hampton, a Colonial-era capital for pirates, the freshly severed head of Blackbeard was displayed at the harbor entrance in 1718; during the Civil War, the battleships *Merrimack* and the *Monitor,* exchanged cannon fire in the bay: An historical marker at the end of my street, Shenandoah Avenue, tells me this. The quaint Victorian homes and the crab and lobster fishing boats that dominate the bayside landscape are a hell of a lot more pleasant to look at than The Buff's abandoned steel plants.

Not only am I distanced from the bleakness that Buffalo has represented for me, but my newspaper job, which entails writing general-interest feature stories and covering local religion news, infuses me with a sense of self worth and purpose that I have been lacking since quitting hockey almost three years ago.

My first day back to work, my motherly editor, Marguerite, sheepishly asks me to cover a breaking story in Virginia Beach at the headquarters of televangelist Pat Robertson's Christian Broadcasting Network. There's a gay-rights protest being led by the Rev. Mel White, a former ghost writer for Robertson who is now demanding that the smiley TV preacher/politician meet with him to discuss "anti-gay" comments Robertson recently made on *The 700 Club*. Marguerite tells me that last week Robertson faxed a letter to the 54-year-old gay minister informing him, "I do not wish to meet to debate the merits of homosexuality. You have chosen your lifestyle, and I hope that God will reveal to you one day what His word says about it."

Noticing that I have been sullen all day long, Marguerite adds, "It might be good for you to get out for a while and think about something else."

I grab my spiral reporter's notebook and head across the bay. I pull into the parking lot that White and his supporters are using as a staging area. A steady drizzle has started falling, so I grab my umbrella and hustle over to White, who is wearing his white reverend's collar, and a crowd of about twenty mostly gay and lesbian supporters. They lock arms and start walking across the street onto the grounds of Christian Broadcasting Network, from which Robertson broadcasts his conservative brand of Christianizing. Not wanting to miss the showdown (and hoping to scoop all the other assembled media), I stuff my notebook into my pocket and scurry into the middle of the pack, locking arms with a couple of supporters. "Welcome aboard, my friend," a skinny middle-aged man says with a smile. I smile back as we march past a wall of security guards warning us through their megaphones: "This is private property. You will be arrested." I overhear White reply, "If I'm arrested, so be it."

I look back and see that the dozen or so other news photographers, reporters and camera men covering the protest have stopped at the entrance gate. I am the only journalist; this will be a *Daily Press* exclusive.

About five minutes later the huddled group, surrounded by Virginia Beach police officers and CBN security guards, reaches the steps outside of Robertson's office.

A stone-faced attorney, flanked by several other men in suits, is waiting for White at the base of CBN's steps.

"You have no business here," the attorney tells White, explaining that Robertson is not going to meet with him today, tomorrow or any other day.

The protesters spontaneously start singing "We Shall Overcome" as a police officer locks handcuffs on White's wrists and shoves him into a police cruiser. "Go with God," White says to his supporters as the cop shuts the car door.

The police inform the rest of us that the only way we can avoid arrest is to disperse and immediately vacate the "private property." A few protesters sit down and are promptly arrested; the rest of us walk away peacefully.

I speed back to the *Daily Press* newsroom to write my breaking story—the headline: **GAY MINISTER ATTEMPTS TO CONFRONT ROBERTSON.**

At Columbia, I was taught that a journalist must always remain impartial, an observer and dispassionate chronicler of people and events. In reality, a journalist is also human and sometimes can't help but become emotionally involved in a story. Later that night, I realize that I had just participated in my first act of civil disobedience, and that the issue—sexual identity—I was de-facto marching for was not entirely coincidental.

I won't reveal this to my friends and journalism colleagues, but the truth is that I can relate to White and his gay and lesbian followers, not to mention anyone else who has experienced the isolation of what it means to be a sexual "other" in our heterosexual, majority-rules culture of man-woman sexiness that pervades everything from television shows to movies to magazine covers. I am an alien confounded by the obsession these humans have with sex and skin and "better orgasms" and "how to please a woman." My well-adjusted, Jimmy Olson appearance belies the alienation that I feel from my own gender tribe. I spend a lot of weekends pondering my alienation. I watch this inane TV show *Studs*. I see a shirtless guy around my age—25—strutting in front of a gaggle of bikini-clad girls on a beach, trying to seduce them with his sweat-buttered biceps, square jaw and washboard abs. The studly sex toy sneaks up behind each of the cooing girls and rubs his manly paws on their backs. I cannot relate at all to any of these Gen X shenanigans.

All through college, I heard feminist professors lecturing on how the sexual objectification of women by men has oppressed women, forcing them to seek approval through their sexual attractiveness more than their intellectual aptitude. Although I agree that our society is overly sexualized, their argument lacks one-half its potency, for never have I heard a feminist concede that the same sexual objectification is practiced by women against men. Just look at *Studs*. You think those girls would be so hot and horny for Joe Stud if his pecs jiggled like Jell-O, or if they knew his dick couldn't get hard? I doubt it. I know from experience that there are a lot of women (and men) who like to intellectualize and politicize the nature of human mating. But, pardon my Buffalo English, these people are full of shit. The reality is that, from my perch of impotence and feminized malehood, I see men and women doing little more than engaging in a mating ritual of sexual selection in which the rules of attraction are hormonal, their behavior primal and too often brutal.

Unlike me, though, Rev. White is brave enough not only to reveal his otherness but also to fight for its dignity.

For the next twenty-three days White sits in a orange jumpsuit in a five-foot-wide jail cell on a hunger strike that he refuses to end until Robertson agrees to meet with him to discuss his views on homosexuality. He could walk out by posting a thousand-dollar bond and promising not to trespass on CBN property. But White has become a prisoner of conscience—his own.

Just about every day I receive a collect call at my desk from the city jail; it is White updating me on his condition. His fast—consisting of a carton of milk in the morning and a Tang-and-water mixture in the evening—has caused him to drop fourteen pounds from his six-foot frame. I tell him that a professor of internal medicine at Eastern Virginia Medical School estimates he will die within four to six months if he keeps up his three-hundred-calorie-a-day diet.

"Ken," White replies, "I believe with all my heart that gays and lesbians are worth dying for. I will not end my strike until Pat comes down here and meets with me."

And I believe him.

Twenty-three days into his hunger strike, on a calm, cool Virginia evening shortly before eight o'clock, White is paid a visit by Pat Robertson, who simultaneously releases a letter he wrote White to the media. "You wanted a media circus to publicize your activities. I could not agree to be taken advantage of by you and your associates," Robertson wrote. "No amount of marches or pickets or hunger strikes by you will force Almighty God to rescind his laws."

My coverage of White's protest ends that day, but Robertson's words will echo inside my head with resonance for several more years to come. I end up thinking a lot about the laws of God of which Robertson had written and how those biblical laws may apply to me, a man who, judging by his thoughts and actions, is neither fully gay nor straight.

Yet, still acting very Larry Baker–like, I don't even seriously consider seeking help from another doctor or a psychologist. Instead, I try to be the Baker Stoic, that brand of man who solo retreats to a mountaintop in order to figure himself out.

There's no male equivalent to the Oprah Winfrey show, where men openly discuss their problems and after tears, an expert dishing out advice and a few hugs, all is well again. Men just don't talk about this stuff. Oh, they might make jokes about not getting it up, but it rarely ever has to do with them. And it's not like I can log into an

America Online chat room especially targeted for impotent young guys who have a depressed sex drive and milky nipples that are sensitive to the touch. Additionally, most of the literature I've read about erectile dysfunction makes it seem as if only old guys and diabetics suffer from it, not young, athletic men such as myself. I am at a loss.

But since part of my job is to write about religion, rarely does a day pass that I don't have to read a passage out of the Bible.

Under the ruse that I am writing a story on the Christian men's movement, I phone a local pastor named Tim. He's a young, hip kind of pastor, the kind of holy man that even kids think is cool. By the end of our conversation, it's obvious that my questions—What does the Bible say about single guys? What about celibacy?—are really for my benefit.

"Ken," Tim levels with me. "Why don't we have coffee and talk about this stuff."

After two cups of joe and much idle chatter, I confess to him that I have been celibate for almost two years and, before that period, I never have really wanted to go out and have sex like most guys. I tell him I have scoured the Bible looking for a passage that addresses what a man is to do if his penis doesn't work, but, alas, I haven't been able to find one.

"To be honest with you," I say, "I feel like a mutant male."

It's kind of embarrassing, but Tim's smile quells any of my fears that he will think I am a freak.

"If you're a mutant," Tim says, "then you are a mutant in the most positive sense of the word. You are unlike most men your age, perhaps, but according to the Bible that makes you a very admirable, Christ-like person. Jesus never had sexual intercourse, and as a Christian I believe he is the greatest man ever to walk the planet. Celibacy is one of the highest Christian virtues. You shouldn't be ashamed of it."

He opens his pocket Bible (young pastors always seem to have a copy on them) and reads from Romans 12:6: "We have different gifts, according to the grace given to us. If a man's gift is prophesying, let him use it in proportion to his faith. If it is serving, let him serve; if it is teaching, let him teach."

"Are you trying to say my not being a sex machine is a gift?"

"Well," he says, laughing, "you can look at it that way if you want. I guess what I'm trying to say is that God has given you gifts, and, Ken, God has a plan for you. His gifts make up all of the person that you are, including your talent for writing, your sensitivity, your sense of humor, your not having sex just because everyone else might be doing it."

"That's easy for you to say; you're married and doing"—I fashion my fore- and middle fingers into air quotes—" 'it.' "

He cracks a sly grin. "Okay, okay. Fine. You're right. But that's what *I* am about. The question is: What are *you* about?"

Glenn, my housemate and a feature writer at *The Daily Press,* is probably the quirkiest, wittiest, smartest journalist I have ever met. With his pale skin, skinny frame, black hair, dry wit and nerdy manner, he is Nicholas Cage and Billy Crystal cross-bred with Ferris Bueller.

Besides the fact that we're in our early twenties and share the same house and that the only thing separating us every night is a half-inch of wall plaster, the main source of our bond is that we both feel like outsiders living in southern Virginia. Glenn is from Colorado and a graduate of Northwestern, just outside of Chicago, where his fiancée is still living. Then why is he working for a tiny local newspaper one notch above the *Mayberry Journal?* Not even Glenn can answer that. It just sort of happened, is how he explains it.

Glenn spends his days two cubicles away from me, hunched in front of his computer screen, writing stories about brilliant teen geeks at Poquoson High School and socially awkward guys who collect antique Atari consoles. Clearly, Glenn's attracted to the region's, shall I say, nerdy underbelly.

Meanwhile, save for the occasional breaking news story surrounding Mr. Robertson's evangelistic empire, I'm mostly writing about potluck dinners at Our Lady of Mount Carmel Church and crafting the occasional *amazing!* local hero story. Needless to say, neither of us is practicing the kind of journalism that has us on the fast track to *The New York Times*—that is, until one day while we're eating stale turkey-and-bacon sandwiches at a Subway sandwich shop.

We've spent the last half hour or so kvetching about how our little *Daily Press* (i.e., *The Daily Depress* or *The Daily Mess*) epitomizes why newspaper circulation nationwide has been falling faster than Hampton tidewater.

I tell him, *Most of it is all boring stories about boring people doing boring things!*

Yeah, for old farts!

All just detached, third-person-voiced news stories that don't relate to young people.

A sad, folded, multicolored excuse to run the comics, weather, horoscopes and the obituaries.

What you said!

By the end of our bitch session, we have scribbled down on a couple napkins an idea for a slice-of-life humor column, cowritten by the two of us, that we have dubbed "The Adventures of Ken&Glenn." Even though Glenn has never done a damn thing I have suggested—including that he cut his ratty black ponytail—he agrees that the column name sounds better with the Ken before the Glenn. I, however, nix his idea that I change the spelling of my name to "Kenn." When we get back to the newsroom, we pitch our idea for the second coming of Huckleberry Finn to Will Corbin, our hard-ass managing editor.

"It's about two guys who go out, do stuff and write about it," I explain to Will. Glenn, the more quiet of our duo, sits silently beside me.

"*Stuff,* huh?" Will says, obviously not buying a single iota of it.

"Yeah, you know, like we'll try out for a professional football team and write about it. We'll see how many Big Gulps a human being can ingest in one sitting. Stuff like that."

"This is starting to sound more sad than funny," he says.

Will is a tough customer, a roughneck from the Deep South whose thick arms and barrel chest suggest he has victoriously wrestled gators into submission. I tell Glenn that if we can sell Will on the idea, we can sell anybody.

"Sounds interesting," he says finally, leaning back in his chair, stacking his snakeskin boots on his desk. "*Twisted*—but interesting. We'll try it out. One day a week. We'll see how it goes."

As we stand, Will smirks. "But this better not be an excuse for you guys to get girls."

"Don't worry, Will," I say. "We wouldn't know what to do with one anyway."

"My point exactly," he chirp-chuckles.

As I leave his office I realize we have tapped into Will's editorial wild side and discovered one of my God-given gifts (humor writing) that Pastor Tim had said I needed to find.

I haven't been this exhausted in a long time. I don't think I have ever felt so spent. I just can't figure out what's sapping me of my energy. It certainly isn't as if I'm working twelve hours a day, six days a week, as I often did at ABC News. Except for when Glenn and I are out late at night experiencing one of our "adventures," my hours are better than a banker's: 10 A.M. to 6 P.M.

I speculate that I have grown lethargic as a result of my not getting any exercise after I quit running, due to headaches. Perhaps I need to boost my metabolism with some huffing and puffing and sweating and body movement, the kind of physical exertion I imagine sexually active guys get every day with their girlfriends. But my weariness has not waned even after I started lifting weights at the YMCA two or three days a week. Moreover, I don't seem to get any stronger. Weight-lifting seems to only make my headaches more severe, forcing me to stretch out on the mats while I watch the beefy rednecks bench-press their pecs into chiseled form. It's so discouraging.

Mom, whom I have begun talking to on the phone regularly since Dad died, suggests that I may be suffering from chronic allergies, which have plagued her all of her life. Virginia, she hypothesizes, may have more pollen and ragweed and airborne particles that are causing my sinus headaches.

When I wake up one spring morning with a throbbing brain-buster of a headache and feel too tired to slide my leaden legs off my mattress and onto the bedroom floor, I go see a doctor in Hampton.

"What are your symptoms," the old doctor drawls.

"Really bad sinus headaches," I say, sitting shirtless (and extremely chest-conscious) on the examination table.

"That's all?"

"No, I guess feel fatigued a lot too. Mostly in the mornings. That's when it is the worst. But otherwise I feel pretty good."

"Hmmm," he says, scribbling some notes on a sheet of paper.

He puts down his clipboard and presses a stethoscope to my chest, then my back, listening. He places his hands on the front of my neck and gently feels my glands with his fingers.

"Where exactly do you feel these headaches?" he asks.

I point to the middle of my forehead.

"So you don't ever feel pain on the sides or in the back of your skull?"

"No, not really."

The doctor, a laconic southern fellow with a shock of white hair, jots down a few more notes as I bite my fingernails. But I'm impatient. I just want to get into work and write a story. I'm not about to tell him about my lactating nipples: It's probably just a gross body quirk, like nose hair, anyway. I don't have time for shin-stroking doctors when I have daily deadlines. *I don't even need to be here.*

"It's allergy season, and I would say there's some stuff in the air that's givin' your sinuses a helluva time," he posits. "This should help."

He hands me a prescription for an antihistamine and asks me to return in seven to ten days if my headaches don't abate.

A month later, the headaches haven't stopped; nor have they become any less painful. Still, I never return.

As Dad said, *You gotta die of something.*

Courtney Love's band, Hole, is playing a club in Virginia Beach and my friend Sam, *The Daily Press*'s pop-music writer, has scored me two free tickets. I invite Melissa, a waitress at Sorry Sarah's tavern in downtown Hampton. I met Melissa recently while playing pool with Glenn while drunken crabbers and lobstermen hit on Melissa and the usual gaggle of redneck girls in cutoff shorts and tight tank tops. I didn't hit on Melissa, a "gentlemanly gesture" that she said she appreciated. Of course, I have heard this you're-a-different-kind-of-guy story before. . . . Melissa's a blue-eyed blonde with just enough of a twangy drawl that she reminds me of the busty girls Dad would ogle on *Hee Haw*. I bet Dad would have liked Melissa.

I haven't kissed a girl in over two years, nor have I even tried. Instead, I have been holed up in a shelter ever since my last flaccid encounter with Claudia on that New Year's Eve. Sure, there have been many lonely nights when I have wondered if I will ever find a woman who will put up with my low libido, but more often I have been enjoying my "gift" of celibacy by working six or seven days a week at the paper.

Melissa, however, may be the one. Maybe she is the girl with whom I will finally feel comfortable enough to have sex. I have gone out of my way to be friendly with her, acting in a nonsexual way in order to prevent any expectations on her part. Judging by how she calls me at least once a day "just to talk," she probably likes me, but I hope I've kept a safe enough emotional and physical distance from her (I gave her a goodbye hug once at Sorry Sarah's) to not have to worry about the possibility of enduring the emasculating horror of not being able to get it up.

A Courtney Love concert, however, is more serious.

The nightclub, aptly called The Abyss, is smoky and dark yet expectant. At least a thousand fans, most of them guys in grungy jeans, flannel shirts and Doc Martens boots, puff joints and chug two-dollar drafts in anticipation of seeing Kurt Cobain's recently widowed wife perform her unique brand of sexy-metal music. Within thirty minutes I have drunk five or six beers—enough to make me less afraid about flirting with Melissa.

Over an hour after their scheduled start, the stage lights pop on. The crowd whoops. Looking very slutty in a short, black baby-doll dress that the front-row guys desperately are trying to peek up, Courtney Love steps to the mike, takes a lazy drag from a cigarette and starts screeching.

They get what they want, and they never want it again. . . . Go on, take everything, I want you to. . . .

Primal drums . . . *Buh-buh-bop* . . .

Screaming guitars . . . *wah, wah, wah* . . .

White strobe lights flash.

Sweaty bodies mosh.

Melissa's lips, her wanting, longing, lustful eyes.

We kiss.

Love wails:

I fake it so real, I am beyond fake. . . . Some day you will ache like I ache. . . .

Two hours later, many kisses and hugs and lustful glances from Melissa later, our songstress stomps her show to a close.

As I turn to Melissa to leave, Courtney dives into the panting mass of horny males huddled six feet below her. The men catch her lithe body, passing her atop their ass-squeezing, bra-tearing hands. The hands roll her to me and—*I am one of the guys!*—so I grip her ivory-white thigh, holding her above my head like she's the Stanley Cup and I'm Wayne Gretzky. Glancing up her skirt, I notice she's wearing black lace panties.

A team of bulky bodyguards elbow their way to the molested rock star and pull her from the crowd and dump her listless body to the stage. Love, her dyed-blond hair strands sprouting in a thousand directions, grabs the mike. Shaking a naughty finger, Love playfully points to the crowd. "Hey," she shouts over the sound system, "which one of you guys stuck their finger in my pussy?"

A hundred whistling and howling men claim responsibility.

I meet Melissa outside the club. Concentrating hard to stay between the yellow highway lines, I drunk-drive her back to her Hampton condo. She invites me in. *Don't be a pussy.* I accept her offer and walk her up to the front door.

Uh-oh. I can't have sex.... I can't have sex.... I can't have sex....

"I'm gonna get ready for bed," she says as we enter, pecking me on the cheek. "I'll be right back."

I plop onto her couch, dropping face-first into a pillow. I pinch my eyes shut, trying desperately to fall asleep. A few minutes later I hear her footsteps coming closer to the living room, where I lay—available, vulnerable, impotent.

I feign snoring. *I can't have sex.*

Kneeling beside me, she rubs my back and strokes my hair. "Come to bed with me," she whispers, unlacing my boots and sliding them off. When she starts to unbutton my jeans, I groan. A leave-me-alone-I-am-sleeping groan.

It works. She flips off the lamp and walks upstairs.

I fake it so real I am beyond fake.

There's this character named "Ken." He's one half of the young-and-wacky writing duo of Ken&Glenn. He is funny and adventurous. Smart. Fearless. Young. Sexy. Cool. Just like the studs on TV.

Every week he, along with his nerdy sidekick, go out and do what all of southeastern Virginia's Walter Mittys only dream of doing. Just for fun. Then this character Ken writes about it, every Thursday, in the LifeStyles section of *The Daily Press,* making a great portion of the paper's more than 100,000 readers chuckle at their brazen hijinks.

• Ken visits a massage parlor to see what it is like to get half naked and have a young woman rub slippery oils that smell like jungles all over his body.
• Wearing a very macho pair of brown-leather cowboy boots, Ken tries to get a date with a twenty-three-year-old Dutch blonde who was chosen to be the queen of NATO's (headquartered in Norfolk, Virginia) annual International Azalea Festival:

> Ken: "So, when you come down, we could take you out. Show you around and stuff."
> Queen Emilie: "I don't know. I don't know how tired I'll be."
> Ken: "There's a lot to do around here."
> Queen Emilie (raising her eyebrows): "Really?"
> Ken (laughing like a knickers-wearing schoolboy): "Not really."

• Ken tries out as a wide receiver for a semiprofessional football team. Despite his valiant effort, he fails.
• Ken and Glenn place a personal ad in the newspaper: **BORED TWO DEATH. Two white, slim, anti-social males seek two females with similar flaws, for dysfunctional fun:**

> Two women—Sherry, who works at an auto-parts store and Rose, a cashier at Wal-Mart—respond by declaring, "We like dysfunctional fun, too!" The date turns disastrous when we arrive at a cowboy line-dancing club to meet our blind dates and they never show. Sherry later calls me and

leaves a message admitting that they in fact saw us at the club. "But," she says, "you and Glenn aren't our kind of guys."

My alter-ego shenanigans continue for nearly a year and a half. Rather than confront my sexual confusion, frustration and befuddlement, I live my life in ink, through the experiences of a semifictional funnyman. I am my own PR rep promoting an image of this wild-and-crazy guy "Ken."

This guy Ken is carefree and horny, willing to do just about anything to get a date (which female readers are explicitly alerted to on the Ken&Glenn Web site. Ken is sexy yet sensitive. "Ken" is the man I wish I was but can only be as a character in a newspaper column.

The real Ken has started eating nothing but salads and Cheerios (with no milk, as not to ingest any more fat that will only then settle onto his bloated boobs, making him look even more freakish and womanly) in an effort to wither his shameful body down enough so that, hopefully, muscle will emerge.

The real Ken is not horny; in fact, he spends most nights alone, wondering why he isn't more sexually driven, concluding that he just may be one of those rarefied shy guys who will only sleep with the girl he ends up marrying.

The real Ken once let the sting of his impotence get him down, to the point where he would cringe at the sight of his swollen nipples and his jelly belly and his dick, which seems about as long as an elevator button; Ken used to be perplexed by women and how they seemed to only want him AND his dick—not just him—and how they would summarily dump him when his dick repeatedly didn't perform. But now he has come to accept his being "different" much like an abused child copes with an alcoholic father. Grin and bear it.

The real Ken is torn between wanting to avoid the unbearable dread that accompanies not being able to get it up in the presence of a woman and wanting to find a woman in whose comforting arms he can be himself. So he compromises. He goes on dates with girls but, rather than get physically intimate, he forges an emotional, platonic bond. He becomes their "friend," a guy unlike any of the other guys, a guy who will listen to them, understand their frustrations with men. He can relate to women because, although he doesn't know it, he is, hormonally, similar to them.

Disgusted by his father's track record and cynical that half of all man-and-woman marriages fail, that statistics show that anywhere from thirty to fifty percent of husbands will cheat on their wives, he has ditched his dream of having 1.85 kids and a pretty wife, of being a "normal guy," because he knows he would never divorce the woman of his dreams, that he would never cheat on a woman who was understanding and caring enough to put up with his penis problems, that he will never be the man that he must become.

To prove his antipathy toward marriage, he even scribbled a note to his doubting editor Marguerite that reads: "I will never get married."

The real Ken can't even read the hockey scores listed in the newspaper because it only reminds him that his lifelong dream will never be realized.

The real Ken wanted to run the DC marathon again, but he had to stop a week into his training because (a) he nearly collapsed from dizziness after just two miles of jogging, and (b) he has been suffering from headaches that pulse so painfully, he must walk gently down flights of stairs because the jarring it causes pinches his brain as if a hockey puck has been implanted three inches behind eyes.

The real Ken keeps secrets that he will never tell a soul. He is hiding behind a mask of newspaper-column humor and an ironic detachment that is a shield of denial from the pain and confusion that is his physical self. The Bible, once a source of inspiration, is now bullshit to him. After reading everything from Jewish Haggadah to a Sufi text, the real Ken views religion as a drug that weak people use to dull the pain and loneliness that is the reality of our bleak human existence. The real Ken is a journalist who focuses on other people and their feelings first; a person who feels his own emotions second.

When a *People* magazine correspondent stumbles upon Ken& Glenn's offbeat adventures on our Internet site, she interviews Ken for a possible story. After the interview, Ken (the real one? the character?) asks the reporter if she can help him flee from the land of y'alls and collard greens (and women who pursue him for sex that he cannot provide, which scares him—although he doesn't mention this part) and into "the epicenter of pop culture."

When Glenn leaves Virginia to live with his fiancée in Los Angeles, Ken—now alone and lacking a newspaper persona to hide behind—wants out even more badly.

The *People* correspondent, impressed with Ken's can-do attitude and charm, gets "Ken" an interview at *People* magazine's Hollywood bureau, in the capital of the American West, the place where, for the last 150 years, young Americans have been journeying to reinvent themselves.

Ken flies across the country to meet the legendary Jack Kelley, the magazine's longtime Hollywood bureau chief. Jack likes Ken. Ken gets hired. Ken gives his two-week notice to Will. "Well, Baker, it makes sense that you'd move to LA," Will grouses. "All wackos eventually end up in California."

Before leaving *The Daily Press*, however, Ken reminds all his friends in Virginia that "chicks dig *People* magazine," which no doubt means he will be quite the stud in La-La Land.

Being as deluded as Ken is into thinking this self-effacing twenty-six-year-old guy is not at all ill, his friends believe him.

I move into an eight-hundred-dollar-a-month bungalow apartment in Brentwood, three blocks from the *People* offices and two blocks from where O.J. Simpson's ex-wife, Nicole, and her friend Ron Goldman were slashed to death almost two years before I unpacked my two suitcases and settled here. I last visited LA four years ago, when I came to see Jenny, whom I don't plan to call or see because I fear it will only remind me of that old doormat Ken.

One day, while I'm walking down palm-lined Bundy Drive, a chubby tourist politely stops me.

"Excuse me," she says, a camera dangling from her neck. "Do you know where the O.J. house is?"

"It's the one with the gate," I say, pointing to the stucco condominium across the street.

Walking away, I am heartened to think that I am now living in such a vast, transient city. After just three days in this smoggy, sunny, car-clogged urban paradise, three time zones and oodles of emotional twilight zones away from the emasculated confusion of my prior, East Coast life, I already qualify as a bonafide local.

Even so, I've got a long way to go before I can be considered a true Hollywood player, a man-about-town.

This transformation, from man-faker to star-maker, will require me to shed all the emotional baggage I've been schlepping around for the last five or six years: Namely, I have to stop being about as sexually active as Pope John Paul II.

Glenn, now living in the Valley with his fiancée and writing for *The Los Angeles Daily News,* agrees wholeheartedly. Having just spent two years watching me celibately traverse my mid-twenties, Glenn says he is tired of seeing my stagnant sex life play out in all its lonely-guy glory. "You need a girlfriend," he says, so often it's really starting to bug me.

One night Glenn and I are vegging out in front of the boob tube, watching a mindless dating show on MTV, when Glenn has an idea how I may be able to turn around my moribund manliness.

"Wouldn't it be cool if you got on TV, dude?" he says, jotting down the number for the show's contestant hotline, undoubtedly hoping that by immersing me in fifty single young women in a TV studio I may—call the wire services!—finally get laid.

"It would be funny," he says. "We'll both do it."

The show, *Singled Out,* is co-hosted by a former *Playboy* model, the bottled-blonde Jenny McCarthy. Glenn and I used to watch this Gen X version of *The Dating Game* all the time on boring and humid Virginia nights. On this boring and arid evening in LA, Glenn dials the number to get us on the show.

A mumbling cool-guy answers the phone. He asks Glenn how old we are.

"I'm twenty-four, and my friend is twenty-six," Glenn replies.

"No-can-do," the MTV coolster says. "Our age range is eighteen to twenty-four. Your friend doesn't *look* twenty-six, does he?"

"Oh, no, no. He looks younger than I do."

"Okay, then. Just make sure he doesn't look twenty-six. Grunge him out in a flannel and shit."

The dude gives Glenn the address of the MTV studio in Burbank, where Glenn and I promptly show up the next morning.

Outside the stucco studio huddle a couple hundred teenagers and twentysomethings. I'm wearing cut-off jeans, a faded purple T-shirt, Teva sandals and a green-and-black flannel shirt tied around my flabby waist. But the predominant wardrobes are more urbane and sexy:

- Guys: baggy jeans, oversize button-down shirts and fat-heeled black shoes.
- Girls: short skirts or summer dresses, open-toe platform sandals, cleavage and lots of hairspray and makeup.

As we're filing into the building, a peppy grunge girl from MTV— "Um, excuse me, sir . . ."—stops a balding guy behind us who looks about thirty-five-desperately trying-to-be-twenty-five. She tells him he has to leave. *Too old. Phew. Coulda been me. That was close.*

They sit us down in a room where another peppy young woman teaches us *Singled Out* 101. She says that one hundred of us—about fifty of each gender—will stand in "the dating pool," a sort of corral located behind a partition, in front of which will be the contestant who, without seeing any of us, will "single out" one of us as the winner of a date with her.

I remember asking Dad what I should do when I'm playing hockey and not feeling like the best. "Fake it," he said. As such, I mingle backstage in line with the super-pretty wannabe actresses and confident, tanned dudes and fake like I know how to play this game. One by one, each of us singletons works our way to the front of a line where we are "interviewed" by a producer. Meanwhile, other MTV'ers roam around us, looking for the most attractive members of the group, then selecting them to stand in the front, closest to the cameras that will be beaming images of beautiful people to the young American masses.

My turn.

"Okay, now, I have to rate you on a few categories," the dating game clinician says. "First of all: wealth. What do you do for a living?"

"I'm a writer."

"Like a screenwriter?"

"No, a journalist kind of writer."

"All right. Fine." She jots something down. "Lift up your shirt," she continues.

"Why?"

"I need to rate the amount of body hair you have. And your chest size."

I suck in my stomach and raise my T-shirt up to my armpits, praying that none of the girls is looking at my boobies.

The judge-lady glances at my torso (*Thank God, I got a tan at the beach yesterday*) for a few seconds that seem like minutes, then she moves on to the next few categories. At the end of her rating session, she hands me a slip of paper that categorizes me.

A few minutes before show time, an MTV hipster in a headset corrals us into the "dating pool." A bouncer-type dude announces the ground rules:

- No nudity.
- No profanity.
- No touching Jenny McCarthy. "If any of you guys lays a hand on Jenny, I will personally kick your ass," he says with I-pity-the-fool gravity.

When Jenny, microphone in hand, slithers onstage and into the middle of our single-guy group, it's apparent to me why the MTV mavens feel obligated to communicate this last rule: Jenny simply looks made for touching. A skimpy orange dress that shows off just enough of her assets to make all the guys around me stare but that contains just enough fabric to get the show past the censors.

Theme music.

Announcer.

We cheer.

"Welcome to *Singled Out*," Jenny's male co-host, Chris Hartwick, tells the camera. "We start out the game with fifty single guys and fifty girls, and, through a series of completely arbitrary decisions, only two of them will get dates. Now let's go to Jenny McCarthy in the dating pool."

"Hello, hello," Jenny coos. "As usual, the men will be the first ones thrown into the fire of love. So, boys, are you ready to fry?"

We men whoop and holler like we're competing in a Delta Upsilon beer-chugging contest, something I never got to do in college but, now that I am a frisky Hollywood guy with no pressuring father, no hockey, I will act like a sex-addicted teenager.

The object of our lust enters. The bachelorette, the reigning Miss America Petite, struts across the stage with a blindfold on.

A *blindfold*. The last girl I saw in a blindfold was Claudia. I had wrapped one around her delicate eyes—a shield keeping her from seeing my limp penis that was not reacting to her gorgeous body, which, though very nice and fit, was not nearly as attractive as the perfectly sculpted physical specimen that is Stephanie Brown, Miss America Petite, whom the announcer informs us is a "twenty-four-year-old Iowa native and dancing instructor" and, he adds, "a bit of a flirt."

Oh, no. This is just the kind of mega-attractive, sexually assertive girl that scares the crap out of me, that sends my penis into retreat at even the thought of having to have sex with her. What if I win? Then I will have to date her, kiss her. There will be pressure to perform. I better not win.

The first category from which she is to start singling out her unwantables is **Age**. A cardboard wall lists her options:

1) Meat
2) Rotten Meat
3) Maggot Infested Meat

"I like a mature man," she says. "So let's get rid of the meat."

About half the guys, excluding me, in the dating pool desultorily walk off stage when Jenny instructs them to.

Next category: **Hair Style**

1) Styles It

2) Could Give a @*#

The dangerously nubile Stephanie ponders her options for a few seconds and decides, "I'm not into the grunge thing, so let's get rid of the could give a shit."

Yes! God bless my skateboarder bangs that have never seen a dollop of gel. I'm outta here.

I walk offstage. With relief, Glenn (also rejected due to his unkempt hair) and I watch the rest of the game from the shadows. A pretty boy with broad shoulders wins the date with Stephanie in the final round by correctly guessing how many pairs of panties she owns (twenty-five).

As Jenny hands Stephanie over to the lucky dude, the rest of us are escorted outside and handed a T-shirt along with a *Singled Out* condom. Glenn gives me his. "I don't need this," says Glenn, just months away from doing what I am more and more convinced I will never be physically, psychologically or emotionally able to do: getting married.

Alhough he's my best friend, even Glenn doesn't know the depth of my sickness. And neither do I.

I'm interviewing rock guitarist Carlos Santana for a special issue of *People* featuring stars "Before They Were Famous."

I ask Carlos if he remembers when he first realized he might become a world-famous musician. "When I decided to be my own man," he tells me. "I was sixteen and living at home. If you want to become a musician you have to go out and get your own stories, away from your parents. You have to go to the streets and get firsthand experience with life."

Like most of my journalistic experiences in my first year as a *People* magazine correspondent, I write down what Santana says, write a short profile of him based on the interview, and then send it to the New York office as soon as possible so that I can quickly move on to my next celebrity story. I don't consider how Santana's commentary on manhood relates to me.

I've long since stopped the obsessive introspection of my youth; instead, extrospection is my preferred practice, my job being the ultimate tool for my outward analysis. Perhaps, I reason, through seeking to understand the lives of others I can untangle the cross-wired circuitry that has strangulated my own manhood. As a journalist covering the personal lives of famous people, week after week I am bombarded with enough headline-grabbing celebrity distraction to keep me from focusing on own problems.

- Margaux Hemingway dies from an apparent suicide.
- Robert Downey, Jr., gets busted for heroin possession and for falling asleep in the bed of his neighbor's child in Malibu.
- Barbra Streisand gets engaged.
- Farrah Fawcett and Ryan O'Neal get divorced.
- Pamela Anderson Lee quits *Baywatch*.

It's common for me to work from 9 A.M. to 9 P.M., sitting in my eighteenth-floor office overlooking the Lite Brite–like sprawl of LA's west side in the evening. Week after week I craft stories about the rich and famous, all for the reading benefit of some thirty-five million readers whom I don't see or speak to. It's impersonal, and I like it. It is a one-way form of mass communication. Me to them. My gaze is outward. I can ignore my pain.

I love my job, and my bureau chief, Jack, a dapper man with Kevin Costner coolness, lets me know he appreciates all my hard work. Dad would be proud of me.

While spending yet another late night at the office making phone calls to sources long after the rest of the staff has gone home to their wives, husbands, girlfriends, boyfriends, dogs, cats, sports—their fun lives—Jack walks by my office on his way to the elevator and does a double take when he notices me banging out a story in the dim light.

"You're still here?" he says.

"Just makin' the doughnuts," I say, ever the good worker bee.

"We appreciate it," he says. "But, for your own sake, get a life, dude."

He's right.

But it's not only because I don't have a life that I work late hours. Often I must work so late because I had to spend a few hours in the afternoon at home lying in bed, waiting for my over-the-counter sinus medication to ease the ever-present throbbing in my skull. Working at night is nice because I don't have to speak to anybody in the office. Talking, especially in the loud, hyperkinetic style that is the norm among correspondents, makes my head hurt even more. At night, when I am alone, I find peace.

Jack is right, though. I do need a life. I'll stand at the window of my office in the evenings looking down on the Brentwood yuppies sipping beer at the pool hall on Wilshire Boulevard and the athletic yuppies playing soccer at the high school. I'd like to play sports, but I am too fucking tired by the end of the day to walk home, let alone go running or play soccer or baseball. (Hockey is not an option; I still can't even watch it on TV without feeling depressed.)

What I could really use is a girlfriend. Not only did my MTV-assisted mating prove to be an exercise in frustration, but so has Glenn's other brilliant idea for getting me laid.

Recently he introduced me to a friend of his, a very sweet and smart staff writer for the *Los Angeles Times*. I had hoped that this time, perhaps benefiting from the transformative experience of moving three thousand miles away from my dark, impotent past, I would just be a normal guy and have sex with this nice young redhead. Before I can talk myself out of it, I decide that I will sleep over at her apartment and "see what happens" from there.

As soon as I sit down on her bed, she pounces on top of me and grinds her vagina against my (perma-soft) penis, which is safely cloaked under a layer of cotton underwear and blue jeans. My leather belt is looped tightly around my waist—a veritable chastity belt.

When it becomes obvious what is happening—or, rather, *not* happening—I suddenly evacuate myself to the bathroom. When I come back, I tell her I have to get home and make a phone call for work—you know, do an interview.

"You can use my phone," she offers.

"No," I say. "I don't have the number on me."

I leave.

While writing a story on actor Ben Stein's new game show, *Win Ben Stein's Money*, I conduct a phone interview with Al Burton, the show's creator. Mr. Burton is a Hollywood legend who has created or produced dozens of the most popular TV shows of the last quarter century, among them *One Day at a Time*, *Diff'rent Strokes*, *The Facts of Life* and the Scott Baio vehicle *Charles in Charge* (for which he also wrote the catchy theme song). Mr. Burton takes pride in having "discovered" an unknown Meg Ryan, whom he cast for a 1984 episode of *Charles in Charge*.

A leprechaun of a man, short and perpetually smiling, Mr. Burton is curious about my background before coming to Hollywood. I tell him that I used to write a humor column called "The Adventures of Ken&Glenn" and describe some of our antics, which amuses him. "Send me over some of your columns," he says. "Sounds like a lot of fun." A few days later he calls me back and invites Glenn and me to lunch at Morton's, his favorite Hollywood haunt on Melrose Avenue.

I figure it will be good for my *People* schmoozing to meet such a respected producer, so I agree. Mr. Burton, however, has his own agenda. After ordering our iced teas and crab cakes and grilled salmons and ahi tunas, Mr. Burton cuts right to the chase.

"Fellas," he says, "the reason I wanted to meet you is that I have an idea for a TV show starring Ken&Glenn. I think the stuff you guys did for that newspaper would translate very well onto television."

"Okay," I say. "We're all ears."

"All right," he says, clearing his throat. "Two words: Chick Magnets."

I look over at Glenn; Glenn looks over at me.

"Come again?" I say.

"Chick Magnets," Mr. Burton repeats.

"Chick magnets?"

"Yes," he insists. "It will be a reality show about two guys who are always trying to get chicks by doing silly, outrageous things. Think MTV. Think *The Real World*. And we would call it *Chick Magnets*."

Ken respectfully nixes the idea (fearing that "Ken" can only exist in the safety of the printed word, not exposed before a camera) and suggests to Mr. Burton that he instead hire someone more chick-magnetic. Someone much more at ease with picking up girls. Perhaps someone who has actually tried to pick up a chick since Reagan left office. Someone like Scott Baio. Though disappointed, Mr. Burton relents, and my opportunity to become a TV star is lost.

The distinction between "Ken" and Ken—that is to say, between "the funnyman with the funny prose" and the real man with the real problems—has grown even more blurry while I have been living and working in Hollyweird, where the convergence of image and reality is a stated goal, not something one should avoid.

There's the "Ken" who invites a Harvard girl he met at a party to accompany him to a comedy showcase at The Laugh Factory. This Ken buys her drinks and says funny things and pretends to flirt with her when she self-consciously crosses and uncrosses her muscular, mini-skirted thighs and brushes her hair off her face. He then pretends he's too cool and has too many sexual options to accept her eyelash-batting invitation to "come into the bathroom and fuck the shit out of me." The real Ken then goes home, disgusted, slaps his jiggly tits and wonders when the fuck he is going to get a life and get laid.... There's the "Ken" who flirts with Drew Barrymore at a party, but then the real Ken rears his fearful head and leaves the premises when the possibility, however slim, that he may be called upon to screw Ms. Drew becomes reality.

Ken has compartmentalized himself for protection against his own self-critical ego that constantly reminds him that *I am the biggest pussy on the planet and don't deserve the dick and two balls God gave me.*

When my boss Jack assigns me a story about the teen rock group Hanson, I enthusiastically begin making arrangements to interview the three blond lads. When I learn that Hanson will only be available for an interview in London, I hastily arrange to fly there and spend the subsequent three weeks traveling through Europe on a much-needed vacation. There, I hope, I will gain perspective on my general malaise and weariness and, in between, walk my slothful body into shape by backpacking everywhere. And I will keep a diary, something I haven't done since college, since before my life became one big series of humiliating sexual encounters that have made rehashing it in print the last thing I want to do.

I arrive at Heathrow Airport on a chilly summer afternoon, and the next day I interview the Hanson brothers on the set of a music video they're shooting in Kensington Station. Practicing the fluff-journalism equivalent of foreign correspondence, I'm having a blast being away from the LA grind. No one knows me. I am invisible.

With my work done, I am set to begin what, in my black, five-by-seven-inch diary, I have dubbed "Ken's European Adventure."

Before jetting off to Rome, I take a train north, to Cambridge, to see the storied university and to relax in the English countryside.

. . . I'm still single and haven't had sex in over three years. Loneliness is a bit of a problem, obviously. I've been very private—defensive, really—ever since my relationship with Claudia fell to pieces. The root of my isolation is a general anxiety I have about sex, particularly a fear of not being able to get it up. Of course, such a fear is as ridiculous and illogical as my phobia of elevators was back in college. I recall thinking that my life would be forever doomed, because I'd always have to avoid elevators! But I got over the anxiety, partly through desensitization and partly by simply making up my mind that I'd rather risk getting stuck in one than live a tortured life. I overcame this past problem through strength and courage—I was a man. It is a good lesson for me now with respect to my sexuality. It's very frustrating that I've been so fucking queer about women the past couple of years; and downright regrettable. I've let good opportunities for clean, fun sex slip away. And why? Because I won't let myself relax and confidently allow my body to enjoy itself.

Now. Right now! I'm vowing to change that. I will ruminate more on my self-imprisonment (sexually) later. Maybe this Europe trip is a turning point.

On the Alitalia flight from London to Rome, I read all 211 paperback pages of Douglas Coupland's novel *Generation X.* I relate to the search for meaning that underpins the book's characters and I feel, for the first time in a long time, that there might be other searching souls just like me out there. *This trip was a good idea.*

The marble buildings and statues and sprawling piazzas of Rome, if not my musty brick hotel near Termini Stazione, are breathtaking. I spend a week walking—everywhere. I never take a bus or a taxi. I walk to the Vatican, to the Spanish steps, across the Tiber River, out to the

Colosseum. I spend long, hot days sight-seeing, alone, existing on little more than water, bananas, espressos and Diet Cokes. I drop at least ten pounds in less than a week, thus shrinking my boobs and love handles to a point where I am not embarrassed to take off my shirt as I sit by a fountain and write in my diary.

6/10/97

This trip had to happen, for I couldn't have continued living as maniacally as I had been for the past year or so. Ever since coming to LA I'd been whizzing around, trying to survive. I landed a great job and now I have fled to Europe. Slowly, I am gaining perspective on myself. Loneliness and isolation in a foreign country does that.

What I can tell is that I relate to the narrator in Generation X, *Andy Palmer, who comes from a large family and thus craves his own personal space. He also is afraid to love, yet he craves it. I, too, feel as though I've created barriers to protect myself from hurt. Physically, I moved to the edge of the continent. My location is no accident; neither is my not having had sex for nearly four years. I am so bloody fearful of the disappointment and loathsome aching that sex—failed—has brought on me.*

The question, of course, is why I have this erectile problem in the first place. The shrink I saw while at Columbia didn't have answers, so I bolted and have been in a self-induced celibacy ever since. The truth, the plain fucking truth, is that I'm sick of it. Sick of avoiding relationships with women, sick of being alone, sick of being controlled by a fear that should not exist any longer.

When I was little, my father constantly told me that women could fuck things up. Now I realize that Dad's view was quite skewed, since his mom was an idiot, and his resentment of my mom for getting pregnant with Kevin was extreme and self-pitying. Still, his whore-i-fication of the female gender was the first brick

lain of my celibacy temple, because I, psychologically, placed women
to the side, so as not to detract from my focus on hockey and life. This
fear stayed with me through my teens and into college—repression
ruled this era. Avoiding women has become a symbolic act of defense;
the problem is now I need not fear women.

The short end of this is that I need to do a psychological house-
cleaning, throw out all those outdated fears that ruled me. In other
words, relax and enjoy.

So, shall I see a hooker? I don't know. Maybe. In one sense it
would be good to practice a bit with a pro. But the ideal situation
is to find a woman I can love and cherish, get intimate with, naked
with, someone who is real and to whom I am emotionally vulner-
able, for that is the true test. I need to overcome this nonsense. It is
a priority. Move on—or check out.

A week after I return from my European Adventure, I am still
feeling rejuvenated, refreshed—and thin. Yet, I am also suicidally close
to "checking out" if I keep on disappointing myself. I am exhausted,
tired of fighting my body. It's not so much that I want to kill myself as
I want to just go to sleep forever, to escape my pain.

"You look so thin," my friend Lizz says. "Good thin."

In Hollywood, there's no such thing as *bad* thin.

All those long days hiking outside in Rome, Florence, Munich,
Paris and London also have given my face a healthy, sun-kissed color,
not the sickly pale hue I've had for over two years. Also, since I returned
I haven't been beating myself up for not having a girlfriend. All that
diary writing and pondering has disposed of my bad attitude and long-
standing she-fensive posture, if you will. I'm confident that it will just
be a matter of time before the future Mrs. Kenny Baker walks into my
life.

The publicist for Hanson, pleased with my *People* story on the trio,
has invited me over to the NBC Studios to view the band's Friday-
night appearance on *The Tonight Show*. Hanson's little drummer, Zac,

gave me a tip on the store in London where I could get a pair of electric-green Doc Martens boots, so I want to say hi and show off my thick-soled beauties.

I sit in the audience as Jay Leno introduces the guys, who then play one of their bubblegum-pop ditties called "Where's the Love?" Although in more bitter times I might have lamented the song's lovelorn message, I happily tap my Doc Martens to Zac's beat, amused at the rabid teenage girls screaming in my ear throughout the performance.

After the show, as I wait backstage for the kids to emerge from the dressing room, my cell phone chirps. It's Jack.

Jack says there's a story about a ballerina who might have starved herself to death. It's getting a lot of attention in the national press, he says, so he wants me to interview the dancer's family in San Francisco ASAP.

Early the next morning I drive to LAX and hop on a United shuttle flight, reading a stack of newspaper clippings about the dead dancer, Heidi Guenther, as I speed northward. *A twenty-two-year-old dancer from San Francisco . . . officials told her to lose weight . . . Heidi kept losing . . . 5-feet-4 inches tall, 93 pounds . . . she died a few days ago of an apparent heart attack while driving with her mom to Disneyland.*

When I first came to *People,* my least favorite stories to report were the tragedies. They still are. The worst part is looking in people's grieving eyes. Eyes filled with a depth of loss and pain I cannot fathom but that I must somehow muster the strength to portray to our readers. Perhaps what makes it so hard is that every time I see those eyes, I think of my dad's in the last few months of his life. Perhaps reporting these disasters is my penance for not being with my dad in the final, ugly days of his life. I nearly threw up as I knocked on the door of a family who had lost their nineteen-year-old son in a TWA crash off the coast of Long Island, then shook as a distraught father handed me a photo of his son and implored, "Please don't lose this. It's all I've got." I blinked back tears as I sat in Emery and Virginia Richter's living room in Oroville, California, listening to them tearfully recall what a smart, pretty girl their daughter Margaret had been before she joined the Heaven's Gate doomsday cult and ended up killing herself a few days earlier, along with thirty-eight other members.

I cry yet again. On a foggy June afternoon in San Francisco, as I press Record on my microcassette recorder and listen to one of Heidi Guenther's best friends, Robin, tell me how a young woman as beautiful and talented as Heidi could practically starve herself to death. As usual, it's the eyes that turn on my tear faucet. In journalism school they taught me to maintain eye contact, no matter how disturbing the words coming from your subject's mouth. This way, the person connects with you as a person, not a journalist, and they will trust you enough to give you the "good stuff." Robin's caring blue eyes tell a story all their own. Tired and red, they belie the youthfulness that must spring from her when not under such duress. I am drawn to Robin's eyes; they are windows into her soul.

"All she wanted to do was dance," Robin, herself a ballerina, says. "She loved it more than anything. She was so focused and driven to succeed, even at a young age. All she wanted was to be a ballerina."

Robin talks of the pressure Heidi felt to be thin, to realize the superthin body ideal that's expected of female ballet dancers. Ex-Lax, diet pills, starvation diets, obsessive exercise regimens. Heidi tried it all. "She didn't want to have breasts," Robin adds. "She wanted to be flat-chested. She hated her body."

I nod and dab a tissue under my runny nose. Before leaving, I give Robin a firm hug. *I can't remember the last time I hugged a girl.*

Driving back to my hotel, I realize that I easily could be as dead as Heidi Guenther. For the past few weeks, in fact, I have been taking an herbal appetite suppressant. Two pills a day. The pills give me the false sense that my stomach is full, so that I don't eat, so that I can be thin and compete with the Hollywood pretty boys I have to write about. Of course, no one knows this about me. Neither do they know that a few months ago I bought a package of "dieter's tea," which, like Ex-Lax, flushes food out before it can be deposited onto my love handles and chest. Like Heidi, all I wanted to do was dance the goalie dance; like Heidi, I panicked when coaches criticized me; like Heidi, I am trying to control my seemingly out-of-control life by controlling the food I eat; like Heidi, I hate my breasts; like Heidi, I hate my body. But, unlike Heidi, I am lucky. To be alive. To have identified the mistakes I'm making, the potentially fatal choices I have made to cope with my haunting self-hatred that I have not shared with anyone, that I have been too Larry Baker macho to admit that it is killing me. To have an understanding soul to call on a lonely northern California night as I stare out my hotel window, desperately wanting my body, my life, my sexuality, back.

I phone Robin and tell her I was thinking of her, of Heidi, of wanting to see her. She admits the same.

Liberated by the realization I'm lucky to be alive, no matter how frustratingly emasculated and androgynous I might feel, the next night I take Robin to an Oakland A's game. I hold her hand the entire time and, taking comfort in the possibility that I have found a kindred soul, I am not nervous.

During the seventh-inning stretch, as the crowd around us rises to their feet and sings a rendition of "Take Me Out to the Ball Game," I turn and face Robin, run my fingers through her sandy-blond hair and, staring into her expectant eyes, kiss her with a genuine, pinched-eyes passion I've never felt before.

It's the kiss that eventually saves my life.

After our first kiss, I return to Los Angeles and start calling Robin every day. I begin sharing secrets with her that I have never revealed before: my impotence (which, I explain, stems from my fear of sexual failure), my not feeling like a normal guy, my periodic depression. I also admit that I having been starving myself to achieve an idealized male body shape, a similar goal to Heidi's. The five hundred miles of California coastline separating us allows me to open up. I have finally found a woman who, unlike Claudia, I will not nickname Monster.

I admit that I have had very little positive experience with sexual intercourse; as such, I don't want to have sex until I feel more comfortable, secure in our relationship. She says she understands this too. "Actually, that's refreshing to hear," she adds. "I've never heard a guy say he wanted to *wait* to have sex. Don't worry. Just get back up here, okay?"

Every other weekend, I fly up to San Francisco to see her. We go shopping at Union Square, roller-blade in Golden Gate Park and walk along the beach, where we often will stop and hold each other as the sun sets over the Pacific horizon.

We play tennis, something I haven't done since college. And the city's cooler, cleaner air seems to make my sinus headaches less painful than in LA. For the first time in many years I have a female companion, someone who understands me, and who, due to having just lost her close friend, understands how devastating it is to lose a loved one.

After one of our romantic weekends in San Francisco, I return to LA and fill Glenn in on where I have been the last few days. "She is so great, dude. She accepts me for the freak that I am," I say, without, of course, telling him half of it.

But we still haven't had sex, and I am not sure I even want to try. Just in case, though, I not only have been preparing mentally (mostly telling myself to relax and not overthink myself into failure) but I also have been popping pills. They are a new "natural remedy" called melatonin. My roommate, Kelly, who works the graveyard shift at a video production house, has been taking melatonin for the last few months because the hormone is supposed to help regulate the body's sleep clock. He returns from work at about nine in the morning, usually about when I am trying to drag myself out of bed, and immediately pops a melatonin pill, which he claims helps him sleep all day long. Kelly tells me that melatonin, which is secreted naturally by the pineal gland inside your brain, is believed to keep a man's testosterone levels high. "I heard a lot of guys are taking melatonin to boost their sex drive," he says.

Bingo! I immediately decide that I, too, will start taking melatonin, not only to help me feel more refreshed when I wake up in the morning but to prepare me for having sex with Robin. I take them every night before I go to sleep. I seem to fall asleep more quickly, rather than stay up past *Letterman* as I obsess over the pathetic state of my life. I don't notice an increase in my sex drive, but, then again, I haven't tried to have sex yet.

A month after we met, I bring Robin to Buffalo to meet my Mom and Norm. While Robin is in the shower one morning, Mom tells me how happy she is that I have finally found someone I love. "You deserve to be happy," she says. My brothers, on the other hand, act shocked that

I even have a girlfriend, let alone someone so pretty. Most of my brothers, I conclude, have spent the last few years assuming I was gay.

Robin is taken on a tour down my memory lane, through my old neighborhoods in Hamburg. I have been back to Buffalo only twice since Dad died a little over two years ago; I still associate Buffalo with Dad. Every ice rink we drive past, every baseball diamond, is a reminder of the most influential man in my life. When I'm not angrily telling Robin how much of a jerk he could be ("He's a big reason why you're the first girlfriend I've had in a very long time"), I am tearfully recalling how supportive he could be, too, how he was my number-one fan, how the best parts of my personality—my ability to relate to all kinds of people, my work ethic, my sense of humor—come from him. I miss him.

We then fly to New York City, where I attend meetings with *People* editors. I treat Robin like a princess, pampering her in an executive suite at the Parker Meridien hotel in Midtown Manhattan. Free room service. Free shoe shines. Free pool and spa on the roof. I use my *People* connections to get us tickets to see the Broadway production of *Rent*.

It is only the second time I have been in New York since I graduated from Columbia over three years ago. Like most places I've lived so far in my life, I have avoided returning to them. I don't like to be reminded of the pain associated with my former homes—Colgate, DC, Manhattan, Virginia and, of course, Buffalo. But I feel better about myself on this trip to New York than I did the entire year or so I lived in Upper Manhattan. Walking hand-in-hand with Robin through Times Square, I actually feel like a normal guy with a normal girlfriend—not the male poseur I have been for so many years. I'm so grateful to be falling in love. Yet, I know I can't put off the inevitable—sex—too much longer. There will come a time when Robin, being a healthy woman with a healthy sex drive, will want to consummate our bond.

On our last morning in New York, I wake to find Robin lying on the couch naked, her lean ballerina legs spread apart. Usually, we will just kiss and, perhaps, I'll bring her to orgasm with my fingers or my tongue (then I will decline her advances to satisfy me). The intensity of her kisses this morning, however, tells me she is eager to do more.

As she kneels on the carpet, sucking and caressing me, thoughts of past sexual failures flash through my mind: Claudia's crying in bed; panicking with college girls; avoiding sexual intimacy by feigning sleep; my hotel disaster in Toronto with Jenny. The racing heart, the sweat, the anxiety, the *psych-out*. The moment is all too familiar.

"No, no," I plead. "Please, don't." I push her off my crotch and hug her, telling her softly, "I'm feeling a little rushed right now is all. I'm sorry."

"But we have all day," she says, annoyed. "I'm not rushing you."

I tear the sheet from the bed and, suddenly uncomfortable being seen naked in front of her, wrap it around me. "I just don't feel like doing this right now," I say.

"Why not?" she says.

"I don't know. I just don't."

She starts throwing clothes into her suitcase.

"I wish I did, but . . ."

I knew this would happen. This relationship was too good to be true.

"Please," I plead. "Don't leave." I start crying—"I love you."

"If you love me," she says, "then why can't you make love to me?"

I don't know, I tell her.

"Maybe it isn't all in your head. Maybe it isn't all your dad's fault."

Maybe, I nod.

"Maybe you are *sick*."

Maybe, I say.

"I mean, there *must* be *some*thing wrong with you. A normal guy doesn't have problems like this. It's just not right."

I know, I say.

"Promise me you will go see a doctor when you get back to LA."

I promise her.

. . .

"Do you have any problems achieving or maintaining erections?" Dr. Trabulus, my physician, asks me as I sit across a desk from him in his Beverly Hills office.

"Um, yeah" I reply. "I actually do."

It's a few weeks after Robin confronted me in New York, and I have just arrived for my first physical examination in over five years. Trabulus, a famously laid-back doctor with a celebrity clientele, proceeds with a clinical thoroughness that belies his cool demeanor. His erection question is about the twentieth of about forty queries ("Family history of diabetes?" "Yes." . . . "Headaches?" "Yes, real excruciating sinus ones." . . .) that he reads off of a rote checklist.

When I answer that I have erection problems, Trabulus, pen firmly in hand, glances up from his clipboard and counters, "What do you mean?"

"Well, you know," I stammer. "I guess I have trouble getting hard sometimes."

"What do you mean by sometimes?"

"Well, I really should say *most* of the time."

"Not all the time?" he asks.

"Yeah. I mean, every now and then, if I concentrate and relax, I can make myself hard, sort of."

I have hated doctors' offices for as long as I can remember. The sterile white walls. The crinkly paper over the examination table. The smell of alcohol. The old doctor feeling my balls for a hernia during elementary school exams. The oldsters in the waiting room, hacking up phlegm. The babies wailing behind closed doors. Everything about doctor's offices recalls my worst childhood memories of accompanying Dad, pale and prematurely frail, to the doctor because my mom didn't think he was well enough to go alone. But now I need to see one. If anything, I need to know that I am a healthy twenty-seven-year-old guy with nothing but sexual hang-ups stemming from a pressuring father and a traumatic romantic history. That way I can focus on the psychological reasons for my impotence; then I can move on and become the sexualized man I desperately want to be.

Trabulus has me strip down to my boxers and lie back on the table. He listens to my heartbeat through a stethoscope, he pinches my nipples.

"You ever have any discharge come from here?"

"Yeah," I say, almost gleefully.

No one has ever asked me this question; I have never heard any guy mention this happening to them. That he would ask, I hope, means that it wasn't as bizarre a bodily function as I have feared. "As a matter of fact," I add, "every now and then a little stuff comes out. Not always. Just sometimes."

"Any soreness around here?" he asks, pressing the tissue around my nipple.

"Yeah," I say. "Especially when I go running or something."

A nurse then draws several vials of blood, and I pee in a cup. Trabulus returns and says he will call me in a couple of days with the results.

The very next morning, Trabulus calls me. He wants me to come into his office to talk about "the results" of my blood tests.

"Can't you just tell me over the phone," I reply. "I'm really busy today, and would rather . . ."

"No," he brusquely interjects. "I want to go over them with you in person."

This is the death call. Where I learn I'm going to die of some dreadful disease. AIDS, cancer. Just like in the movies. Just like Dad.

An hour later I'm sitting in Trabulus' office. I'm gnawing my fingernails.

"First of all, I think you're going to be fine," he begins, his grave expression suggesting otherwise. "But you could have a problem."

Rigid as a tongue depressor, I sit up in my chair.

"Because of some of the symptoms you reported to me, I went

ahead and ran an across-the-board check on your hormones. They all looked okay. Except for one."

He places a sheet of paper in front of me. It's the laboratory report for my blood test. "I tested the level of prolactin in your system. You probably don't know what prolactin is; don't worry, most guys don't," he continues, explaining that prolactin is a milk-producing hormone secreted by the pituitary gland, a pea-sized gland at the base of your brain. "Most men have just trace levels of prolactin in their blood system."

He taps his finger on the report, and I look down. Just above his index finger reads the number **1578**.

"One thousand five-hundred and seventy-eight," he says. "This is your prolactin level."

"What should it be?" I ask.

"Anywhere from 2 to 18." He adds, "Even women who are lactating—you know, breast-feeding—usually have a prolactin level lower than 200."

I glance up, straight into his eyes. He says, "I think you might have an adenoma, or a tumor. In most cases, the prolactin level is so elevated because a tumor, attached to the pituitary gland, is oversecreting that hormone. But—and I emphasize the *but*—we can't know for sure until we see it on an MRI."

I sit with an unflinchingly stoical stare. A hockey stare. A tough-motherfucker stare. A Larry Baker stare. I don't cry, nor do I feel scared. I feel nothing. I am numb.

"You told me yesterday that you sometimes can get an erection," Trabulus says. "When's the last time you had one?"

"Within the last few months, I'd say. Not a real hard one. But it was an erection."

"Really?" he replies, his eyes widening with surprise. "With that high a prolactin level, I'm surprised you've been able to have one in the last five years." *Fake it, Dad liked to say. If you believe it, you can achieve it.*

I learn that autopsy studies suggest that as many as five percent of the general adult population is walking around with benign tumors feeding off their pituitary gland, a pea-shaped nub of tissue at the frontal base of the brain known as "the master gland" because it secretes the hormones that, chemically at least, make men men and women women. The overwhelming majority of these pituitary tumors, however, remain so small that the person feels little or no symptoms. But in rare cases, such as mine, the tumor grows so big that it can short-circuit your endocrine system, disrupting the biochemical balance that is one's natural state.

I pull a pen and reporter's spiral notebook out of my black leather shoulder bag; rather than emotionally confronting this grim news, I do what I have been doing my entire journalism career: I hide behind my journalistic shield and seek from him the cold, hard facts.

What's it called? A prolactinoma. Because it is a growth, a tumor, that is secreting prolactin.

Are these malignant, cancerous kind of tumors? No. They're usually benign.

How big is it? Hard to say, but, judging from the high prolactin level, it could be quite sizeable.

How many people get these kinds of pituitary tumors? There are studies that say about five percent of the general population, but, again, there's a lot we don't know about these things.

Will I need surgery? Maybe, but there is a powerful anti-tumor medication called bromocriptine that can shrink prolactin-secreting pituitary tumors.

Will these pills allow me to have erections? They should.

So this explains my erection problems? Yes.

Can this explain why I feel sort of fat? Well, your pituitary gland does control your body's metabolism. It's possible that in addition to not having enough testosterone, your body is not readily burning fat.

My milky nipples and the headaches? Yes, probably.

Could I die? These tumors are rarely fatal. But we need to get an MRI as soon as possible. I recommend first thing tomorrow.

Driving down Wilshire Boulevard back to the *People* office, I finally began to feel the hit. I dial Robin on my cell phone.

"Robin," I begin. "I'm scared."

The MRI report describes the cause of the emasculating misery I have endured my entire adult life as a 2.3-centimeter-wide "pituitary adenoma occupying the right and central portions of the enlarged sella turcica" and " there is evidence of tumor extension to the right cavernous dural sinus." This clinical description lacks any mention of how psychologically disturbing, physically debilitating and sexually disorienting a "pituitary adenoma" (a.k.a. "tumor") can be to a young man trying to understand why his mind and body have pulsed with androgyny. I don't know half the terms in the report, but just reading it I know it's not good.

The enemy appears as nothing but a dark circle on black-and-white MRI film. Trabulus translates all the medical jargon into lay terms. "You've got a tumor about the size of a chestnut sitting a few inches behind your right eye, at the base of your brain," he says. "The bad news is that it is pressing against your sinus tissue and the base of your brain. The good news is that it doesn't appear to be compressing your optic chiasm. If it were, you could go blind."

More bad news: The tumor not only is pressing against my tiny pituitary gland, but it has grown into my right cavernous sinus, which Trabulus explains is a blood-filled cavity housing the carotid artery, the main blood pipeline between the heart and the brain. Should the tumor extend a few millimeters further to the right, I could suffer a stroke.

Thanks to the Internet and a stack of brochures from the Pituitary Tumor Network Association, I learn that prolactinomas grow very slowly, meaning that, using prolactin like a plant does water, the tumor might have been expanding at the base of my brain for as long as the last ten or fifteen years. I also learn that, in addition to producing breast milk, prolactin suppresses one's level of "free testosterone," which fuels a man's sex drive, grows body hair, makes him more aggressive than passive, helps him build muscle. Essentially, prolactin deprives a man of the biochemical brew that makes men men.

As I read the information, I am glued to the pages, for the symptons they describe of a prolactinoma patient sum up my life to a tee. More than any Bible passage or Zen Buddhism guide, and certainly more than any newspaper profile of me, the medical information I'm reading is the most compellingly relevant literature of self-discovery I've ever encountered.

So this explains why, as young as fourteen or fifteen, I felt sexually unmotivated. So this explains why, despite my growing older and more mature and more comfortable with the notion of having sex with women, my penis became softer and softer, my sex drive less active. I have a hundred and fifty times the normal level of a *female* hormone saturating my body's every tissue. A tumor has been growing more and more every day, pressing against my cranial tissue, which explains why I've suffered excruciating headaches, why my body has refused to grow muscle, hair. This may explain why all along I have often felt, in what some may say the stereotypical sense, more womanly than manly—that is, more passive than aggressive, more nurturing and sensitive than tough. These weren't in and of themselves bad qualities, but I knew my body wasn't right. And as it turns out, my male engine has been chugging through life on a bad tank of gas.

I flash back through my history of sexual frustration and failed romances, and I conclude that had I known about the throbbing lump of female hormone-secreting tissue inside my head, I wouldn't have been so hard on myself. Maybe I wouldn't have beat myself up. I also realize that while the existence of the tumor wasn't my fault, the size to which it grew without my revealing the pain it was causing me *was* my fault. In a sense, I had repeated the mistakes of my unhealthy, doctor-hating father. Yet, now I have a second chance.

I feel as much relief as grief. I no longer need "Ken" to protect me from Ken. I can face my demons. I have just learned that the cause of my male inferiority complex, of all my sexual failures, is not Dad's fault, my brothers' fault, Jenny's fault, Claudia's fault or society's fault. Perhaps the greatest relief of all, it is not *my* fault. I can stop running away from myself.

(PROLACTIN LEVEL: 13 NG/ML)

After discovering the tumor, Dr. Trabulus immediately refers me to a specialist, Dr. Glenn Braunstein at LA's Cedars Sinai Medical Center. I'm familiar with the hospital; it's where most celebrities deliver their babies. A genial, bespectacled man in his fifties, Braunstein is one of the world's eminent endocrinologists. He wants me to try shrinking the tumor with drugs for the next few months. "If that doesn't work," he explains, "you'll probably need to have surgery. But let's see how it goes."

It goes like a freight train. Within a week of taking four bromocriptine tablets a day, my prolactin level plummets from 1,578 to just above 10. The tumor is no longer acting as a dam preventing my pituitary gland from sending male steroids throughout my body. My legs feel sturdier, my mind sharper. The first morning after taking the pills, I wake up with an erection so hard it feels as if it may break the skin. I realize that my penis had not gotten that hard since I was thirteen or fourteen.

Braunstein informs me that, at age twenty-seven—and virtually overnight—I have undergone the biochemical equivalent of puberty. This means that for the first time in my adult life I can experience true biological maleness, the way I'd imagine God has it planned for men *without* prolactinomas.

The only downside of all this testosterone is that zits have popped up all over my back and my face. Like a teenager.

It's a small price. In addition to feeling an overall sense of power, my penis can get hard quite easily, and I am suddenly aware that I have an organ dangling between my legs that, at any given moment, is capable of transforming into a rigid instrument of sex that can be inserted into any willing vagina. Whereas I once thought my sex life would be forever doomed, I now seek sex out with frequency and passion. Whereas just a month ago I liked having a girlfriend who lived far enough away that I didn't have to feel the pressure of having sex with her, I am now frustrated that I can't have Robin with me; I masturbate almost every day, just to relieve all my pent-up sexual energy.

A week after I begin taking the bromocriptine tablets, I drive up to San Francisco to see Robin. In three days I manage to have sex on the floor, on the bed, on the couch, in the stairwell. I say that "I" managed to have sex, because it was all about me.

It's Halloween and, lacking real costumes, we dress as bowlers. I throw on a bowling shirt and a pair of bowling shoes I bought at a thrift store in Oakland. Robin paints her face with blue eyeshadow and bright-red lipstick and dons a white-trash outfit of tight jeans, old sneakers and a bowling shirt. We head over to a party in a Victorian apartment off Haight Street. The place is packed with twentysomethings, drunk and in costume. A few beers later, in walks a trio of attractive girls in high heels. They're dressed as hookers, wearing hot pants and short skirts and vinyl bras, and I can't stop staring at their bodies. *Look at her smooth skin. . . . Wow, no underwear! . . . What a sexy mole on her left hip.* I'm having thoughts and noticing things with unprecedented appreciation. *Nice legs. Holy shit, I can't believe I'm getting a boner.* Luckily, I'm wearing baggy jeans.

That next week, at a follow-up visit with Dr. Braunstein in which he tests my prolactin level to make sure it is remaining low, he asks me how I am feeling. "I can't stop thinking about sex," I say. "It's so strange. I feel like there's something wrong with me."

Braunstein chuckles. "There's nothing at all *wrong* with you. You're experiencing what's called 'testosterone storm,'" he explains. "What you describe is essentially an accelerated puberty. Normal puberty takes about five years to complete—and you've done it in a month or so. You've experienced in a matter of weeks what a teenage boy undergoes gradually over the course of several years."

And it is dizzying. Unlike when you're a teenager, I have no one my age who is going through the same thing: the obsessive thinking about sex constantly, the zits, the boundless energy. Perhaps I would better handle this adult-onset puberty if I weren't afraid that it could all end any second. Every erection, I fear, could be my last. I am fully aware that the bromocriptine tablets are to my dick as spinach was to Popeye's arms. I am reminded—hauntingly—of the movie *Awakenings,* in which Robin Williams played a psychiatrist who revived a group of elderly catatonic patients with the drug L-dopa. The patients had lived in a comalike stupor for several decades, but the drug enlivened the elderly men and women with youthful vitality. They danced, kissed, listened to their favorite records. But, sadly, when the drug's effectiveness wore off, so did their new lease on life, and they slipped back into their vegetative state. I am desperately afraid the same will happen to me.

Freed from prolactin's chastity belt, I realize that I am now controlled by a hormonal condition marked by an obsessive fascination with all things female.

When Braunstein prescribed me a bottle of prolactin-inhibiting bromocriptine pills, it was as if he had handed me a loaded gun. Yet, there was no license or instructions telling me how to use it responsibly, how to avoid hurting myself and others. Hormonally those pills have made me a male; but they haven't made me a man. But I don't yet realize this.

Unable to concentrate on anything more than sex and exercise ever since my medication kicked in, I often leave work early. At home I strap on my rollerblades and skate down to the bike path at Santa Monica beach, where I head south toward Marina del Rey. My strides are powerful and hard. The pavement passes under my feet in a blur. *I've never gone this fast.* As I round a corner at Venice Beach, I gaze up and spot something that I have somehow neglected to notice in the hundreds of other times I have skated here. She is tan and sleek. She is smooth and graceful. And she is blond. My male eyes detect the stimuli and my hormonally healthy brain instantly analyzes the data, at which time it sends its conclusions to my groin—as well as my euphoric inner voice.

Nice tits. Nice shoulders. Nice legs. Nice smile. Nice eyes looking into mine.

She passes by me; I twist my neck back.

Nice ass.

I keep skating, farther than I ever have before, all the way down past LAX, past Manhattan Beach, all the way to Palos Verdes. Over thirty miles later I return to my Brentwood apartment, drink three glasses of water, put on my sneakers and jog a mile up to my gym. I slide two forty-five-pound plates onto each side of the forty-five pound bar. One-hundred and thirty-five pounds. I haven't pressed half this much in years.

I rub chalk into my palms and lie back on the bench. I take a deep breath. As I exhale, my hands clutch the metal bar and I push it skyward, and then slowly lower it to my chest. I suck in some more air and . . . grunting, I push the weight up. *Shooooo.* One. Light as plastic. Again. *Shooooo.* Two . . . and three . . . and four. Fifteen reps later, I stop. A minute later I add ten pounds and do it again.

A few days later, while browsing through the newsstand down the street from my apartment one night, I spot the words **SLUTTY BAD**

GIRLS on the cover of a magazine, speaking to me from the top row of the rack like Sirens luring sea-weary Odysseus from atop a Mediterranean cliff. I used to come into the store late at night and notice the middle-aged guys standing in the porn section, thumbing through *Penthouse* or *Barely Legal,* careful not to make eye contact with anyone else. Those guys have always struck me as pathetic loners who pay five bucks to get their rocks off by looking at bimbos with fake boobs and fake tans. They seemed so foreign, so unlike me. But this time as I thumb through the magazine I feel like I sort of understand what those guys were always doing. *They lust for women's bodies.* For the first time in my life, I buy a pornographic magazine.

In order not to seem like too much of a sex-crazed masturbator, I toss a pack of gum onto the counter next to the magazine. When the scruffy male clerk, from whom I have been purchasing *The New Yorker, Us* magazine and *The Atlantic Monthly* for the past year, hands me my receipt with a sly grin, I feel as if I have just joined a fraternity that has been in operation, invisible to my asexual eyes, around me all of my life. As a teenager and, to some extent, in college, I used to notice the profound difference between Them and Me, between sex-crazed men and my nonlibidinous self. But now—no longer ensconced in my celibate world of headaches, milky nipples, heightened emotional sensitivity and an absent sex drive—I have finally stopped being a different kind of guy and am just a guy.

Long-distance rollerblading, weight-lifting and masturbation can pacify only so much sexual energy; and watching the red-bikini–clad *Baywatch* actresses film their bouncy scenes on the Pacific Palisades beach can only satisfy so much of my sex drive. With Robin, who is always busy studying for a grad school exam *and* is a six-hour drive away, I often find myself restless and horny. But alone.

During my prolactin-saturated days, I was intimidated by Hollywood parties, fearful of girls hitting on me. Now that I am hormonally healthy, I enjoy the exercise of donning a nice shirt and jeans and flirting with pretty girls, who, judging from the attention they've started to pay me, seem drawn to some sort of invisible, pheromonal scent from my body. But I have a girlfriend.

Thus my mating game is a frustrating and guilt-inducing one. Here I am, blessed with a fully functioning penis and a sex drive, but I have someone to whom I have pledged fidelity and devotion, whose patience and understanding and love made it safe for me to seek medical help. In fact, she probably saved my life.

Yet, the everyday reality is that I see her only a few days a month, and she has not been able to keep up with my body's changes because she is not around to know how horny I am, how much happier I am, how much lighter my body feels. And I am starting to build muscle. When I do sit-ups, I can immediately feel my stomach getting harder. Veins are starting to bulge from my arms. My dick actually seems to have grown larger from the influx of all the blood.

I have been granted this gift of physical, psychological, social and sexual liberation, but I rarely get to celebrate it—have sex. I don't want to be one of those testosterone-poisoned men who cheats on their girlfriends. I don't want to be the kind of man who allows the raw forces of his primal nature—not love and respect—to guide his sexual behavior. But I find that my idealism seems powerless next to my newfound desire to engage in the single most important human behavior keeping our species alive and that I was deprived of for so many years.

Later that winter I attend a birthday party at a home in the Hollywood Hills. There I meet up with Jane, a journalist who had been gazing at me across from premieres and press conferences. Although Jane has a boyfriend, that doesn't stop her from stroking the back of my hands and rubbing my thigh as we chat on the living-room couch.

By about two in the morning, most everyone has left except for a couple of attention-seeking women wearing tight black leather pants and T-shirts. They're dancing provocatively with each other to a techno CD. I cuddle on the couch with Jane as she passes me a joint, which, for the first time since college, I take a drag from. I manage not to cough.

Watching the dancing girls grind against each other, Jane places her hand over my crotch and gently squeezes my penis, which immediately starts creeping down the inner leg of my jeans, ready for action.

"I've always wondered what it would be like to kiss you," she says.

"Oh, really?"

"Uh-huh."

"What about your boyfriend?" I say. "Where is he?"

"Vegas."

"I see."

I have never acted like such a player, but here I am toying with a very attractive girl who, just a few months earlier, would have scared the crap out of me; in her hip-huggers and push-up bra, she would have made me so nervous and intimidated I'd rather have rushed home than risk the embarrassment of going limp in front of her. Not now, though.

"That means we could kiss and he would never know about it, right?" I say.

"I was thinking the same thing," she gleefully replies.

With the marijuana buzz uninhibiting me and my penis leading me, I take her hand and walk her out outside. I thrust her body against the side panel of her car and start kissing her, pressing my erection against her pubic bone. "Mmm, hmmm," she moans.

She is Claudia, Tonya, Amy, Jenny, Melissa, Jenny McCarthy, Jennifer Aniston. She is Drew Barrymore.

Kissing, groping. Hot breath. Hand under skirt.

"Let's go home," Jane whispers.

I should just take her home and fuck her, take out all these years of sexual frustration out on her wet vagina. Act out the graphic scenes in my porno mag, use this throbbing gift of manliness that's engorged with blood, my life force. But . . . there's Robin. So sweet and gentle, so caring, so committed. Robin. So cute and petite, Robin is probably lying in bed in her pajamas on a chilly San Francisco night. Sleeping like a princess. Content, devoted, loving. I can't do this. I am an asshole. A fucking two-timing asshole! A cheater. I've become one of them—a guy, a dude, a stud, the kind of jerk who used to disgust me with all his macho, dick-swinging posturing. Haven't I learned anything from all those years of emasculated pain and frustration? Haven't I learned that a man is made of more than a hard dick, a square jaw and sex drive? A man possesses what I did all those years: inner strength, sensitivity, thoughtfulness, bravery, resiliency, convictions. A man is not a weak person willing to compromise his convictions—and betray a woman—for a few seconds of ejaculatory pleasure.

"No, I can't," I tell Jane, pulling away.

"Why?"

"I have a girlfriend."

"So?"

"I can't," I say. "It's not right."

No matter how potent it makes me feel, bromocriptine is no cure-all. In about 85 percent of patients with prolactinomas, bromocriptine not only lowers their prolactin level but it also shrinks the tumor, thus making risky tumor removal surgery unnecessary. For some patients, though, their prolactin level lowers but the tumor doesn't shrink. Mounting as aggressive a pharmacological attack as possible, Braunstein has had me taking eight bromocriptine pills a day, plus a new anti-prolactin drug called cabergoline, waging a two-pronged attack on the tumor. It's a last-ditch effort to avoid my having to undergo brain surgery.

But eight months into my drug therapy, another MRI shows that my tumor is just as big and perilously close to my optic nerves, my carotid artery, my infection-prone sinuses and my brain's speech and language center as it was before the bromocriptine, of which I am ingesting eight pills a day, nearly the maximum dosage considered nontoxic.

Though sexually liberating, the pills make my tongue dry as cotton, speed up my metabolism so much that I can sleep only six hours a night and give me constant nausea. And my headaches, which are being caused by the tumor pressing against the surrounding cranial nerves, have not gone away at all. My penis may be able to get hard, and my once dichotomous *Ken-and-"Ken"* identity may be morphing into a more confident, self-assured, integrated Ken, but the chemicals are taking a toll on my body. I have lost ten pounds on a five-foot-eleven-inch frame that didn't have much weight to lose to begin with. Ever since college I have had circles under my eyes because, I assumed, I didn't get enough sleep. I didn't realize that the reason was that I had a tumor forcing my body to fight against itself, which meant no matter how much sleep I got, my body was exhausted from the battle. Now that I am swallowing so many pills every day, the circles are even darker and ring my eyes like Halloween eye paint. I can't live long like this. What at first seemed like the solution is now creating its own set of health problems. It turns out that getting diagnosed was only the first half in my marathon of recovery.

"Surgery is always the last option," Dr. Braunstein tells me during one of my biweekly visits, "but it's looking as if drugs aren't going to get rid of the mass. It's time to plan for surgery."

Braunstein sends me over to the hospital's Skull Base Institute to consult with its top surgeon, Hrayr Shahinian, a no-nonsense kind of doctor who immediately clips my MRI film onto an illuminated plastic board and shows me just how dangerous it is for me to keep living with this tumorous chestnut a few inches behind my eyes. If the tumor expands a few millimeters one way, he points out, I could go blind. Should the tumor extend a few more millimeters to the right, I could have a stroke and die.

"You have a grenade inside your head," he says. "You can't afford to wait any longer. Surgery is the *only* option."

"But couldn't I die from having the operation?" I ask.

"I'm not going to lie to you: yes. But for a young guy like you there's a less than one-percent chance of that happening."

Shahinian, his black hair clipped as short as his speaking style, then concedes all of the "potential" risks. A smidgen of a slip to the right? A stroke. An errant microscopic slice to the left? Eye paralysis, brain damage or worse. Shahinian is confident that none of these things will happen.

I appreciate his candor, and I trust him, but, still, I can read between the lines: This surgery could make me brain-damaged. If successful, though, the procedure will free my body, and, he explains, my testosterone and other hormones will pump to perfection without the need for nauseating medication. As for my sexual function, he adds, "It should be better than it is on the drugs."

Ever the journalist, while scribbling notes onto a pad, I glance at Shahinian's hands. They look solid, manly. His fingernails are perfectly manicured.

"I don't mean to sound arrogant," he says, "but I have never lost anyone on the table. But if you don't get this operation, the tumor could eventually kill you."

Luckily, Robin is on summer break from school. She has moved in with me, in case I need help following my surgery, not to mention to see if we can get along while living together. Her visit, we have decided, will be a test to see whether we will take our relationship to the next level—that is, whether one of us will move permanently to be with the other.

We start failing the test. I soon find that some of the qualities I admired in her from afar—her tireless dedication to her work, her shyness, her almost childlike sensitivity—are not so attractive when I see her every day. I start thinking not only that we are too different but that we are in two different stages in life. She has dated numerous men and, after playing the field, now wants to settle down; I have spent my entire adult life in a sexual stupor. Although I am wracked with guilt, I can't stop myself from craving someone who laughs more, who is more goofy, who, well, isn't as intense as she is.

As clichéd as it sounds, though, it really isn't about her. It's me. I have changed. But while Robin likes the new Ken even more than the old Ken, the new Ken feels a need to confront these doubts of his by seeing what else is out there. This is a conclusion I would rather not have to make. I wish I could overcome this health problem and find a way for us to live happily ever after in the same city together. I have never been strong enough to even think of breaking up with a woman, especially someone as attractive, kind and perceptive as Robin. Her urging is what saved me from becoming a victim of my own denial. I waited so long, suffered through so much self-doubt and loneliness, to find a woman who would accept me for who I am; she not only did, but she made me stronger with her love. With her I learned that there is hope that I could someday have that wife and a home and kids and a dog and all the romantic dreams I have had for as long as I can remember.

As much as I wish I could silence these competing voices inside my head, I owe it to myself and to Robin to acknowledge my conflict.

It finally becomes clear to both of us that I don't think Robin is "the one" when we're walking along the beach in Santa Monica the day before my surgery. It's a scary time. Neither of us knows what is going to happen to me when the surgery is over, whether it will make me whole or make me worse.

"Do you think we'll get engaged after the surgery?" she asks me.

"I don't know, Robin," I say, stopping to hug her. "Let's just take things one day at a time."

"I know, I know," she says, the corners of her lips curling downward in disappointment. "But it would just make me feel a lot better if I had that to hold on to when you are in surgery tomorrow. That's all."

I easily could just tell her yes—and not tell her the truth, just like I had lied to myself for so many years. I could keep going out with her and having sex, using her body while constantly eyeing other women like those lecherous old men and wondering if I am just settling for something that isn't right for me. I could be "a player" and cheat on her while telling her everything is fine, then one day dump her like I have seen two-timing guys do so many times before that it has became a male cliché. But I don't want to become a prisoner of my strong sex drive just as easily as I was imprisoned by my lack of one. Even though I feel these sexual urges, desires that can make an American president seem like little more than a two-timing sex addict, I want more.

I don't just want sex; I want to fall in love. Ever since I dreamt of building a family with Jenny away from Buffalo, I have always longed for a woman with whom I could share a marriage. I have witnessed the disintegration of my parents' marriage, heard the horror stories of my grandparents' failed marriages, seen men tell lies that ultimately ruin relationships, and now I want to succeed where so many men have failed. And I am willing to be alone until that time comes.

I have just spent my entire adult life lying to myself and others. Now it's time to be a man.

"I love you, Robin," I say, "but if I told you right now that I believe you and I will be together forever, I would be lying. I appreciate you so much—you're so sweet and caring. I am a lucky man. But right now I'm just enjoying this moment with you and I thank God you're here with me. I love you."

And I mean it.

The next day, a surgical-masked nurse wheels my body into a chilly operating room on the eighth floor of Cedars Sinai Medical Center. Before the anesthesiologist injects me with a sedative that in seconds will knock me out, I take a deep breath and say a prayer. *God, I go with You.* And I close my eyes, prepared to cope with any complications when I wake up, ready to cope with whatever outcome.

Shahinian usually enters through the nostrils in his "transphenoidal"—through the sphenoid sinuses—approach to the brain. But my nose is narrow, "not like my Armenian nose," he explains. As a result, Shahinian uses my upper gum as a portal to my brain, making an incision just above my teeth, forcing open an accessway. He then widens the incision with a metal instrument resembling a vise. He bores through several layers of skull tissue and bone like a surgical subway tunneler, finally reaching the tumor, a throbbing blob of white tissue. Despite all the high-tech medical procedures doctors can employ these days, the procedure is manual and primitive. Shahinian carefully scrapes the mass off my pea-size pituitary gland with a blunt metal tool roughly the width and length of a pencil.

Five hours later, he concludes the operation, sealing the circular hole he created in my skull bone with a cut-to-fit slice of yellow fat he has taken from my lower abdomen. If the fat plug doesn't successfully seal the hole, I could leak brain fluid and die from the ensuing infection.

AWAKENING

The steady, high-pitched beep of a heart monitor tells me I am alive. The complex of intravenous tubes and temperature-, pulse- and oxygen-monitoring wires tells me that I am lucky to be so.

A plastic catheter is carrying urine from my bladder into a tube that empties into a bedpan on the floor. The gauze in my nose makes nasal breathing impossible, so I inhale through my mouth, despite the discomfort of swallowing the constant drip of blood leaking from my skull-base wounds.

I can't sleep. Every time I nod off, the dripping blood chokes me awake. Every minute or so, I must gasp for air.

As I once did while playing goalie in front of thousands of taunting, screaming college hockey fans, I focus on the task at hand. Yogic breathing; easy in, easy out.

The clock above the nurses' station says it's six o'clock. It must be morning. Robin walks in and pets my matted, blood-stained hair. I open my mouth and she places tiny ice chips into my parched mouth; unable to chew, I let them melt on my tongue.

I'm too concerned with breathing to talk; the oxygen mask will muffle my voice anyway. I strain my eyes over to Robin, who is lightly stroking my hand. Our eyes lock and, realizing the trauma I have just endured, I begin sobbing uncontrollably.

I start choking. Robin runs to get a nurse, who rushes into my room to settle me down.

"Just relax," the nurse says, eyeing my vital life monitors. "You're going to be okay. Just relax."

She drops a couple of ice chips into my mouth.

"Are you scared?" the nurse asks.

I nod.

Later that morning, I'm feeling less groggy, my thoughts are clearer. It will be a long two days before I can stand up; another two days before I can walk without assistance. Lying in bed, staring up at the white ceiling tiles, I wonder if what I have just endured will be all worth it. Will I reap the reward that surgical removal of my prolactin-secreting tumor promised: unimpaired manhood?

The orange Southern California sun is just starting to fill my room as Dr. Shahinian, my surgeon, steps in with my charts in his hand. He's beaming as he lifts the oxygen mask off my face.

"Everything went well," he says. "I got the tumor."

"You're a fucking stud," I mumble.

"No," he says. "You are."

About three months after my surgery, I began feeling a little sluggish. I had a harder time waking up in the morning and sensed that I had lost that energized feeling that had catapulted me into a state of euphoria after surviving a brain surgery that had promised a drug-free and normal hormone level for the rest of my life. Also, my hunger for sex—ravenous immediately following surgery—had declined and my erections weren't as hard.

It proved to be the first test of my new manhood. Instead of ignoring the symptoms as I had before, I immediately went to see Dr. Braunstein, who administered a blood test. It showed that my prolactin level had jumped up to 80 ng/ml—eight times the normal level. An MRI the next day confirmed his suspicion: a crumb-sized fleck of tumor, secreting prolactin, remained lodged in my right cavernous sinus. *Here we go again.* Just when I figured I could get on with the rest of my life, I find out that Dr. Shahinian, despite his valiant effort, was unable to extract the entire mass. It remains lodged dangerously close to my carotid artery. For Shahinian to have poked around this bloody crevice just inside my temple would have been too risky. There's a sound biological, if also disturbing, reason why people commit suicide by shooting themselves in the temple: If he had gone for that last bit of tumor and severed my carotid artery, I could have hemorrhaged and died.

So now I must take two pills a week—perhaps for the rest of my life—in order to keep my prolactin level at a normal level of about 10 ng/ml, and to keep the tumor from growing any larger, thus requiring me to have the same surgical procedure again. So delicate is my drug-enabled balance of hormones that if I fail to take just one pill in a week, I have a lower energy level and less of a sex drive.

Yet, rather than viewing the stubborn tumor as a burden, I believe it is a gift—a daily reminder not only of the fragility of life but of the fragility of healthy hormonal maleness. Because of what I have been through, I am infused with an incredible lightness of being. I will never take my health for granted, nor will I squander it by acting like anything less than a man who respects its power.

Which is what I now try to do every day. But it is not without the emotional intensity that my health allows.

Several weeks after my surgery, Robin and I still had neither committed to each other nor broken up. What we did know was that our long-distance romance was no longer feeling romantic or like much of a relationship. I agreed to see a couples counselor with her. I flew up from LA on a Friday afternoon and drove straight to the therapist's office in Oakland. The therapist was a graduate student working on her Ph.D. who had been counseling Robin one-on-one for the last several weeks. It was the therapist's idea to invite me to their sessions.

Robin and I uneasily sat next to each other on a couch across from the woman, who first asked Robin to voice her frustrations and concerns, a list that was longer than the printout of my phone bill for the past few months, a measure of how Robin and I had been desperately trying to make things work.

Robin told the therapist that she believed we had a generally healthy relationship that would thrive once we lived in the same city. Robin explained to the therapist how committed she is to me, accurately telling how she stuck with me before and after my surgery, how she took care of me when I was recovering and how I am now repaying her by doubting our compatibility.

Tears welled up in my eyes as she spoke. Because she was right, and because she was wrong. Yes, she had been there for me when I needed her most, but the truth is that I now wanted to break up with her more out of my own need for self-discovery after my tumor was treated than due to her not being a good and loving human being.

Robin, herself amidst a stressful graduate-degree program, added that I was being insensitive and inconsiderate by "dumping all of this" onto her during such a busy time of her life.

Finding her cue, the therapist fixed her gaze on me. "You have to admit that you don't have very good timing," she said.

"Timing?" I angrily snapped back. "You're trying to say that *I* don't have good timing?"

The old, passive Ken, the one who always avoided conflict, might have reacted to her comment with solemn sympathy, perhaps even apologizing for his behavior. But I was the new, testosterone-charged Ken. I had just endured a biochemical revolution and survived a surgical trauma. I leaned forward and shot needles into the therapist with my eyes.

"Timing, huh? It wasn't good *timing* when I found out I had a tumor that was strangling my masculinity. It wasn't good *timing* when a surgery that was supposed to make my life better has only made it more complicated. And it's not good *timing* right now, when someone—who has no fucking idea what I just went through—is blaming me for dealing honestly and up-front with a health crisis that, frankly, hasn't exactly been a piece of cake. Do you have any idea what it's like to undergo a complete hormonal transformation overnight? Well, do you?"

"No," the therapist replied. "I don't."

"Well, then the next time you go and suggest that this situation was somehow bad *timing*, just stop and think about the hell I just went through."

Robin promptly paid and we left.

I wasn't used to lashing out like that. Prolactin had always kept my temper cool. I was embarrassed by my outburst; yet, I didn't regret it. *At least I have passion.*

For the first ten minutes of our ride back to her San Francisco apartment, neither Robin nor I uttered a word. I think we both knew we were being pulled apart by a masculinizing force perhaps as strong as the one that had emasculated me for all of my adult life. Nature was in its own cruel way separating us.

Halfway across the Bay Bridge, Robin broke the deafening silence.

"It's just not fair," she said, staring out her window at the choppy waters. "Just when you've become a healthy man, I can't enjoy you."

The ancient Greeks had a saying: "The suffered is the learned." Here is what I have learned: Both nature and nurture make the man. Manhood is about an inner, intangible essence. Maleness is about biology; manhood transcends biology. A drug or the removal of a tumor can make someone more male, but it makes him more of a man only like breast implants make someone more of a woman.

For better or worse, manhood—the approved way of being a male in our society—is something that a male is expected to prove. Yet, he is given no guide, no handbook offering a checklist of accomplishments. Instead he culls his understanding of what's expected from the personified icons of manhood—fathers, brothers, friends, teachers, rock stars, underwear models, religious figures, politicians, TV personalities, comedians, athletes, movie stars—that form his collective male unconscious. He endures a series of rituals—among them losing his virginity, exhibiting physical, mental and sexual potency, working hard, amassing resources—in an effort to achieve his culture's idealized state of manhood. It took me years of suffering through a male inferiority complex before I realized that the resilience and courage I employed in order to survive my ordeal had made me more of a man than, given my hormonal handicap, I ever thought possible.

My recovery made me feel blessed to enjoy sexual health and the ability to share love with a woman. But rather than using my strength by only looking outward for satisfaction, I first turned inward and got acquainted with my new self. I realized that I don't have to be alive; I am here by the grace of a force stronger than any hormone. I returned to the spiritual texts that I had abandoned in frustration. The Buddha's writings now made sense: *Though he should conquer a thousand men in the battlefield a thousand times, yet, he indeed who would conquer himself is the noblest victor.*

Not long after my breakup with Robin, I began dating someone who shared as much passion and joyful appreciation for life as I now did—only she didn't need to have a brain tumor short-circuiting her endocrine system to be that way.

Her name is Brooke. An athletic California girl with a wit as quick as her foot speed, Brooke worked one floor below me in the advertising department of my former employer, Time Inc., for a year without our ever meeting. But we eventually did meet, as yuppies often do, in the photocopying room. With Brooke, my male health became cause for celebration, not conflict. I no longer was hurting anyone—myself included—by merely being myself. With Brooke, I didn't need to explain who I was and what I was thinking; Brooke already seemed to know. Indeed, I had forged a bond as magical as the miracle of my renewed life.

Two years later, on a brilliant Saturday afternoon in the romantic wine country of Sonoma, California, I stood in a silver-vested black tuxedo before the people in the world who mattered to me most and pledged my lifelong devotion to Brooke. My mother, her hair perfectly coiffed, stood beside her husband, Norm, still a good man after all these years. I looked out and saw my old Colgate friends, who had stuck with me even when I was hiding my real self from them. My three older brothers, all of whom have children and jobs, strapped paychecks and bills to pay, couldn't afford to make the trip to California. But to my left stood my little brother, Kris, my best man; as a twenty-four-year-old college student and record-store manager, Kris had spent the five years since our father's death searching for purpose in his life. Now that I had found mine, I vowed to help my not-so-little brother find his. I wish Dad could have seen that, as he had requested in his last days, my mother and I have taken care of Kris. If Dad had been there, I know he would have been proud of us, his two youngest boys looking so dapper and strong: survivors.

I also wish my father—from whom I learned so many lessons, both good and bad—could have seen the man I have become. Finding that my postsurgical sinuses had grown more sensitive to the smog, I had left LA for the cleaner air just north of San Francisco, in the shadow of Mount Tamalpais. I had stopped trying to escape my personal pain by packing up and moving before I could get close to anyone—from Buffalo, to Washington, DC, to New York, to Virginia, to Los Angeles. I soon began telling people, without shame, what I had learned through my ordeal, and eventually I started putting those thoughts onto paper, the result of which fills the pages of this book.

I have also learned how to celebrate my body. My arms and legs are sturdy from training for a marathon to raise money for pituitary tumor patients. My calves, chest, torso and shoulders are firm from riding my mountain bike and playing hockey. When I let in a goal, I don't hate myself; rather, I love myself and am grateful for having the great fortune to play. My body feels whole. My mind, no longer a prisoner of a tumor, is teeming with creative energy and wonderment. My spirit is emboldened.

I am a man—made of the experience of my life.

AUTHOR'S NOTE

The characters and events in this book are real. Names and identifying characteristics of some individuals have been changed or altered to protect their privacy. Where my memory of specific details or dialogue has failed me, friends and family members have filled in the gaps; where those sources have failed me, I have relied on a combination of my own reportage and best memory. The prolactin levels featured at the beginning of each chapter are estimates based on calculations by me and my doctors.

ACKNOWLEDGMENTS

My story would never have made it into print were it not for the love, support and genius of many people, all of whom I owe heartfelt thanks.

Jane Dystel, my literary agent, and Miriam Goderich indelibly shaped early versions of this manuscript, as did Samuel G. Freedman of Columbia University's Graduate School of Journalism. But it was Ben Stein, the smartest man in Hollywood, who first told me I had no choice but to write this book.

The wunderkinds at Tarcher Putnam—Joel Fotinos, Ken Siman and especially my editor, Mitch Horowitz—have worked so hard to make me look good.

Throughout the writing process, my team of doctors—Hrayr Shahinian, Glenn Braunstein and Joshua Trabulus—generously provided me time and information, without ever billing my insurance company. (A portion of the royalties from this book will be donated to The Ken Baker Pituitary Tumor Fund, which I have established at Cedars Sinai Medical Center, a house of earthly angels in the heart of the city of angels.)

I'm also indebted to David Groff, John E. Friberg, Jr., Glenn Gaslin, Mayrav Saar, Kevin Joyce, Sean Delgado, John Marrin, Joyce Maynard, Jennifer Mendelsohn, Ron Murphy, Mark Erickson, Sam McDonald, Marguerite Hargreaves, the Schlossers, Will Corbin,

Melissa, Sarah, Drew Barrymore, Brandi Chastain, Duncan Sheik, Jerry Maguire, The Depot, Café Kaldi, Jerry Weltsch, Paul Wilner, Don Snyder, Bic Tran, Al Burton, Steve Bellamy, Sam Donaldson, Nekisha Mohan, Troy Body, Stan Evans and the staff at *The Buffalo News,* Kris Hicks, the Dupont Circle posse, Gary Ross, Jason Greyerbiehl, Melanie, Tamara, Katie, Cyrill Walter, Dana Richie, YONiYUM, the Fury Frisbee girls, Todd Gold and the *Us weekly* crew, Elizabeth Leonard, Jack Kelley, Monica Rizzo and *all* the *People* people. These dear friends (and everyone else I have forgotten to mention) helped me in their own ways and kept me laughing even through the most un-funny of times. *Namaste,* guys.

Every writer needs a muse who barks when protecting your computer from being stolen, and luckily I have the amazing Arthur Fonzarelli. Likewise, every writer should take a class from Sandy Padwe at Columbia University, who showed me that a story is only as compelling as the size of its heart.

Heidi Guenther helped me choose life, and her spirit lives on in these pages.

Dad, I wish we could have talked all this out before you left us.

My brothers—Kris, Kyle, Keith and Kevin—and I have been through so much, and I will always love them, even though I don't call them nearly often enough. My mother, Marcia Seiflein, and her husband, Norm, have reminded me that faith—in yourself, God, family and friends—is the key to happiness. Steve and Paula, Jack and Judith, and the entire West Coast family have taken in this East Coast stray, which he appreciates.

Brooke Baker is my ultimate friend and lover. I speak to you, the reader, only by standing on her shoulders.

Thanks, God.

ABOUT THE AUTHOR

Ken Baker (www.kenbaker.net) is a senior writer for *Us weekly* and a former nationally ranked ice hockey goalie. He lives in the San Francisco bay area.